MW00461330

THE COSMOPOLITAN SELF

MITCHELL ABOULAFIA

The

Cosmopolitan

Self

George Herbert Mead

and

Continental Philosophy

UNIVERSITY OF ILLINOIS PRESS

URBANA AND CHICAGO

Library of Congress Cataloging-in-Publication Data
Aboulafia, Mitchell.
The cosmopolitan self : George Herbert Mead and
continental philosophy / Mitchell Aboulafia.
p. cm.
Includes bibliographical references and index.
ISBN 0-252-02650-0 (alk. paper)
1. Mead, George Herbert, 1863–1931.
2. Philosophy, European—20th century.
I. Title.
B945.M464A62   2001
191—dc21   00-011806

For Lauren and Sara
Hymns of Compassion
Songs of Insight

Contents

Acknowledgments   ix

Introduction   1

1. Mead and the Social Self   7

*2. Judgment and Universality in Arendt's Kant
and Mead   28*

3. Universality and Individuality: Habermas and Mead   61

4. Levinas and the Other Side   87

*5. Pluralism, Radical Pluralism, and the Perspectives
of Others   105*

Notes   129

Bibliography   147

Index   155

Acknowledgments

Of the many tasks involved in publishing a book, writing the acknowledgments clearly is the most pleasant. And yet in many ways it is also the most difficult. How does one thank so many in so few words? I suppose that one simply begins.

I want to thank my all my colleagues in the philosophy department at the University of Colorado at Denver for helping to create an exceptionally supportive academic environment. Specifically, I am grateful to Myra Bookman, Brian Lisle, Robert Metcalf, Candice Shelby, Mark Tanzer, Sam Walker, and Glenn Webster for dialogue and friendship over the years and to Andrew Barber for being a great administrative assistant.

I wish to express my appreciation for commenting on parts of the manuscript to Joe Esposito, Joe Margolis, Hilary Putnam, Ruth-Anna Putnam, and Tom Rockmore and to Jürgen Habermas for exchanges during visits to Houston and Denver. A special word of thanks to John Stuhr for the time and effort he spent (beyond the call of duty) reading and commenting on the entire manuscript. I also wish to acknowledge members of the colloquium held in Prague at the Institute of the Czech Academy of Sciences for their comments on an early version of chapter 3, the Continental Theory Workshop at Rice University, and members of the Society for the Advancement of American Philosophy for providing a home for those interested in sustaining and nurturing American philosophy.

Richard Martin, my editor at the University of Illinois Press, has been a pleasure to work with and deserves a heartfelt word of thanks for supporting this project, as does Carol Anne Peschke for her efforts as copy editor.

I am very grateful to my daughters, Lauren Hana Ellman Aboulafia and Sara Frances Ellman Aboulafia, for being troopers during some very difficult times these past few years. It is to them that I dedicate this book. To Cathy Kemp, my deepest gratitude for being colleague and companion, and a lasting source of inspiration and vitality and love and for an additional small thing: helping me bring closure to this project by threatening to burn the first chapter if I checked over the quotations one more time.

Thank you one and all.

———

Chapter 1, a few brief passages from chapter 2, and a substantial portion of chapter 3 are drawn from the following sources. I am grateful to the publishers for permission to reprint this material in revised form.

"George Herbert Mead and the Many Voices of Universality," in *Recovering Pragmatism's Voice: The Classical Tradition, Rorty, and the Philosophy of Communication,* ed. Lenore Langsdorf and Andrew R. Smith, 179–94. © 1995 by the State University of New York. All rights reserved. Reprinted by permission of the State University of New York Press.

"Habermas and Mead: On Universality and Individuality," *Constellations* 2:1 (April 1995): pp. 94–113. © 1995 by Basil Blackwell Publishers Ltd. Reprinted by permission of Blackwell Publishers.

"Was George Herbert Mead a Feminist?" *Hypatia* 8:2 (Spring 1993): 145–58. © 1993 by Mitchell Aboulafia. Used by permission of Indiana University Press.

THE COSMOPOLITAN SELF

Introduction

For most of the last half of the twentieth century, classic American pragmatism was viewed by the majority of philosophers as little more than a historical curiosity. It was interesting to intellectual historians, perhaps, but surely not capable of supplying the philosophical grist needed for the analytically charged mills of the times. George Herbert Mead, one of the half-dozen most important classic American philosophers, suffered under the weight of this prejudice more than most. Late in the century, however, pragmatism was resurrected and brought to center stage, and themes closely associated with Mead's work began to appear in very different philosophical circles. Mead's ideas came to play a central role in Jürgen Habermas's theory of communicative action, and several important books appeared that addressed his thought. Yet the vast majority of philosophers remained unaware that ideas that have become the common currency of our times can be found in or illuminated by Mead's work. This is unfortunate because in addition to Habermas there are numerous points of potential contact between Mead's ideas and contemporary currents, notably Hannah Arendt's work on Immanuel Kant's political philosophy, postmodernism's decentered subject, new analyses of Kant's third *Critique*, Richard Rorty's linguistic pragmatism, Hilary Putnam's deepening engagement with pragmatism, Joseph Margolis's historied thought, the recovery of Ludwig Wittgenstein's later philosophy by Continental theorists, the renewed interest in Adam Smith, and Emmanuel Levinas's concern for the other. The list could go on. In short, if one is interested in advancing an enduring exchange between pragmatism and other contemporary trends in philosophy and social theory, then one would be advised to turn to Mead. His concerns are in many respects our concerns, and this is especially true with regard to questions of pluralism, universalism, and the fostering of a democratic temper.

If there is a theme woven through Mead's work, it is that the self is integrally related to society, and if there is one goal that animates his intellectual projects, it is the realization of a democratically organized political system in which individuals can flourish. One of Mead's underlying assumptions is that a democratic temper entails a capacity for both universalism and pluralism, in particular, for locating the common and appreciating the different. These are themes that link Mead's work to contemporary debates in philosophy, and they are explored in this work. Drawing on Mead, I argue that the self emerges through taking the perspectives of others, and because it emerges in this fashion the individual can accommodate both the universal and plural when they are understood in a certain fashion. To be more specific, *The Cosmopolitan Self* offers a model of the social development of the self that shows how a democratically inclined subject embodies both a universalistic dimension and a sensitivity to particular others, and in the process it examines several different contemporary approaches to universalism and pluralism, namely those of Jürgen Habermas, Hannah Arendt, and Emmanuel Levinas. In doing so it considers how a socialized self can become a critical political actor whose interests do not defeat its reasonableness and good judgment. This, in turn, raises questions about the nature of individuality. Finally, in addressing the previous points, *The Cosmopolitan Self* attempts to support the cause of pluralism by advancing the dialogue between Continental thought and classic American philosophy.

The Cosmopolitan Self begins with a presentation of George Herbert Mead's ideas on the self and society. From the vantage point of those attuned to the cluster of sensibilities that have come to be called postmodern, Mead would be classified as a modernist. He promoted an ideal of social progress that drew on a host of notions typically associated with the Enlightenment. For instance, Mead was a booster of the empirical sciences, and he thought that their procedures and accomplishments could help develop and sustain democracy. He was a central figure in the history of pragmatism, and like many pragmatists he viewed himself as actively committed to important features of what might be called the modernist agenda. Yet certain elements of Mead's thought—for example, his antifoundationalism and perspectivism—hold much promise for building bridges between conflicting contemporary orientations. This is far from accidental. Mead's commitment to the Enlightenment was filtered through the lens of romanticism, and many of the most troubling tensions in his thought parallel a host of fractures that plague and inspire contemporary speculative and ethical impulses. Mead's pragmatism is examined from a number of different perspectives in this book, including its relevance to pluralism, democracy, and the question of how socialized agents become political actors capable of criticizing the status quo. Chapter 1 presents a comprehensive overview of Mead's ideas on the self and society against the backdrop of his political concerns, specifically his commitment to women's rights.

Kant stands behind much of what we have come to classify as modern, and figures such as Habermas continue to develop their positions in his shadow. One does not usually associate the work of the transcendental philosopher Kant with the naturalist Mead. Yet several of Mead's central ideas show striking affinities to specific claims in Kant's *Critique of Judgement,* a work that served as a fulcrum between Kant's Enlightenment roots and the romantic philosophers who followed in his wake. Chapter 2 opens with an exposition of Kant seen from the vantage point of Hannah Arendt's political reading of his aesthetics. My goal in this chapter is to draw from her reading themes that are central to Kant's version of the Enlightenment, themes that prove surprisingly topical when viewed and transformed in light of Mead's insights. In this chapter several of Mead's ideas, such as his concept of the generalized other and his claims about international-mindedness, are compared with Arendt's and Kant's views on *sensus communis* and the enlarged mentality of the cosmopolitan.

Mead's enlightened perspectivism not only parallels Arendt's and Kant's in important ways but also has certain affinities to Habermas's theory of communicative action. Turning to Habermas is natural at this juncture because his theory is indebted to Arendt and Kant and because he looks to Mead for support of his position. Specifically, chapter 3 addresses Habermas's reading of Mead, a reading that seeks to explain how modernity has contributed to the growth of individuation. Viewed by many as the most distinguished living champion of modernity's quest for universals, Habermas has been criticized for failing to do justice to the unique, in both cultural and individual terms. His reading of Mead is striking in this regard: The manner in which Habermas modifies Mead's position reveals a great deal about the limitations of his own work for coming to terms with various contemporary notions of community and irreducible individuality.

Habermas excessively formalizes Mead's position and misses the links between Mead's notion of the social subject, his Christian roots, and Adam Smith's concept of the impartial spectator. Mead's concept of universality, contra Habermas's reading, was not grounded in the formalisms of Kant's moral philosophy but in something much more like the direction in which Arendt moves Kant's *Critique of Judgement*. Her reading of the third *Critique* is in certain respects very close to positions found in Adam Smith's *The Theory of Moral Sentiments*. The connections here are intriguing. Presumably Kant was familiar with Smith, and the latter in all likelihood influenced Mead and Mead's contemporary, pioneering sociologist Charles H. Cooley. If my intuitions are correct, then what Arendt has managed to do is tease from Kant ideas that he may have drawn and modified from Smith. Thus the connection between Mead and the third *Critique* becomes all the more plausible.

Although I cannot hope to prove or provide a definitive account of these historical connections in this work, I hope they will interest the reader. However, what is most telling is not the direct historical connections, interesting as they may be. The philosophical importance of these connections lies in what their traditions represent and how they are being received and understood. Smith and Mead form an interesting pair in this regard in that they tend to approach questions of morality through the psychological and empirical, whereas Kant and Habermas seek transcendental ground. But although Smith clearly was a precritical thinker, Mead was not. The latter was quite familiar with German idealism and the philosophical currents that followed in its wake. As a matter of fact, Mead's social psychology reveals a certain kinship to such contemporary trends as neo-Hegelianism, communitarianism, and postmodernism, although it would be misleading to append any of these labels to him. For example, Mead would insist on a type of universality that would be unacceptable to many postmodernists. It is this notion of universality and its connection to pluralism that is illuminated when Mead is read in light of Smith, even if Mead remains something of a neo-Hegelian.

Having addressed ideas central to Mead's work and their connection to universalistic sensibilities stemming from the Enlightenment, I turn to challenges from Levinas, who is moved by very different ethical impulses. I suggest that Mead's understanding of individuality and particularity must confront the words of Søren Kierkegaard, Martin Buber, or Levinas to reveal whether and to what degree his project and pragmatism can speak to the dignity and uniqueness of the self and the other. Although there is little doubt that pragmatism—at least in its Deweyan and Meadian incarnations—has more to teach us about political transformations than does Levinas, what is at stake in such a confrontation is how we should view the relationship between the ethical, political, and individual. Or, to be more specific, what is at stake is how we are to understand pluralism and whether true pluralism is unalterably at odds with all forms of universalism. It is in this domain that Levinas poses a formidable challenge to Habermas and perhaps even to Mead. From Levinas's perspective, Mead's framework fuels and is fueled by violence, and the Kant of the third *Critique* feeds the same flames. One does not do the other a service by taking his or her perspective, as their work suggests; one transgresses, usurps, the transcendent otherness of the other in an act that is driven by ontological narcissism. We must see whether Mead and his version of universalism, one in which social and ethical life entails taking and appreciating the perspectives of others, can meet the challenges of such claims.

What is most striking about Western monotheism is how often the ethical has been viewed in terms of the singularity of the other. It is no accident, then, that postmodernists such as Jacques Derrida and Jean-François Lyotard have been intrigued by Emmanuel Levinas and that Levinas is not only a phenomenologist but a Jewish thinker. Western theology has no doubt provided grounds for believing in the importance of universalistic spiritual communities—for example, in the work of Hegel—but its prophets have time and again sought to remind us of the uniqueness of the individual, the otherness of the singular other, and have often done so in the name of God. Although many postmodernists would be loath to define their concern for the other in religious terms, the ethical impulses running through their work often bear a striking resemblance to those that can be considered religious. I do not prove that thesis in this book. Rather, I show that by engaging Levinas and Habermas, as well as Smith and Arendt, Mead's pragmatism can speak to the issues of pluralism, sociality, democracy, identity, and individuality that are at the core of much of our ethical and political lives. I hope that such an approach will widen the increasingly important dialogue between classic American philosophy and other vital traditions and sensibilities.

1 Mead and the Social Self

To introduce many of George Herbert Mead's most seminal ideas, I will explore a topical question: Was Mead a feminist? And I will use a letter Mead wrote to his daughter-in-law to provide an answer. I take this tack not only because it addresses an important contemporary issue but also because it frames Mead's philosophical and psychological insights in terms of his politics. It is impossible to appreciate fully the implications of Mead's approach to the social self, pluralism, and universalism without understanding the political dimensions of his thought, and this aspect of his thought has often been overlooked.[1] I hope that this route will entice those familiar with Mead the social psychologist to read yet one more account of his ideas. Mead's letter is an excellent point of entry into his thought because it contains several of his key terms and ideas in a setting that speaks to an important social issue of our day. Although it is possible that he was using these terms in a colloquial fashion, their juxtaposition and context suggest that his philosophical understanding of them was close at hand.

In 1920 George Herbert Mead, while on vacation in Honolulu, received word from his daughter-in-law, Irene Tufts Mead, that she had been warned against beginning her studies in medical school. The advice had come from her young son's pediatrician, who presumably held some old-fashioned views on maternity. The doctor's words, arriving with the birth of her first child, must have given rise to a good deal of consternation. Mead was not amused. He had long supported and worked for numerous progressive causes.[2] A close friend and colleague of Jane Addams,[3] he joined with her to oppose "the segregation of the sexes at the University of Chicago in 1902."[4] Mead had marched with suffragists and over the years had defended the contributions of harassed female colleagues.[5] When the time came to respond to his daughter-in-law, he could draw on a good deal of experience.

> First of all, in regard to Dr. Hoffman's views. The fundamentals in the matter I take to be the following:—for the most normal situation a woman as well as a man should have the training for a social calling apart from the family life, this for the sake of the best family life but principally for the independence of mind and self which every one legitimately craves.[6]

> Do not let the dependence on others which we all have for those whom we love carry with it intellectual dependence and you cannot have real intellectual independence, that which gives one the fundamental self respect on which one builds, without competence in some field of the society which is responsible for the very existence of ourselves. Cultural training never gives this—only training for a practical end.[7]

The specific advice Mead gave to his daughter-in-law was to attend medical school part-time. Although "society is not organized for this now . . . the fortunate situation in which you and Henry [Mead's son] find yourselves makes this more normal expression for a woman possible for you."[8] The fortunate situation seems to have been that they could afford servants. Irene Tufts Mead did go to medical school, took nine years to become a physician, and later studied with Carl Gustav Jung and practiced psychiatry in Chicago. One of the obvious points to be made in Mead's favor is that he was not engaging in an abstract discussion of women's rights; rather, he was telling the wife of his only son and the mother of his first grandchild that she should have a career.

As progressive as Mead's solution may have been in his day, it would not appeal to many contemporary feminists because Mead did not suggest that his son stay home part-time instead of his daughter-in-law. But if one examines the language of Mead's comments in light of his philosophy and social psychology, his response reveals a radically progressive approach to social issues, an approach that not only can be used to challenge questionable assumptions about sex and gender but may very well make an important contribution to feminist literature and political practice.[9]

Mead did not write a treatise on feminist theory, although he was actively involved in civic groups that sought to promote women's rights. He probably would not have thought it necessary to devise categories outside the ones he had developed in his philosophical and social psychological work to address the plight of women. This was not because he thought their plight unworthy of discussion—quite the contrary. But he would have argued that his categories could be used as conceptual and political tools to help overcome subjugation. Doing justice to the progressive possibilities of Mead's position entails coming to terms with much of his thought because so much of it is pertinent. One would also have to address how Mead might respond to contemporary feminist literature, from the neo-Freudian approaches to postmodern tracts.

Mead was a firm believer in what is often loosely described as participatory democracy. For democracy to flourish, Mead would tell us, society must recognize that it has an obligation to assist its citizens in the actualization of their potential. A society that does not is simply less than a just society. For Mead, it is also one that will fail to realize a truly democratic order, for such an order requires an active, flourishing, and engaged citizenry. Of course, these are the very sorts of general claims we might expect from many liberals writing in the context of twentieth-century U.S. politics. However, Mead has an intersubjective theory of mind and selfhood that can be used not only to ground aspects of liberal theory but to deepen and transform it. Yet he no doubt adhered to certain beliefs that we associate with liberalism. For example, Mead would not have hesitated to use the currently unfashionable term *progress* to describe what he thought we should work to achieve: "The obligation which the charitable individual feels is the demand that these restrictions [economic, feudal, and cultural class distinctions] should be removed. It is not a demand which society as it is now organized can enforce against him. It is a part of the growing consciousness that society is responsible for the ordering of its own processes and structure so that what are common goods in their very nature should be accessible to common enjoyment. We vaguely call it 'progress.'"[10]

In his letter to his daughter-in-law Mead asserts that there should be "training for a social calling apart from the family life, this for the sake of the best family life but principally for the independence of mind and self which every one legitimately craves." The terms *mind* and *self* have very specific and crucial meanings for Mead. Before turning to them, however, I would like to call attention to the phrase *social calling*. Mead was raised in a puritanical Christian household with long-standing academic affiliations. His father taught homiletics at Oberlin Theological Seminary; his mother served as president of Mount Holyoke College and taught at Oberlin College. Mead attended Oberlin, which in his day was becoming a hotbed for progressive ideas.[11] As a young man Mead seriously considered becoming a Christian social worker. In 1884 he wrote to his good friend Henry Castle about this option, "I shall have to let persons understand that I have some belief in Christianity and my praying be interpreted as a belief in God, whereas I have no doubt that now the most reasonable system of the universe can be formed to myself without a God. But notwithstanding all this I cannot go out with the world and not work for men. The spirit of a minister is strong with me and I come fairly by it."[12]

Mead's ameliorationist impulses remained with him through his many years as a professor at the University of Chicago and expressed itself in his involvement in city affairs. His interest in city life and politics was evident early in life. In another letter to his friend Castle he declared, "We must get into politics of course—city politics above all things, because there we can begin to work at once in whatever city we settle, because city politics need men more than any other branch, and chiefly because, according to my opinion, the immediate application of principles of corporate life—of socialism in America must start from the city."[13] And it may very well have been that his lifelong political and community involvements were in part responsible for the fact that with the exception of a coedited volume on vocational training, he never published a book.

When Mead refers to "the independence of mind and self which every one legitimately craves," mind and self must not be thought of as merely personal attributes, for they are social phenomena. Yet as we shall see, the social nature of the self does not deny the independence of individuals. For Mead, independence suggests not isolation from others but the self-respect and dignity that a social being acquires by virtue of the acknowledgment of others. To understand his concepts of mind and self, one must understand their genesis in linguistic interaction: "Mentality on our approach simply comes in when the organism is able to point out meanings to others and to himself. This is the point at which mind appears, or if you like, emerges. . . . It is absurd to look at the mind simply from the standpoint of the individual human organism; for, although it has its focus there, it is essentially a social phenomenon; even its biological functions are primarily social."[14]

Mead viewed mind as emerging through the use of gestures. Gestures are used by many species; for example, a dog growls at another dog and the second dog runs or growls back. In this context the first dog's growl is a gesture that means "run or growl back" because meaning is defined in terms of the responses that gestures elicit. But for human beings a different sort of gesture is possible because of our ability to vocalize and the sophistication of our nervous system. When using vocal gestures, human beings can hear themselves as others hear them. For example, say you are about to walk out in front of a moving car and I shout, "Stop!" I hear the vocal gesture as you do, and I tend to heed my own gesture. Thus I might feel myself stopping under the circumstances that prompted my gesture.

Mead tells us that "the critical importance of language in the development of human experience lies in this fact that the stimulus is one that can react upon the speaking individual as it reacts upon the other."[15] For language to evolve, one must be able to respond covertly or implicitly to a gesture as the other responds overtly or explicitly. It is by taking the position of the other, responding as the other does to vocal gestures, that one learns a language. And with language comes what Mead calls mind. It is worth noting that hand signs can serve the same function as vocal gestures; they allow individuals to see (and feel) their own gestures as they see the responses of others to their gestures. Gestures that can serve this reflexive function are called significant symbols.

> It is by means of reflexiveness—the turning back of the experience of the individual upon himself—that the whole social process is thus brought into the experience of the individuals involved in it; it is by such means, which enable the individual to take the attitude of the other toward himself, that the individual is able consciously to adjust himself to that process, and to modify the resultant of that process in any given social act in terms of his adjustment to it. Reflexiveness, then, is the essential condition, within the social process, for the development of mind.[16]

Mead subscribes, as do those in the German idealist tradition, to the centrality of the notion of reflexivity for comprehending the nature of mind. But he provides a new twist by arguing that we can give a social behaviorist account of how this capacity arises in linguistic interaction. To simplify matters for the purpose of introducing Mead's orientation, we can say that the anticipatory dimension of using vocal gestures is directly tied to a form of self-consciousness. By self-consciousness here I mean not an awareness of personhood or selfhood, which I discuss later, but an awareness of meaning, that is, an awareness of the possible responses to what one is saying. I can be said to be self-conscious in this sense when I am explicitly aware of the possible implications of my (linguistic) behavior, sufficiently aware of them, for example, to modify what I am saying or doing. The development of these sorts of linguistic skills allows what we call mind to arise. Mind itself must be understood as a social phenomenon that depends on communicative interaction for its development.

Obviously, many questions can be raised about Mead's social behaviorist account of the development of language and mind. There are structures and usages of language that some would claim Mead never adequately addressed.[17] For example, Habermas argues that Mead's model must be augmented if we are to understand how our ancestors moved from dealing in gestures that merely provided similar (functional) responses to stimuli to situations in which identities of meaning are established (in other words, I want to know that you understand a gesture in a way that is identical to my understanding, as opposed to merely responding in a similar manner to the gesture). To fully understand how this is possible, Habermas tells us that we must appeal to a notion of linguistic rules that define and confirm meaning as well as address the ways in which rules are generated. He believes that Wittgenstein's understanding of rules can be used to complement Mead's model, and Mead's approach can be of assistance in explaining their development.[18]

To generate identities of meaning, according to Habermas, individuals must have developed a facility for anticipating the responses of others and must have learned to take yes-or-no positions with regard to the actual responses of others. I must be able to say that you have or have not violated my expectation of a certain behavior, a certain response. And you must be able to do the same. In intersubjective give and take, in the testing entailed in the taking of yes-or-no positions toward expectations of behavior, identities of meaning arise in the context of evolving linguistic rules. Oral discourse is privileged over written discourse here, at least with regard to the evolution and maintenance of identities of meaning, for it seems that one can never question a text in quite the same way in which one can question and be questioned by another. (Of course, sophisticated grammatical structures allow certain presumptions of meaning with regard to written texts.)

Habermas notes that Mead fails to address the evolution of language from the (merely) symbolically mediated to the grammatically nuanced but instead "goes abruptly from symbolically mediated to normatively regulated action,"[19] in which the existence of language with sophisticated rules is presumed. And no doubt Mead appears interested in understanding the basic mechanisms of self-conscious language usage to move on to what holds the most interest for him: the complex social psychological, normative, and political life of human beings. The latter entails sets of attitudes that are not solely linguistic, and this proves to be an important source of difference between Mead and Habermas's theory of communicative action and the linguistic neo-pragmatism (or nominalist contextualism) of Rorty.[20]

Returning to the discussion of Mead's understanding of mind, we can say that mind entails an awareness of socially significant symbols and matures through their use. We develop the capacity to take the position or perspective of the other as we become linguistically capable creatures, and being able to take the position of the other with regard to linguistic symbols is a prerequisite for more complex sets of behaviors. These more complex sets, which may entail both nonverbal and verbal behaviors, are called roles by Mead: "The child says something in one character and responds in another character, and then his responding in another character is a stimulus to himself in the first character, and so the conversation goes on."[21] Roles are complex sets of responses that we can learn only by taking the position of the other, and in so doing we learn to anticipate what the other will do and what is expected of us.

Mead's account of gestures and role taking is only the beginning of his social analysis of the genesis of the self. Although we need specific others to learn to take specific roles, Mead tells us that we need a generalized other to have a self. Mead tries to explicate the distinction between mere roles and selfhood by talking about "the game." When involved in an organized game one learns more than roles; one learns to take the positions of the various players on the team and learns the implicit rules of the game that unify the activities of all agents. The well-known example Mead used was of a ball team, but this example can be somewhat misleading. As Mead explains it, "The organized community or social group which gives to the individual his unity of self may be called 'the generalized other.' The attitude of the generalized other is the attitude of the whole community. Thus, for example, in the case of such a social group as a ball team, the team is the generalized other in so far as it enters—as an organized process or social activity—into the experience of any one of the individual members of it."[22]

Perhaps it would be best to leave aside the sports analogy and emphasize that the generalized other arises when we internalize the expectations of an organized group. Groups of this sort can be thought of as systems. We are capable of viewing ourselves as part and parcel of these groups, and when we do so, selves emerge that correspond to them. Examples of such groups include "political parties, clubs, corporations,"[23] but they might also be families.

> In any co-operative process, such as the family, the individual calls out a response from the other members of the group. Now, to the extent that those responses can be called out in the individual so that he can answer to them, we have both those contents which go to make up the self, the "other" and the "I." The distinction expresses itself in our experience in what we call the recognition of others and the recognition of ourselves in the others. We cannot realize ourselves except in so far as we can rec-

ognize the other in his relationship to us. It is as he takes the attitude of the other that the individual is able to realize himself as a self.[24]

Through our interactions with others in a specific context, we arrive at a system of responses that unifies various roles. When we see our responses from the perspective of this unified group, we are said to be taking the position of the generalized other. By taking the position of the generalized other, we become aware of the unity of our behaviors; that is, we become conscious of having a self. For Mead, the self is a cognitive object that is viewed from the perspective of the generalized other. In short, selfhood and self-consciousness go hand in hand: "The self-conscious human individual, then, takes or assumes the organized social attitudes of the given social group or community (or of some one section thereof) to which he belongs . . . [and] he governs his own conduct accordingly."[25] This does not mean that one is always directly aware of having a self when functioning in a group. For Mead, much of our activity is nonreflective and habitual. I return to this theme later.

So Mead has us viewing ourselves not only from the perspective of an other but also from the perspective of groups that provide us with generalized others; what we view are selves that correspond to them. In a certain sense, then, individuals can be said to have more than one self because they participate in numerous communities that give rise to generalized others. This is by no means the end of the story. Mead suggests that some generalized others are more universal than others. Claims that these more universal communities make on us can (and should at times) override the claims of what he would describe as narrower and parochial communities. I return to the question of Mead's universalism later.

The self I have thus far described can be called a "me." But Mead also tells us that there is an "I," and at times he refers to the combination of the "I" and "me" as the self. The "I" is the home of the individual's novel responses and the source of one's awareness of the social "me." It is because there is an "I" that we can become self-consciously aware, that is, aware of having a "me." Although the "I" is a necessary presupposition of the "me," it is never presented directly in conscious experience.[26] "If you ask, then, where directly in your own experience the 'I' comes in, the answer is that it comes in as a historical figure. It is what you were a second ago that is the 'I' of the 'me.' It is another 'me' that has to take that rôle. You cannot get the immediate response of the 'I' in the process."[27]

If the "me" is thought of as an empirical ego that one can be aware of, then the "I" can be viewed as its transcendental counterpart, for we presuppose an "I" as a "source" of activity and awareness. In one place

Mead even says, "The 'I' is the transcendental self of Kant."[28] However, almost in the same breath he adds, "The self-conscious, actual self in social intercourse is the objective 'me' or 'me's' with the process of response continually going on and implying a fictitious 'I' always out of sight of himself."[29] Kant would never have considered referring to the transcendental ego as fictitious.

Despite possible parallels to the transcendental versus empirical dichotomy, it must be emphasized that Mead treats the "I" and "me" as functional distinctions, not ontological ones. Together they describe what he calls the personality, although he sometimes calls their combination the self, as mentioned earlier. Following William James's analysis of the stream of consciousness, Mead understands them as phases of experience so that the "I" is not a transcendental subject "behind" the "me" and somehow ontologically different from it.[30] If the "me" is thought of as the phase of experience that is socially constituted, then the "I" is the phase that responds to this social constitution through impulses and novel responses that use previously learned repertoires of behavior.[31] If the "me" is understood as directed to the past and the just-past present, then the "I" is directed to the future, although it must draw on the past and present in its spontaneous responses. Furthermore, "the 'I' gives the sense of freedom, of initiative. The situation is there for us to act in a self-conscious fashion. We are aware of ourselves, and of what the situation is, but exactly how we will act never gets into experience until after the action takes place."[32]

Mead's introduction of the "I" helps prevent him from falling into an overly socialized conception of personality because one can never fully determine one's responses to social situations based on previous behaviors. Responses have varying degrees of novelty. I may have made a certain play in a ball game many times or I may have driven my car along a road many times, but even in these activities some degree of novelty intrudes, and my responses this time around are not exactly like my prior ones. In most circumstances, however, my present responses can be viewed as functional equivalents of earlier ones, that is, as the same responses. Habermas uses Mead's notion of the "I" to help explain modern processes of individuation, and I address the nature of the "I" again when I turn to his interpretation of Mead in chapter 3. In later chapters I also address features of Mead's model that should offer a richer account of the individual than has thus far been presented. However, an additional aspect of the individual warrants mention here.

No doubt Mead was a naturalist. Yet his naturalism is laced with a commitment to the existential. The latter dimension manifests itself in a passage in which Mead addresses what he calls the biologic individual. It is a rather striking passage because it shows that even when directly appealing to the biological, Mead is not presenting a reductionist vision.

> This immediate experience which is reality, and which is the final test of the reality of scientific hypotheses as well as the test of the truth of all our ideas and suppositions, is the experience of what I have called the "biologic individual." The term refers to the individual in an attitude and at a moment in which the impulses sustain an unfractured relation with the objects around him. . . . I have termed it "biologic" because the term lays emphasis on the living reality which may be distinguished from reflection. A later reflection turns back upon it and endeavors to present the complete interrelationship between the world and the individual in terms of physical stimuli and biological mechanism; the actual experience did not take place in this form but in the form of unsophisticated reality.[33]

This passage reveals a thinker whose naturalism would be seriously misunderstood without an appreciation for his sensitivity to experience. The latter sensitivity, one that he shares with John Dewey and William James, bears comparison with thinkers who have been called existentialists.[34]

The "I" is not an afterthought for Mead but follows from deeply held convictions about nature. He argues time and again that novelty is part of the fabric of the universe and can be observed in the evolution of life, for example. That human beings give novel responses to stimuli is a fact that can be observed and studied.[35] As we have seen, he goes so far as to suggest that we can never be absolutely certain how we will respond to a stimulus until after we have done so. The uncertainty here is not simply caused by ignorance but follows from the nature of the human organism and the worlds it inhabits. Furthermore, Mead tells us that natural and social worlds are made up of dynamic systems that undergo transformation. In fact, the "me" should be viewed as a type of system, which may undergo transformation due to the I's novel responses.

Mead appeals to what he calls sociality to characterize a crucial feature of the transformations that occur when novelty is introduced into an established system. For example, if one has a functioning ecosystem and there is a mutation of an existing organism, the old system may be transformed through the endurance of this emergent organism. If it is transformed, then there must be a period between the old and the new systems. Sociality is the phase between the systems, when an emergent has one foot in the old and another in the new: "If emergence is a feature of reality this phase of adjustment, which comes between the ordered universe before the emergent has arisen and that after it has come to terms with the newcomer, must be a feature also of reality."[36]

For Mead, there is no question that emergence and sociality are prevalent in nature. But with the advent of the human social world a curious thing occurs. There is now an organism who has the capacity to reflect on its own sociality and the sociality of the world around it. In so doing it recognizes that not only does it take various perspectives—which is another way of saying that it inhabits different systems—but that a good deal of its life is spent moving between perspectives or learning new ones. And new perspectives are not just added arithmetically to a prior repertoire; coming to terms with them often entails modifying prior systems (i.e., who we were). This is a common experience that occurs, for example, when a role we have taken (e.g., that of the parent of one child) must be redefined in the face of a new situation (e.g., the birth of a second child). In this case the family, viewed as a system of relationships, has undergone a transformation, and so has our place in it. Much of our experience takes place as situations change and "me" systems are modified or as we move from one established "me" system to the another (i.e., from one perspective to another).

Human beings have learned how to use the in-betweenness of sociality to buy themselves time to reflect on changes that confront them. The in-betweenness of sociality can be thought of as a space that arises with the advent of novel events and allows the possibility of new reactions to these novel events before they have solidified into some new system.[37] The "I" gives us a "sense of freedom, of initiative"; it can do so because it responds in novel ways. Individuals can then reflect on these responses in the space of sociality and decide whether to accept or modify them.[38] If imagination can be thought of as a condition for the possibility of critical judgments for Hannah Arendt, in that it allows us to distance ourselves from the immediacy of the present and the undue influence of those around us, sociality can be said to perform a parallel function for Mead.[39] Because there is sociality, even ordinary folk can avoid being consigned to Nietzsche's unthinking herd.

So central are the terms *mind* and *self* to Mead's worldview that it is difficult to believe that his invocation of them in his letter to his daughter-in-law did not have deep resonances for him. We have seen that for Mead, without others and language the development of mind would be impossible, and without organized social groups selves would not emerge. One might wonder why family life would not have been enough to satisfy his daughter-in-law's need for a self, especially because I suggested earlier that a family might be viewed as a system with its own generalized other. Why couldn't Mead simply have suggested that she stay at home to have independence of mind and self?

Part of the answer lies in understanding the historical currents Mead had to contend with at the University of Chicago. As Mary Jo Deegan points out, there was a strong push at the University of Chicago during Mead's tenure to change coeducational classes to segregated ones, a move he resisted.[40] The ideological underpinning for the segregation of male and female students was the doctrine of separate spheres.

> Women were expected to remain within their "special sphere," even though educated in an advanced manner. This "Doctrine of the Separate Spheres" was the dominant attitude towards women's place in society at this time. Each sex was expected to be distinct. Women "managed" the home, emotions, culture, morality, and children. Men "governed" the family, social and political institutions, especially the economy, and were more rational than women. Thus Chicago made a forward step by including women within the university structure, but retained its belief in a "separate sphere" for women within this structure.[41]

Mead had to endure colleagues who supported the doctrine of separate spheres and the segregation of the sexes. More congenial to his taste, and to many of his colleagues who were pragmatists, must have been social planners and social scientists who expressed an interest in finding new scientific paths to help improve interpersonal relationships and the management of the household. From Mead's vantage point, women who were "persuaded" to remain traditional mothers could lose out on two fronts: They would be cut off from opportunities for personal growth found in nontraditional careers (or spheres), and they might be turned into merely passive recipients of scientific developments (or even miss out on them altogether). It is with these concerns in mind that we must evaluate Mead's remarks to his daughter-in-law. He advised, "It is a difficult thing you are undertaking but worthwhile things are all difficult. Being a wife and a mother is no longer a calling in itself, because the exercise of intelligence in those activities has passed out of the home and involves scientific method at every point. You must be a part of this intellectual world to which this method belongs, or you must accept the judgments of others without feeling competent to criticize them."[42] Mead follows these words with the previously quoted remark on intellectual independence, in which he mentions the need for "competence in some field of the society which is responsible for the very existence of ourselves." One reaction to Mead's reference to the scientific method might be to view him as a parochial positivist who wants his daughter-in-law to be in tune with the powers that be. However, Mead's understanding of science was decidedly nonpositivistic and closely linked to his views on the nonhierarchical nature of democracy. He viewed the scientific method not as an esoteric methodology but as an extension of day-to-day problem solving, reflective thought. For Mead, reflection is a mode of thought that is directly linked to our ability take various perspectives, and one uses the perspectival nature of mind when solving problems at hand. The modern world has given rise to a methodical deployment of this capacity in science. "Scientific method . . . is nothing but a highly developed form of impartial intelligence," Mead argues. "[It] is not teleological in the sense of setting up a final cause that should determine our action, but it is as categorical in insisting upon our considering all factors in problems of conduct, as it is in demanding the recognition of all of the data that constitute the research problem."[43] Mead's view of science would call on practitioners to reflect on their personal investments in paradigms and modes of operation.

For Mead, the sciences are clearly social activities closely affiliated with many other kinds of social activities. When properly used and understood in terms of his perspectivism, the scientific method is an inherently democratic one. Mead's good friend John Dewey put it well when he wrote, "No scientific inquirer can keep what he finds to himself or turn it to merely private account without losing his scientific standing. Everything discovered belongs to the community of workers. . . . The scientific attitude is experimental as well as intrinsically communicative. If it were generally applied, it would liberate us from the heavy burden imposed by dogmas and external standards."[44] That the practitioners of science have not always lived up to Mead's and Dewey's expectations goes without saying, and we must leave open here the question of whether all the sciences can be understood as extensions of common skills. But Mead's attitude toward science allows us to begin to understand how he could link his daughter-in-law's well-being to the claim that she "must be a part of this intellectual world." Yet to fully understand Mead's remark, another aspect of his thought must be introduced.

Mead was a dedicated internationalist. No doubt he was led to this position in part through his early commitment to certain religious and moral ideals. Jane Addams may also have had some influence on Mead's commitments.[45] He argued that because of numerous factors in the modern world, such as the increasingly interdependent nature of the modern economies, enhanced possibilities for contact and communication with others, and the growing self-destructive nature of modern warfare, international-mindedness would eventually become the wave of the future. "We all belong to small cliques," Mead observed, "and we may remain simply inside of them. The 'organized other' present in ourselves is then a community of a narrow diameter. We are struggling now to get a certain amount of international-mindedness. We are realizing ourselves as members of a larger community. The vivid nationalism of the present period should, in the end, call out an international attitude of the larger community."[46]

When Mead says to Irene Tufts Mead that she "must be a part of this intellectual world," he is concerned about her personal growth and not merely about the fragility of her position in terms of the power held by the practitioners of science. Certainly he wants her to be able to respond when criticized. However, this is not simply a statement about power relations. Credible responses to criticism require that we become aware of more expansive communities. "The only way in which we can react against the disapproval of the entire community is by setting up a higher sort of community which in a certain sense out-votes the one we find," Mead observed.[47] Because selves correspond to communities, to be cut off from wider communities, such as an international community of the scientifically minded, is to be blocked from the realization of one's potential (i.e., the self one could become). It is to be isolated in a separate sphere. It is to be cut off from the kind of enlarged mentality that helps one place one's own situation in perspective, which, as discussed in the next chapter, Hannah Arendt strongly advocates.[48] These wider communities should be understood in terms of generalized others that are more inclusive, and they can be more inclusive because they operate at higher levels of abstraction. Generalized others can be thought of as connected with groups such as "political parties, clubs, corporations," but they can also be thought of in terms of more abstract groups, such as classes of creditors and debtors.[49] An individual's participation in several abstract groups can lead to

> definite social relations (however indirect) with an almost infinite number of other individuals . . . cutting across functional lines of demarcation which divide different human social communities from one another, and including individual members from several (in some cases from all) such communities. Of these abstract social classes or subgroups of human individuals the one which is most inclusive and extensive is, of course, the one defined by the logical universe of discourse (or system of universally significant symbols) determined by the participation and communicative interaction of individuals.[50]

Instead of the generalized other of, for example, a ball team or a family, we can have generalized others (and selves) that correspond to complex ethical or political systems of interaction. As Mead explains, "In the community there are certain ways of acting under situations which are essentially identical, and these ways of acting on the part of anyone are those which we excite in others when we take certain steps. If we assert our rights, we are calling for a definite response just because they are rights that are universal—a response which everyone should, and perhaps will, give."[51] But we cannot assert our rights unless we are viewed and view ourselves as active participants in the communities that observe these rights. The doctrine of separate spheres is a threat to just this sort of participation. Needless to say, such a doctrine would violate Mead's egalitarian impulses, which are directly linked to his commitment to the actualization of everyone's socially redeemable potentialities. However, given Mead's commitment to the latter, he could easily defend voluntary segregation (e.g., at a woman's college) if it contributed to individual development (e.g., by building self-confidence and critical skills). But such segregation would be a means for Mead, never an end in itself, never an excuse for permanent separate spheres.

For Mead, as for Habermas, greater socialization leads to more, not less, individuation.[52] Membership in various groups enhances one's individuality by increasing the range of one's experience. Modern democracy's promise is that it will provide these new possibilities for self-development, not for the few but for the many.

> It is often assumed that democracy is an order of society in which those personalities which are sharply differentiated will be eliminated, that everything will be ironed down to a situation where everyone will be, as far as possible, like everyone else. But of course this is not the implication of democracy; the implication of democracy is rather that the individual can be as highly developed as lies within the possibilities of his own inheritance, and still can enter into the attitudes of the others whom he affects.[53]

To keep Irene Tufts Mead at home would have been to deny her the self that was clearly within society's (and therefore her) powers. Mead would have viewed such an occurrence as a form of injustice, for readily realizable potentials were being denied. Like Marx, Mead drew on a set of Aristotelian assumptions about the relationship between potency and act.[54] In the democratized hands of Mead and (especially the young) Marx, the relationship between potency and act was articulated in terms that allowed them to condemn societies that prevented the actualization of socially redeemable potentialities.

Before moving on to address in more detail Mead's notion of the generalized other, I would like to offer a modification of Mead's approach, one that is in keeping with the tenor of his position and may help to answer the question of whether he was a feminist. As self-conscious, perspectively oriented creatures, human beings become aware not only of the selves they experience in terms of generalized others but also of the limits and privations they suffer in relation to current historical possibilities. In so doing they can define themselves in terms of what they perceive as denied and absent. And these perceptions can provide a certain kind of selfhood, one that looks to what one could become.[55] As we will see in chapter 2, if Arendt were to address this process she would want to bring in the notion of imagination, that which can make the absent present. In making the absent present, solidarity with like-minded individuals becomes possible through an awareness of shared deprivations.

Before proceeding, however, I should note the obvious danger here. Women have long been defined in terms of what they lack, especially in relation to men. And many voices have sought to avoid approaches that are grounded in this assumption. But part of the problem lies in who is determining what potentials are unfulfilled and what is lacking. Also, I am not suggesting that the only path to solidarity is through deprivations. It is one of a number of live options, as William James might say.

There are a number of interesting advantages to seeing one's self in terms of privations. First, it provides solidarity with others in terms of demonstrable and shared inequities. Even in the face of disagreements— for example, over the degree to which gender and sex overlap or over the notion that gender is solely a linguistic construct—individuals can still feel a sense of shared selfhood in relationship to a perceived lack. Political action thrives on such perceptions.

Second, it highlights differences that make a difference, as pragmatists might say, in part by readily confirming some very down-to-earth intuitions about differences between men and women and among women. The time-worn question of whether there can be male feminists, for example, can easily be put to the test here. Women, and various groups of women (e.g., black and Latina women), can genuinely claim that in one sense men (and other women) cannot experience what they are experiencing. The felt privations that help define the selves of members of particular groups are uniquely their own. They are their own because of present-day circumstances, that is, because of how people relate to specific generalized others (or their absence), and also because selves have histories. One doesn't necessarily forget the felt privations of one's past even when these privations are overcome. So in this sense no man can ever be a feminist.

But given the multiplicity of selves and aspects of selves that exist in the modern world, and the breadth of certain generalized others, individuals participate in groups whose domains overlap. People belong to different political parties or work for different corporate entities, but there are generalized modes of action that members of these organizations follow that are similar and interchangeable. There are patterns and selves that can be shared at different levels of abstraction, and these are (seemingly) becoming more prevalent in the modern world. Mead would tell us that we can and often do learn how to operate within these different levels of social abstraction.

Although I may not have experienced your specific form of privation, I may have experienced something analogous, and I can see it as analogous because I can abstract from the particulars of my situation. I have learned how to abstract (in part) from the activity and experience of taking the positions of a multitude of generalized others and through learning how to manage the transitions between them. In the process I may have had my own experiences of forced privation or at least have developed a capacity to sympathize with those who have had them[56] (I imagine what it would be like if . . . ; in Arendt's terms, I enlarge my mentality). I come to appreciate how it feels to be arbitrarily denied and to understand the danger that such arbitrariness would pose for my own development and, hence, the development of any individual. In this sense men can indeed be feminists. And George Herbert Mead was surely in such a circle.

———

Before turning to Arendt's reading of Kant and its ties to Mead, I would like to address more fully the links between the generalized other, community, and universality. To do so I call on the work of a group of thinkers known as systematic pluralists, who in turn owe a great deal to the insights of Richard McKeon.[57] According to the work of Walter Watson and David Dilworth, there are four basic levels at which authors and texts must be examined if we are to make clear-headed comparisons between them.[58] We should investigate authorial voice, method, ontological focus, and governing purpose or principle. To focus on texts in this manner seemingly inverts the deconstructionist paradigm. Texts are seen to function in terms of principles that guide or work through signifiers, as opposed to being at their mercy. No doubt there are dangers in drawing on metaphilosophical orientations of this sort, such as ahistoricism. But they can serve legitimate pedagogical ends if their limitations are recognized. For heuristic purposes only I appeal to Watson's and Dilworth's notion of authorial voice.

Texts can be written in four basic voices according to this model.[59] Dilworth summarizes the four voices as follows:

> *Personal.* This is the self-referent, idiocentric presence of an author or authors—in the first person singular or plural—that shapes his world view. . . . *Objective.* This authorial perspective dispassionately observes the world's objects and their practical effects. . . . *Diaphanic.* This is the standard voice of religious texts. It bears witness to a higher wisdom or the revelation of an absolute knowledge. . . . *Disciplinary.* The disciplinary perspective presupposes an ideal community of like-minded readers; it typically takes the form of the first person plural.[60]

Much ink has been spent in recent years debating whether Mead was actually a hard-headed scientist, using an objective perspective as did Peirce, or whether he was more of a Jamesian, biased to the personal and idiosyncratic.[61] (In the latter case he would be seen as emphasizing the importance of the "I" over the "me.") I suggest that there are indeed elements of both present in his thought depending on which Mead you are reading: the more scientifically attuned pieces emphasizing social behaviorism or those stressing the dynamics and importance of spontaneity in the life of an individual and culture.

But both of these readings miss the mark. Mead's real bias, if we are talking of authorial voice, is in the direction of a disciplinary perspective: expert knowledge and communities of knowers and interpreters.[62] Although he sings the praises of the scientific method, which appears to suggest an objective perspective, a closer reading reveals that often he is only talking about a general method of problem solving. When we actually look to different subject matters, we find that there must be different approaches. Consider the following:

> The difference between the physicist and the biologist evidently lies in the goals which their sciences contemplate, in the realities they are seeking. And their procedure answers to their goals.[63]

> Outside this field of appreciation and criticism, the method of study in the field of the humanities is just as scientific *as the subject-matter with which it deals allows.* . . . The ideal of modern education is the solution of problems, the research method. And this research method is no less

dominant in the humanities than it is in the natural sciences *so far as the subject-matter permits.*"[64]

The phrase "so far as the subject-matter permits" is just the sort of qualification one would expect from someone attuned to a disciplinary perspective, as was Aristotle, the preeminent disciplinary voice of his day. But it is not only the voice in Mead's texts or his way of thinking about "specialists" that is worth noting. What is really interesting here is the connection between the voice of his texts and the way in which he sees and describes the social world, particularly his analysis of the generalized other. The generalized other orders our experience in terms of groups, and we become cognizant of ourselves in terms of groups. We speak (or eventually must speak) with the voice of a group when we communicate in a self-conscious fashion—which means that we speak to recognizable audiences—and this holds true for scientific matters. Of course, generalized others may undergo transformation, but this need not lead to the purely personal or idiosyncratic, for they are then reconstituted as new disciplinary voices. In Mead's terms, an "I" transforms a "me," but we become aware of the work of the transforming "I" only through the new (social) "me" that arises.

The fact that we are dealing with groups and perspectives does not eliminate the possibility of a form of universalism for Mead. Recall that for Mead significant symbols arise in the interactions of agents. Symbols become universals for him because they can be shared, but they do not actually have to be shared by everyone to be universals. "But signification is not confined to the particular situation within which an indication is given. It acquires universal meaning. Even if the two [individuals] are the only ones involved [in using a symbol], the form in which it is given is universal—it would have the same meaning to any other *who might find himself in the same position.*"[65] We can call universals of this type functional universals, and their universality rests on the fact that they are shared and can potentially be shared by any one else "who might find himself in the same position." There is a deep connection between Mead's view of the capacity of symbols to be universals and his form of political universalism. This subject is addressed in chapters 2 and 3. Here we can say that Mead understands universals and uses them in a fashion that clearly suggests his disciplinary orientation, which views the world in terms of "we" who define terms—not subjectively—but in a manner that would be true for anyone who can stand in our place. It is the perspective of groups, groups that are skilled at interacting with the world in particular ways and organized in terms of generalized others.

The very nature of functional universals is such that they raise for their users the possibility of being shared in wider circles. This claim doesn't necessarily suggest an imperialism of usage—quite the contrary. It calls on us to remain open to the manner in which others use signs and asks us to anticipate and consider their perspectives in evaluating meanings. It suggests that meanings (and attitudes) are potentially available for everyone. Of course, this possibility is an idealization. But it is grounded in the manner in which (at least certain types of) similarities of meaning are generated.

Communities, whether they are seen in political or scientific terms, define themselves by a common voice, the voice of a generalized other. Scientific communities define themselves in terms of the common perspectives of the different sciences—for example, biology, sociology, and physics—and knowledge is understood in terms of the perspectives of the investigators. Because it is so understood, there is more knowledge, not less. The reason for this is that limits are seen here as allowing richer experience by revealing what would not have been seen without them.[66] (This by no means denies the possibility of disciplinary cross-fertilization. For Mead, limits are not impenetrable boundaries. Perspectives can be shared. New disciplines can emerge. After all, he was a preeminent interdisciplinary thinker.[67]) It is also worth noting that the notion that limits provide fuller insight into the world, as opposed to somehow violating it through essentialist structures, extends far outside the scientific domain. Communities live through their generalized others, their defining limits, for Mead. The issue, then, is whether this manner of seeing the world enriches or violates (or perhaps sometimes enriches and sometimes violates) the other according to fixed and arbitrary categories.[68]

Mead, no doubt, would not have seen himself as a defender of totality and a despoiler of the other. He clearly would have wanted to claim that it is wrong for social groups to violate the reality of others simply because they possess enough power to do so. The question is, of course, on what grounds it is wrong. One obvious objection Mead would make, though by no means the only one, is that such a course would eliminate possible perspectives for understanding and appreciating the world; in short, it would reduce the realizable potentialities of humanity. More abstract groupings should not seek to eliminate the more restricted voices but should maintain them as the means through which individuals can hear aspects of themselves and thus continue to be or become themselves. Mead would have defended this right on both ethical and political grounds. Serious difficulties are raised by the existence of groups that believe that their survival depends on excluding others or who believe that the very existence of other groups and universally minded folk is a nonnegotiable threat to their way of life that must be defeated. I cannot hope to do justice to these concerns in the context of this chapter. But I hope that I have at least begun to show how Mead's international-mindedness was not a call to do away with difference per se but to find commonalities that would allow diversity to flourish in a nonthreatening fashion.

In one respect communication for Mead is limited by the generalized others that help constitute the self. We must speak through group voices if we are to be heard and if we are to remain intelligible. But groups are increasingly less isolated. The assumption of growing collective interdependence that allows truly international sorts of communities to arise is basic to Mead's vision. There will be increased interaction in the years to come, and new skills and forms of communication will have to develop to meet new needs. We will have to learn to take the perspective of the other more frequently.[69] International-mindedness will go hand in hand with new and often wider-ranging (disciplinary) perspectives. Again we see that Mead looked forward to concrete conditions conspiring to fulfill his prescriptive aspirations.

Mead was aware of the importance and power of nationalism.[70] He lived through World War I, and he knew that nation-states would not disappear in the foreseeable future. As a matter of fact, the problem of nationalism was in part a problem of insecure national identities for him. "For at this period of the world's history there is no point of national honor and peculiar interest which is not open to reasonable negotiation in a community of self-respecting nations as any of the so-called justiciable and negotiable issues, if we were sure of ourselves. But we are not sure of our national selves. . . . We cannot attain international-mindedness until we have attained a higher degree of national-mindedness than we possess at present."[71]

Until nations and other social groups are allowed to determine and define their own voices, speak their own interests, we will continue to live in a world of parochialism that breeds hostility, not international-mindedness. The growth of universality in international terms depends on the flourishing of particular social groups, whose interests must be acknowledged. For Mead, particularists need not fear his sort of universalism, but they had best keep a wary eye on their parochial neighbors. The nature of Mead's universalism, and whether it truly has a human face, is explored in the pages ahead.

2 Judgment and Universality in Arendt's Kant and Mead

We have seen that Mead links his vision of the self's genesis through taking the perspective of others to a political agenda that supports democracy and a form of cosmopolitanism. For Mead, both democracy and international-mindedness depend on a capacity to move from one's own concerns to more generalized interests. This capacity originates in our ability to situate ourselves in relation to other individuals and different social groups. In learning to pass from one perspective to another, we avoid the potentially parochial confines of an isolated perspective. But cosmopolitanism cannot simply be a matter of wearing many different hats. And democracy cannot simply be a matter of stepping into the other individual's shoes. Presumably both also entail a capacity for political and moral judgment that can transcend an uncritical relativism, that is, an uncritical movement from one perspective to another. Citizens of the state and world must be able to evaluate and judge, for without the latter Plato's vision of democracy triumphs. Hence, we are brought to a central theme of this book: the relationship between pluralism, universalism, and good judgment and their connection to a democratically inclined social self.

Good judgment in political and ethical matters, as well as fair judgment, appears to entail some degree of impartiality. If one is buried too deeply in his or her own concerns, one cannot achieve sufficient perspective on the given to evaluate reasonably courses of action or the words of others. Some traditions have thought of impartiality in terms of a spectator who can stand outside his or her own interests to avoid being influenced by them. And this sort of spectator's position seems to breed a kind of universalism, the view from nowhere that is for everyone. However, pragmatists do not believe that individuals can be expected to distance themselves from their own interests to this degree, and they criticize spectator models of knowledge and politics. Yet there must be some degree of impartiality, not only in our judgments but in our relationships with others, for without it we would not be able to move beyond the confines of our most immediate and pressing concerns to the concerns of others and to society at large.

Mead was convinced that without a concern for and a sensitivity to the interests of others, true democracy becomes impossible. Democracy depends on political dialogue to inform and assist actors in selecting courses of action, and dialogue rests on a willingness of citizens to engage the opinions of others and not simply dismiss them. Totally egocentric actors, if one could imagine such individuals, would fail at this engagement. Such actors would not be able to take the perspective of others, except perhaps in a purely strategic fashion.[1] In other words, pragmatists such as Mead and Dewey insist that any true democracy needs a sense of community to flourish. We need some form of impartiality for good judgment and for engaging others, and democracy needs both good judgment and engagement if it is to survive.

Mead surely thought that good judgment in social and political matters was possible. He would argue that good judgment—which depends in large measure on the ability to critique the given—is situated in a specific social and historical context. But this should not be understood to mean that good judgment is determined by the status quo. How then are we to understand the genesis of good judgment, which is historically situated and yet must allow a critique of the unexamined? In this chapter I explore Arendt's answer to this question. In chapter 3 I address how Habermas understands the nature of the critical posture, which for him must be understood in terms of reason. In both chapters we will see just how close Arendt and Habermas are to Mead and where they differ. In the process I clarify Mead's orientation to the question of good judgment, which entails elucidating his understanding of the relationship between universalism and pluralism. Many of the differences between these thinkers—Mead, Arendt, Kant, and Habermas—can be understood in terms of the degree to which an agent must be an impartial spectator in order to be a critical or moral actor. These chapters are followed by a challenge from Levinas, for whom appeals to universality deny the uniqueness of the individual and for whom impartiality must be absolute in the moral

realm. We will want to ask whether a democratic temper can be founded on his form of moral absolutism.

This chapter begins with an account of Arendt's reading of Kant on
judgment; it then introduces Smith's notion of the impartial spectator,
addresses Mead's position on universality, and finally contrasts Arendt
and Mead on judgment and impartiality. After the latter comparison there
is a brief excursus on Derrida, Mead, and Kant.

One would be very hard pressed to place Hannah Arendt, who influenced Habermas and was a dedicated student of Kant, in any of the
so-called postmodern camps. Yet she focuses a good deal of energy on
challenging one of postmodernism's worst nightmares, the metanarrative,
and defending her own version of one of its icons, the unique. In addition, she is as skeptical as many postmodernists about the implications
of certain accounts of the idea of progress. For Arendt, Kant was not
merely an advocate of perpetual progress; he was also the sober thinker
who recognized the dangers that the idea of the march of history presented
to the integrity of the individual.

> In Kant himself there is this contradiction: Infinite Progress is the law
> of the human species; at the same time, man's dignity demands that he
> be seen (every single one of us) in his particularity and, as such, be seen—
> but without any comparison and independent of time—as reflecting
> mankind in general. In other words, the very idea of progress—if it is more
> than a change in circumstances and an improvement of the world—con-
> tradicts Kant's notion of man's dignity. It is against human dignity to
> believe in Progress.[2]

George Herbert Mead's work, like Arendt's on Kant, can be read as
an attempt to grapple with the relationship of the unique to the general
or universal. Although Arendt's Heideggerian and classical predilections
place many of her sensibilities in a very different world from those of
Mead the pragmatist, there are a number of intriguing points of conver-
gence; for example, they both emphasize individual initiative and pluralism. As a matter of fact, so basic are the latter themes for their work
that we cannot begin to appreciate either Arendt's or Mead's political
views without appealing to them. Richard Bernstein tells us that for
Arendt,

> Human plurality is the basic condition of action and speech; without this
> plurality, there could not be any action or speech. By human plurality
> Arendt does not merely mean that there is "otherness," that there is

something that thwarts one's desires, ambitions, passions, or goals. Rather there is a unique distinctiveness about each and every human individual. . . . It is a potentiality which is to be actualized—a potentiality rooted in what is distinctive about the human condition—the capacity to begin, to initiate, to act.[3]

There is much in this passage that Mead would have found congenial, for creative activity was a central theme in his work.[4] Additional points of comparison will surface once we have examined Arendt's interpretation of Kant's *Critique of Judgement*.

Arendt passed away before she could write the third part of the *Life of the Mind*, which was to deal with judgment. So in lieu of this work we must draw on her posthumously published lectures, as well as her essays, for her position on Kant and judgment. My intent in this section is not to provide a definitive analysis of Arendt's understanding of judgment, which given the complexity of the issues involved, as well as the tensions in her own thought, would require a work unto itself.[5] Nor is it my intent to provide a critique or a defense of her position at this juncture. Several of my reservations are woven into discussions later in this chapter. Rather, my goal is to provide a commentary on Arendt's work that suggests connections to several of Mead's most compelling ideas and political insights.

The *Critique of Judgement* is clearly one of the most curious works in history of Western thought. Notorious for its repetitiveness and for what appears to be Kant's ad hoc use of his own architectonic sensibilities—as well as for the awkward attempt to locate what some have viewed as separate works (on teleological and aesthetic judgment) under one cover—it nevertheless has had a profound influence on a number of distinguished thinkers, most notably in the German idealist tradition. Its impact has not been confined to the circles of professional philosophers; Goethe, for instance, was moved by the manner in which the work reconciled the natural and aesthetic worlds.[6] Although some have viewed it as the unedited ramblings of an old man, noted thinkers, such as Cassirer, have argued that it extends and deepens the work of the earlier *Critiques*.[7] Of course, it is also a seminal work in field of aesthetics.

Hannah Arendt thought that she had found in the third *Critique* the missing core of the political philosophy that Kant never developed. Woven into his analysis of taste were compelling insights uniquely suited for application to the political realm, such as those regarding plurality, impartiality, and dialogue. Perhaps the foremost of these were his views on the relationship of the particular to the universal. Instead of subsuming particulars under universals in determinant judgments, in the man-

ner of the first *Critique,* the third *Critique* sought to respect the particular as particular—for example, the beauty of *this* flower—in what Kant
called reflective judgments. As opposed to depending on an approach that
subsumes particulars under general rules, the third *Critique* promoted a
method of reflection that could move from the particular to the universal (or to the general, in Arendt's preferred translation of *allgemein*).[8] The
particular is not to be addressed by humbling it before the general or
universal but by treating it, as well as the processes of communication
necessary to confirm the validity of universals, as worthy of respect in
their own right. Yet it must be emphasized that reflective judgments do
not make idiosyncratic claims; rather, they make universalistic ones for
Kant and generalizable ones for Arendt.[9] This particular flower, if it is
beautiful, must be beautiful for all, according to Kant.[10] That I can appreciate its beauty is because I possess taste, and taste—good taste—is
clearly not personal. Richard Bernstein succinctly summarizes what is
at stake:

> Taste is a kind of *sensus communis*. It is a "community sense"—the
> sense which fits us into human community. What Arendt is struggling
> to discriminate and isolate for us is a mode of thinking that is not to be
> identified with the expression of private feelings, nor to be confused with
> the type of universality characteristic of cognitive reason. It is a mode
> of thinking which is capable of dealing with the particular in its partic-
> ularity but which nevertheless makes the claim to communal validity.
> *For this is precisely the mode of thinking that is essential to political
> life.*[11]

Turning to Section 40 of the *Critique of Judgement* may be of some
assistance here, for it addresses a number of points that help to clarify
Kant's approach to taste and Arendt's claims about the merits of the third
Critique. In this section Kant seeks to elucidate basic propositions of his
critique of taste (and to a degree his entire corpus) by specifying what he
calls the maxims of common human understanding. "They are these: (1)
to think for oneself; (2) to think from the standpoint of every one else;
(3) always to think consistently. The first is the maxim of *unprejudiced*
thought, the second that of *enlarged* thought, the third that of *consistent*
thought. . . . We may say: the first of these is the maxim of understanding, the second that of judgement, the third that of reason."[12]

The maxim of enlarged thought—to think from the standpoint of
everyone else—is the key to reflective judgment for Arendt. In her article "The Crisis in Culture," she notes that both Western morality and
logic can be viewed as having closely hewn to the goal of noncontradic-
tion through the ages, a goal that hearkens back to Socrates' claim that

because he is one he must be in agreement with himself and that is at the heart of Kant's third maxim. She goes on to say,

> In the *Critique of Judgement*, however, Kant insisted upon a different way of thinking, for which it would not be enough to be in agreement with one's own self, but which consisted of being able to "think in the place of everybody else" and which he therefore called an "enlarged mentality" (*eine erweiterte Denkungsart*). The power of judgment rests on a potential agreement with others, and the thinking process which is active in judging something is not, like the thought process of pure reasoning, a dialogue between me and myself, but finds itself always and primarily, even if I am quite alone in making up my mind, in an anticipated communication with others with whom I know I must finally come to some agreement. From this potential agreement judgment derives its specific validity.[13]

But this is not the end of the story, a story that has obvious affinities with Habermas's *Theory of Communicative Action* and Mead's cosmopolitanism. Arendt goes on to say in the same passage that the idiosyncratic, which is very naturally woven into each of our private lives, must be left by the wayside once we enter the public realm. "And this enlarged way of thinking, which as judgment knows how to transcend its own individual limitations . . . cannot function in strict isolation or solitude; it needs the presence of others 'in whose place' it must think, whose perspectives it must take into consideration, and without whom it never has the opportunity to operate at all."[14]

Given the importance of an intersubjective domain in Kant's *Critique of Judgement*, at first blush it seems extraordinary that this work should link one's capacity to be discriminating in matters of beauty to the sense of taste, a seemingly private and idiosyncratic sense. Nevertheless, this is just what the work does. Taste is the sense that Kant associates most closely with judgment.[15] Yet of all the senses, taste and smell appear to be the most personal and idiosyncratic and the least communal. How does Kant, in Arendt's reading, manage to link the most private of all senses to judgment, which requires an appeal to a public of some sort? That is, how are we to understand the relationship of *sensus communis* to taste?

In her explanation of Kant's position Arendt claims that sight, hearing, and touch deal with objects of the external world, whereas taste and smell are inner sensations. She presumes that the experiences of external objects—those given by sight, hearing, and touch—can be shared through language and that we can recall our experiences of them. We can *re*present them to ourselves in their absence.[16] This is possible because of the faculty of imagination. Taste and smell, on the other hand, are neither part of a shared world nor susceptible to being represented. They are discriminatory senses in which "the it-pleases-or-displeases-me is immediate and overwhelming. And pleasure or displeasure . . . are entirely idiosyncratic."[17] They relate to the particular solely as particular and do so in an immediate fashion. Why should we look to this most private sphere to help us understand the ground of judgments that are general and nonidiosyncratic? "Because only taste and smell are discriminatory by their very nature and because only these senses relate to the particular qua particular, whereas all objects given to the objective senses share their properties with other objects, that is, they are not unique."[18]

Kant wants to be able to respect the beauty of the particular in its uniqueness. He also wants to appeal to a standard of evaluation that transcends the capriciousness of the immediate response. Yet Arendt tells us that taste as a sense is immediate, subjective, and not communicable. There can be no debate about one's sense of taste. How then do we move from the immediacy of the sense of taste to matters of aesthetic evaluation, which clearly has an intersubjective component? Arendt turns to the role of imagination here. "The solution to this riddle is: Imagination. Imagination, the ability to make present what is absent, transforms the objects of the objective senses into 'sensed' objects, as though they were objects of an inner sense. This happens by reflecting not on an object but on its representation. The represented object now arouses one's pleasure or displeasure, not direct perception of the object. Kant calls this 'the operation of reflection.'"[19]

On one hand, we find that the sense of taste is by nature idiosyncratic and too immediate to allow disinterested analysis, which is necessary if we are to achieve judgments that are general (universal) and truly acknowledge the beautiful. On the other hand, that which is simply shared with others through the objective senses cannot escape the attachments, the public pressures, that preclude disinterested evaluation. So neither the inner nor the outer senses by themselves can provide us with a disinterested response. Imagination allows one to take an absent (shareable) object and make it present, so that one can then turn it over, so to speak, in one's mind in an act of reflection that is evaluative. Or, stated in another way, that which was originally public did not allow judicious assessment because the pressures of the crowd prevented circumspection, whereas that which was originally inner was too immediate to allow evaluation. Through the use of imagination the "external" can be judged "internally," that is, with some distance from its publicness. "One then speaks of judgment and no longer of taste because, though it still affects one like a matter of taste, one now has, by means of representation, established the proper distance, the remoteness or uninvolvedness or disinterestedness, that is requisite for approbation and disapprobation, for evaluating something at its proper worth. By removing the object, one has established the conditions for impartiality."[20]

However, this removal of the object cannot in itself explain impartiality, for once the object to be evaluated has been internalized through the imagination, I may still find myself reacting to it in terms of immediate approval and disapproval. I find that it simply pleases or displeases me. Although I might not be mimicking the public's view, I seemingly have an immediate relationship to the object rather than a critical one. How am I to achieve a critical distance from the immediacy of my response of pleasure or displeasure?

Imagination makes an object present so that one's inner sense can discriminate. The latter sense "is called taste because, like taste, it *chooses*. But this choice is itself subject to still another choice: one can approve or disapprove of the very fact of *pleasing*."[21] I see a painting or some flowers that many call beautiful. I feel pleasure, but I must evaluate whether the object "pleases universally."[22] To do so I judge whether the pleasure I originally received meets with my approval or disapproval. In evaluating the pleasure I determine whether I ought to have been pleased by the original object. But why should this second-level response make a difference? The process appears to entail an infinite regress in which the grounds for making the next level's decisions appear no better than the first's, that is, "X" pleases, and then the pleasure it provides pleases or displeases. "The very act of approbation pleases, the very act of disapprobation displeases. Hence the question: How does one choose between approbation and disapprobation? One criterion is easily guessed . . . it is the criterion of communicability or publicness. One is not overeager to express joy at the death of a father or feelings of hatred and envy. . . . The criterion, then, is communicability, and the standard of deciding about it is common sense."[23]

We arrive back at the central role of the *sensus communis* in Arendt's treatment of Kant. To do so we have moved from the shareable objects of the senses, through the imagination, to choices entailing approval and disapproval. The pleasure of the original it-pleases-me is judged, and this judgment entails a communal moment. We must appeal to the *sensus communis* to transcend the idiosyncratic. Arendt quotes at length a key passage from Section 40 of the third *Critique* in her discussion.

> Under the *sensus communis* we must include the idea of a sense *common to all*, i.e., of a faculty of judgment which, in its reflection, takes

account (*a priori*) of the mode of representation of all other men in thought, in order, *as it were,* to compare its judgment with the collective reason of humanity. . . . This is done by comparing our judgment with the possible rather than the actual judgments of others, and by putting ourselves in the place of any other man, by abstracting from the limitations which contingently attach to our own judgment.[24]

We should strive to foster, in Kant's terms, an enlarged mentality, in which we put aside our own idiosyncratic sensibilities. Disinterested appreciation marks those who have correctly judged the universality of the beautiful. Although Arendt appears to be freewheeling in interpreting Kant's third *Critique*—for example, in *not* emphasizing the *a prioristic* character of the beautiful—in certain passages she is quite close to the spirit, if not the letter, of Kant's method for overcoming the idiosyncratic by enlarging one's mentality. Arendt, like Kant and Mead, emphasizes how the move toward a more general standpoint entails placing oneself in the "standpoint of others."[25]

One can communicate only if one is able to think from the other person's standpoint; otherwise one will never meet him, never speak in such a way that he understands. . . . Finally, the larger the scope of those to whom one can communicate, the greater is the worth of the object. . . . One judges always as a member of a community, guided by one's community sense, one's *sensus communis.* But in the last analysis, one is a member of a world community by the sheer fact of being human; this is one's "cosmopolitan existence."[26]

To support her view of the crucial importance of the intersubjective for making judicious assessments, Arendt quotes passages from two letters Kant wrote to Marcus Hertz, a disciple and friend. These letters emphasize the connection between impartiality and taking the viewpoints of others. Here is the passage she quotes from the first letter: "You know that I do not approach reasonable objections with the intention merely of refuting them, but that in thinking them over I always weave them into my judgments, and afford them the opportunity of overturning all my most cherished beliefs. I entertain the hope that by thus viewing my judgments impartially from the standpoint of others some third view that will improve upon my previous insight may be obtainable."[27]

Arendt responds by giving her characteristically pluralistic interpretation of Kant: "You see that *impartiality* is obtained by taking the viewpoints of others into account; impartiality is not the result of some higher standpoint that would then actually settle the dispute by being altogether above the melée."[28] In the second letter, Kant makes this even clearer. "[The mind needs a reasonable amount of relaxations and diversions to maintain its mobility—H.A.] 'that it may be enabled to view the object afresh from every side, and *so to enlarge its point of view* from a microscopic to a general outlook that it adopts in turn every conceivable standpoint, verifying the observations of each by means of all the others.'"[29] Arendt goes on to tie the notion of the mind enlarging itself that we find in this passage to the enlarged mentality of the *Critique of Judgement.* By so doing she hopes to mark as quintessentially Kantian the seemingly innocuous truisms of liberal thought that we find in these letters. And there is clearly some merit in her position.

One of the intriguing aspects of Kant's letters is that they were written to Marcus Hertz in 1771 and 1772, and that in 1771 Marcus Hertz wrote a letter to Kant in which he speaks of "the Englishman Smith, who, Mr. Friedländer tells me, is your [Kant's] favourite [*Liebling*]."[30] The Smith referred to in this letter is Adam Smith, author of the acclaimed *The Theory of Moral Sentiments.* (*The Wealth of Nations* was published almost five years after Hertz's letter.) The account of morality in *The Theory of Moral Sentiments* involves a protodevelopmental and social conception of the self, and there is some evidence that Kant's third *Critique* may have been influenced by this book. It is clearly the case that Kant's notion of an enlarged mentality, in Arendt's reading, would have been quite congenial to Smith. This historical footnote is all the more intriguing in this context because Mead was familiar with Smith, and certain of the latter's ideas bear a striking similarity to notions Mead developed. In other words, Adam Smith's work on moral philosophy may have influenced both Kant and Mead and through Kant may have indirectly influenced Arendt's political thought. I wish to examine briefly this set of connections before considering in further detail Arendt's position. The reason for this examination is twofold: The possible historical connections are interesting, and addressing Smith's notion of the impartial spectator at this juncture will help set the stage for its use later in this work.

Although there has been scholarly debate about whether Kant could read English, there is reason to believe that he could not do so.[31] If this is true, it is significant that a German translation of the third edition of *The Theory of Moral Sentiments* appeared in 1770,[32] the year before Herr Hertz noted that Smith was Kant's favorite.[33] Smith's book achieved a good deal of notoriety in Great Britain at the time of its original publication in 1759. Given the importance of the work and Kant's interest in English thought,[34] it seems reasonable to conclude that Kant's keen interest in Smith—if we can trust Hertz's letter—would have reflected some acquaintance with his most famous work to date.

Central to the discussion of moral judgment in *The Theory of Moral*

Sentiments is the connection between the notion of an impartial spectator and the process of viewing ourselves from what could be called the
perspective of others. Speaking of the genesis of moral criticism in a passage that could easily have influenced Mead and may well have been the
source of Charles H. Cooley's well-known notion of the looking-glass self,
Smith states, "We begin, upon this account, to examine our own passions
and conduct, and to consider how these must appear to them, by considering how they would appear to us if in their situation. We suppose ourselves the spectators of our own behaviour, and endeavour to imagine
what effect it would, in this light, produce upon us. This is the only looking-glass by which we can, in some measure, with the eyes of other people, scrutinize the propriety of our own conduct."[35] This scrutiny entails
a level of generality that rises above the immediate encounters we have
with others. In one passage, which suggests a certain kinship to Kant,
Smith says that our approval or disapproval of conduct must have "some
secret reference, either to what are, or to what, upon a certain condition,
would be, or to what, we imagine, ought to be the judgment ["sentiments," in the first five editions] of others. We examine it as we imagine
an impartial spectator would examine it."[36] And in another passage Smith
states that such a spectator is "neither father, nor brother, nor friend . . .
but is merely a man in general. . . . This inmate of the breast, this abstract
man, the representative of mankind, and substitute of the Deity, whom
nature has constituted the supreme judge of all their actions, is seldom
appealed to by them [i.e., the weak, the vain, and the frivolous]. They are
contented with the decision of the inferiour tribunal [the approbation of
their companions]."[37]

It may very well be that in struggling to find a way to characterize
the process needed to confirm the universality of one's aesthetic judgments, Kant drew on his familiarity with Smith's account of moral judgments. Kant needed a way to think about universality and impartiality
that did not command the assent of everyone in a categorical manner.
Both Kant and Smith appeal to a level of social experience that transcends
specific others but has a recognizably social component to characterize
impartiality. Interestingly enough, it appears that in his *Reflections on
Anthropology* Kant actually used Smith's phrase "the impartial spectator" to describe the individual who looks on matters "not just from his
own point of view but from that of the community."[38] David Hume, who
was of course known to Kant, spoke of a spectator in his moral theory,
as did Francis Hutcheson, whose work Kant also knew quite well.[39] But
their work did not provide a detailed explanation of the genesis and character of conscience—that is, how one comes to judge one's own actions—

and neither used the phrase "impartial spectator."[40] There is further evidence that Kant was familiar with and influenced by Smith's book. Samuel Fleischacker, for example, has mounted an interesting case in relation to Kant's moral thought.[41] He has also noted some connections to the third *Critique*. "Smith details wonderfully how we come up with general rules out of specific cases, in aesthetic as well as ethical matters, arguing in advance of Kant for something very like 'disinterested satisfaction' (in the sympathy of the impartial spectator itself) and 'purposiveness without purpose' (in his notion that what we find beautiful is not utility itself, as Hume had said, but an apparent *suitedness for* utility that might in fact not be useful—*TMS* IV.i.3)."[42]

A good argument can also be made that a number of Arendt's insights were anticipated in Smith's book. This would make a good deal of sense if Kant had been influenced by Smith's empirically and psychologically minded text and if Arendt had managed to home in on this thread in Kant's work.[43] If we follow Arendt's path through Kant's work—in particular the manner in which she emphasizes taking the perspectives of the others—the possibility of Smith's influence becomes even more apparent.

Mead appears to have been familiar with Smith. At least as early as 1910, before he published some of his most seminal articles, he linked Smith to his own insights.[44] But there is another connection. Mead was clearly familiar with the work of Charles H. Cooley, who was his colleague at the University of Michigan, and Mead refers to him in several places, including in one his most important articles, "The Social Self."[45] Cooley is known for his for his phrase the "looking-glass self," which he used as early as 1902 in a context that clearly resonates with Smith's ideas.[46] Of course, this is not proof of Smith's direct influence on Mead, but I think it does begin to point to the fact that the kinship between many of their ideas may be more than accidental. (There is no question that Mead owed a large debt to British empiricism.) In other words, it would not be unreasonable to presume that important aspects of Kant's third *Critique*—those brought into relief and channeled in her own pluralistically inspired direction by Arendt—can be linked to Mead through a specific historical antecedent, Adam Smith. I return to Smith later in this work. I mention these possible connections not just because they are intrinsically interesting and may prove true but because they highlight in a preliminary fashion conceptual links that I intend to stress. But perhaps I have invoked Mead a bit too early here, for there are some further points to be made about Arendt's position before turning to Mead's view of universality and his relationship to Arendt.

One of Arendt's most striking claims is that questions of truth should be banished from the political world, a claim that relates directly to her vision of pluralism. The beauty of a painting, the correctness of a political evaluation, are not questions of truth and falsity.[47] For the political world is a world of opinion and ongoing debate, and cognitive truth puts an end to this world when it oversteps its bounds with claims to permanence. Whatever kind of universality or generality we find in the political realm, it cannot be the universality of truths and concepts. One simply should not seek to discover truth in political or aesthetic spheres. But although truth is not the goal, these spheres no doubt require thought, and Arendt acknowledges that thinking involves generalizing. Her challenge is to find a way to think about the particular and the general without simply subsuming the particular under the general.[48]

In attempting to articulate how one can think about the particular without appealing to given principles or laws, Arendt suggests that Kant came up with two solutions. The first entails the idea of purposiveness, in which purposeless art objects are evaluated in terms of their "'purpose' of pleasing men, making them feel at home in the world."[49] But this was not the solution that appealed to Arendt; she looked to Kant's notion of exemplary validity.

To explain this notion, Arendt suggests that we reflect on how we recognize particular objects, and she uses the example of a table to explain the possibilities. One way of approaching the matter is to say that we can recognize a table because we possess a concept. A Platonic idea, for example, provides my mind's eye with a formal table, which allows me to determine whether the object in front of me is in fact a table. A second alternative would have me abstracting from all the tables I have ever encountered, leaving by the wayside the superfluous or idiosyncratic features of specific tables and retaining the properties they all have in common. This would provide an abstract table that has features in common with all tables. "One more possibility is left, and this enters into judgments that are not cognitions: one may encounter or think of some table that one judges to be the best possible table and take this table as the example of how tables actually should be: the *exemplary table* ('example' comes from *eximere*, 'to single out some particular'). This exemplar is and remains a particular that in its very particularity reveals the generality that otherwise could not be defined. Courage is like Achilles. Etc.," Arendt says.[50]

We do not arrive at a valid judgment in the political realm through an act of cognition that applies rules to particular cases, that compels assent in the manner of geometric deductions. Truths of the latter sort are simply not to be found in the domain of the political. The general reveals itself in the exemplar that imagination helps to supply, for "imagination, which provides schemata for cognition, provides *examples* for judgment."[51] "When judging, one says spontaneously, without any derivations form general rules, 'This man has courage.' If one were a Greek, one would have 'in the depths of one's mind' the example of Achilles. Imagination is again necessary: one must have Achilles present even though he certainly is absent."[52]

Arendt was intrigued by the possibilities of exemplars because they permitted evaluations without recourse to laws of history or notions of progressive development. By using them we can reclaim the dignity of individuals and their actions in the face of the march of history, a march that tends to pay homage to the successful and in so doing dismisses exemplars worthy of respect. It is in this context that we can understand Arendt's fondness for the words of Cato, "The victorious cause pleased the gods, but the defeated one pleases Cato."[53]

Arendt tells us that a "judgment has exemplary validity to the extent that the example is rightly chosen."[54] But how do we know whether an example is rightly chosen?[55] We can be certain that whatever is truly exemplary would appear as such to any disinterested observer. How does one become a disinterested observer? We already have part of the answer. We must judge only after considering multiple standpoints; not to do so binds us to the local and idiosyncratic. As a matter of fact, one has an obligation to judge from multiple perspectives, for this promotes an enlarged mentality. "One judges always as a member of a community, guided by one's community sense, one's *sensus communis*. But in the last analysis, one is a member of a world community by the sheer fact of being human; this is one's 'cosmopolitan existence.' When one judges and when one acts in political matters, one is supposed to take one's bearings from the idea, not the actuality, of being a world citizen and, therefore, also a *Weltbetrachter*, a world spectator."[56]

We strive for a disinterested evaluation in the political realm just as we do when we judge the beautiful. When I say that this painting is beautiful, I am not merely saying it is beautiful for me. I am presuming that all disinterested spectators would find it so. When I say that Achilles is courageous, I presume that all who evaluate him in disinterested manner would find him so. And when I judge whether Tom, Dick, or Harry is courageous, I view each in the light of the exemplar Achilles. In presuming universal agreement here we are implicitly (or explicitly) appealing to the communicability of our claims because "the less idiosyncratic one's taste is, the better it can be communicated."[57] Yet our reflective judgments do not have the universal validity of propositions in mathematics, and they are valid only for those who are engaged in the activity of judging. We cannot presume that they will be valid for those who do not ask our questions or engage in the same sorts of affairs that we do. "Judgment is endowed with a certain specific validity but is never universally valid," Arendt says. "Its claims to validity can never extend further than the others in whose place the judging person has put himself for his considerations. Judgment, Kant says, is valid 'for every single judging person,' but the emphasis in the sentence is on 'judging'; it is not valid for those who do not judge or for those who are not members of the public realm where the objects of judgment appear."[58]

We have spent a good deal of time addressing the intersubjective conditions that make valid judgments possible. But in so doing we have left an important facet of Arendt's thought by the wayside: the capacity "things" or events have for revealing their status as exemplars. For if "things" did not have the power to show themselves forth in a certain manner, no one would be able to recognize their exemplary validity. And as Arendt thinks about this capacity, her thought takes a decidedly Heideggerian turn. In the distance we gain from our interests, through an enlarged mentality, a "space" opens through which political and aesthetic phenomena can show themselves forth.[59] Ronald Beiner, in his commentary on Arendt's *Lectures*, summarizes her sensibility: "For Arendt, politics is defined by phenomenality, as self-disclosure in a space of appearances. Political things, as Arendt conceives them, are phenomenally manifest: 'great things are self evident, shine by themselves,' the poet or historiographer merely *preserving* the glory that is already visible to all. . . . Judgment discriminates among the self-disclosive phenomena and captures phenomenal appearance in its fullness. . . . The objects of our judgment are particulars that open themselves to our purview."[60]

Arendt appeals to what we might call a form of essentialism here. There are indeed exemplary acts, and the universal (or general) manifests itself in them, but such "essences" should not be confused with Platonic ideas or the secondary substances of Aristotle. They are phenomena that reveal themselves if we have eyes to see (and a willingness to test what we have seen by taking the perspectives of others). Unfortunately, for Arendt, modern consumer society threatens to bury our vision. This is perhaps most obvious in terms of artistic works. What we fail to realize is that "to become aware of appearances we must first be free to establish a certain distance between ourselves and the object. . . . This distance cannot arise unless we are in a position to forget ourselves, the cares and interests and urges of our lives, so that we will not seize what we admire but let it be as it is, in its appearance."[61]

In forgetting these cares we can approach Kant's disinterested joy. I doubt Arendt would have thought that Mead could experience very much of the latter. In all likelihood she would have viewed him as a dangerous instrumentalist who could not appreciate the importance of the spectator and the true nature of art or the political. However, it does not appear that Arendt studied the pragmatists in any depth. Had Arendt studied Mead she might have been surprised by how much they had in common. Turning now to Mead on universality, universals, and the cosmopolitan may help to clarify the extent of their agreement.

Contrary to Habermas's claims, addressed in the next chapter, Mead's views on universality were only to a limited degree Kantian. No doubt the third *Critique* would have held some attraction for Mead but for the most part as a transitional work, one that led away from the first two *Critiques* to the romantic and intersubjective in G. W. F. Hegel. Mead was well aware of the importance of the third *Critique* and the nature of its influence. It is worth noting in this context that when he does address the third *Critique* in his posthumously published *Movements of Thought in the Nineteenth Century*, it is not in his central chapter on Kant but rather in one titled "Kant and the Background of Philosophic Romanticism."[62] In the latter work Mead refers to Kant as the philosopher of the Revolution.[63] And he reads Kant in light of Rousseau, claiming that he took Rousseau's insights and generalized them and hence came to deserve the aforementioned title.[64]

Mead understood that the quest for universality in political forums could not and should not be understood solely in terms of the aspirations of rationalistically minded philosophes or transcendentally inspired Kantians. As a matter of fact, when addressing the genesis of the modern self— in particular the pivotal importance of placing oneself in the perspective of others—Mead turns not to Kant and his enlightened protégés but to the romantics.

> What the Romantic period revealed, then, was not simply a past, but a past as the point of view from which to come back at the self. One has to grow into the attitude of the other, come back at the self, to realize the self; and we are discussing the means by which this was done. Here, then, we have the makings of a new philosophy, the Romantic philosophy.[65]

It was because people in Europe, at this time, put themselves back in the earlier attitude that they could come back upon themselves. . . . As a characteristic of the romantic attitude we find this assumption of rôles.[66]

For Mead, the German idealists who followed Kant—Johann Fichte, Friedrich Schelling, and Hegel—were best understood as romantic philosophers, a reading that shows the influence of Josiah Royce, his teacher for a time at Harvard.[67] Mead's understanding of the self, and his own self-understanding of his model of the self, is indeed indebted to this tradition.[68] He sought to reconcile certain elements of the Enlightenment and romanticism by consciously incorporating insights from evolutionary biology and the behavioral sciences into a romantic conception of the self's development.[69] Mead argues that we grow as individuals to the extent that we take various roles, engage in different social interactions, and learn to navigate between them. It is to this developmental process that we must turn to understand his notion of universality.

Although Mead would agree with many of Arendt's observations on the place of universals (generals) in social life, he would have serious reservations about the consequences of thinking about them in terms reflective and determinant judgments. And contra Kant, he would argue that although we can use the term *universal* to refer to certain provisional laws that satisfy certain hypotheses or to classify specific linguistic interactions, the universality of such laws and interactions is not of the *a priori* variety. Mead's position is that even if only two individuals are involved, we can speak of the universality of a significant symbol.[70] "But signification is not confined to the particular situation within which an indication is given. It acquires universal meaning. Even if the two [individuals] are the only ones involved, the form in which it is given is universal—it would have the same meaning to any other who might find himself in the same position."[71]

Notice that it is the potential generalizability of a response to a specific symbol that allows Mead to speak of it as a universal. Similarities of response are potentially available to all who stand in the same (or similar) social role or position. This is especially easy to grasp if we are speaking of similarities in the responses of members of organized groups. To return to the game analogy of the last chapter, a game such as basketball or baseball harbors universalizable or generalizable responses. Everyone who plays the game must follow the implicit and explicit rules of the game or its patterns of behavior; that is, there must be a generalized other guiding their responses.[72] Mead goes on to say,

How does this generalization arise? From the behavioristic standpoint it must take place through the individual generalizing himself in his attitude of the other. . . . The generalization is simply the result of the identity of responses. Indeed it is only as he has in some sense amalgamated the attitudes of the different roles in which he has addressed himself that he acquires the unity of personality. . . . Group solidarity, especially in its uniform restrictions, gives him the unity of universality. This I take to be the sole source of the universal. It quickly passes the bounds of the specific group. . . . Education and varied experience refine out of it what is provincial, and leave 'what is true for all men at all times.' From the first, its form is universal, for *differences of the different attitudes* of others wear their peculiarities away.[73]

We need not turn to *a priori* truths or propositions about universality to move us away from provincialism, but we can turn to varied experience and education. To understand how we can be so moved, we must look to the way in which the self arises and how it is sustained by environments (both social and biological), which it also helps to transform. I want to stress that in his comments on overcoming provincialism Mead speaks of the attitudes of others, not just the meanings of significant symbols. Attitudes prepare the way for action and must be understood in terms of the physiological and habitual in addition to the cognitive. What one shares with others is not simply linguistic meanings but preparations for action. Under the right conditions (for example, when problems arise) one can become cognitively aware of attitudes or sets of attitudes, but more often than not we remain on a nonreflective level. (Consciousness of self requires a reflective turn, one that depends on the generalized other.) I return to the importance of the sharing of attitudes when I discuss Habermas's interpretation of Mead. At this juncture I simply want to note that Mead's cognitivism is not identical to Habermas's and that he would not be pleased with a good deal of Rorty's linguistic contextualism.[74]

For Mead, as for Arendt, there is an intimate connection between the activity of taking multiple perspectives and becoming an "impartial" spectator sensitive to the positions of others. Mead would argue that a person becomes more internationally minded to the extent that he or she learns to take multiple perspectives. He appears to presume that the taking of multiple perspectives not only increases our appreciation of the specific positions of others but lends itself to the development of a kind of internationally minded impartiality. Although no doubt this claim ultimately warrants empirical assessment, it also requires a more precise characterization of Mead's notion of impartiality, a notion that I attempt to explicate later in this chapter and in chapters to follow.[75] Here we can say that the essence of political and social life is to be found in the moving in and out of perspectives for Mead, and for Arendt this process is crucial for the type of communication judgment requires. Mead writes, "It is the ability of the person to put himself in other people's places that gives him his cues as to what he is to do under a specific situation. It is this that gives to the man what we term his character as a member of the community; his citizenship, from a political standpoint; his membership from any one of the different standpoints in which he belongs to the community."[76] And Arendt declares,

> One can communicate only if one is able to think from the other person's standpoint; otherwise one will never meet him, never speak in such a way that he understands. . . . Finally, the larger the scope of those to whom one can communicate, the greater is the worth of the object. . . . One judges always as a member of a community, guided by one's community sense, one's *sensus communis*. But in the last analysis, one is a member of a world community by the sheer fact of being human; this is one's "cosmopolitan existence."[77]

I suggest that we interpret the generalized other as Mead's social behaviorist version of *sensus communis*. If we view common sense in this manner, Mead can be understood as providing a (quasi) scientific path for fleshing out the sources and nature of common sense. Such an approach would see it originating in the process of taking the attitudes of others, attitudes that cohere in shared networks of responses, that is, generalized others. This hypothesis would allow us to address the question of why *some* interactions or evaluations feel so matter-of-fact. We respond to them in this manner because they depend on shared frameworks (generalized others) for their intelligibility, and as the ground of intelligibility these frameworks are always already given every time they are invoked; the conscious evaluations they make possible then appear in the same light. (It's just common sense, after all.)

Attitudes that constitute common sense originate and are sustained by the collective experience of a community and therefore can translate into practical wisdom. Or, to be more accurate, we should say they translate into practical *wisdoms* because for Mead we must speak of multiple common senses that correspond to different generalized others. Although we should speak of multiple common senses and their communities, there is an impetus in the modern world to expand the horizons of particular communities in a manner that leads to a "common sense" that can transcend provincial biases. We can understand international-mindedness in terms of individuals who can abstract from their experience in specific communities to see how different communities might be related. However, international-mindedness does not arise just because one has been a participant in many communities. It arises because the process of moving from framework to framework entails learning how to readily accept novelty and what Mead calls the state of sociality, the condition of in-betweenness that occurs as one moves from one system to another. The cosmopolitan is one who has not only experienced numerous communities but understands and can anticipate how the movement from one social situation to another requires being prepared to live with unrealized expectations and novel events. In other words, an ability to grapple with novelty clearly is part of the enlarged mentality for Mead. It is also part of a democratic sensibility, one that entails being prepared to take novel and different opinions seriously.

It is conceivable that Kant's cosmopolitan individual could be at home in one of Mead's internationally minded communities, at least until he or she discovered that such communities are not absolutely universal and do not rest on *a priori* moorings. Although for Kant the exact nature of common sense's relationship to reason is open to speculation,[78] there is no question that common sense is invoked to clarify the *a prioristic* processes of the mind that allow beauty to appear and to suggest how we might confirm the validity of a judgment about the beautiful. So we find Kant arguing that "under the *sensus communis* we must include the idea of a sense *common to all*, i.e., of a faculty of judgment which, in its reflection, takes account (*a priori*) of the mode of representation of all other men in thought, in order, *as it were*, to compare its judgment with the collective reason of humanity."[79]

It is not an *a priori* mooring that intrigues Mead and Arendt but the process of arriving at universals (or generals). Both would prefer a turn to what Kant says about how a reflective judgment is validated: "This is done by comparing our judgment with the possible rather than the actual judgments of others, and by putting ourselves in the place of any other man, by abstracting from the limitations which contingently attach to our own judgment."[80] By looking to this process Arendt is able to affirm her commitment to viewing the political world as the land of opinion in which one is able to avoid finality by continually placing oneself in the standpoint of others. In the political world the activity of exchanging viewpoints is more important than any closure brought about through or with the assistance of the *a priori*, and in emphasizing this she is clearly very close to an important aspect of Mead's position. But by no means would they be without disagreements, to which we now turn.

It seems that in at least one crucial respect Arendt would be critical of Mead's orientation. If we link community, the generalized other, and common sense as we have, haven't we once again subsumed the particular beneath the universal? Doesn't such a suggestion amount to saying that if general rules are part and parcel of the generalized other, then particulars are once again being subsumed under a certain type of cognitive umbrella? And if this is true, then the attempt to remove the political from the domain of the cognitive has once again failed. But this way of framing the situation is misleading. For Mead, a generalized other is not simply an object or resource for cognition, although it can be both. It is a set of attitudes, preparations for action, and as such it is not merely a device for subsuming particulars under universals in the manner of determinant judgments. The term *rules* must not be narrowly construed here. (Perhaps the phrase "patterns of behavior or interaction" would reduce the chances of misconstrual.) Furthermore, and more to the point, Arendt's criticism presumes a separation between cognition and judgment that Mead would find unacceptable.

There are numerous issues here, more than we can reasonably hope to address in this chapter. And I am hesitant to engage in an extended response to or critique of Arendt's thought from Mead's perspective, or of his from hers. Nevertheless, a few salient points can be noted if we keep in mind their provisional nature. Arendt, as we have seen, wanted to keep cognitive truth and political judgment apart. However, the pragmatist would be suspicious of such a stark division, a suspicion that could only be confounded by Arendt's tendency to import notions that pragmatists associate with spectator models of cognition into the realm of judgment. A turn to the tension in Arendt's thought about the nature of those who judge should be of assistance in clarifying what is at issue here. We can begin by asking whether it is the historical actor or the spectator of events who is in the best position to judge. According to Beiner, "On the one hand, she is tempted to integrate judgment into the *vita activa*, seeing it as a function of the representative thinking and enlarged mentality of political actors, exchanging opinions in public while engaged in common deliberation. On the other hand, she wants to emphasize the contemplative and disinterested dimension of judgment, which operates retrospectively, like aesthetic judgment. Judgment in the latter sense is placed exclusively within the ambit of the life of the mind."[81]

One could argue that Arendt eventually came to see judgment as more closely aligned with the spectator than the actor. Proving this here is unnecessary, for it is not crucial to the point I want to make: Arendt did at times view judgment in terms of the individual who detaches herself from the scene to judge rightly. Bernstein notes, "She loved to cite the parable ascribed to Pythagoras and repeated by Diogenes Laertius: 'Life . . . is like a festival: just as some come to the festival to compete, some to ply their trade, but the best people come as spectators [*theatai*], so in life the slavish men go hunting for fame [*doxa*] or gain, the philosophers for truth.'[82] But as she interpreted this parable, it was not the quest for truth the she emphasized; it was the quest for meaning and understanding which is manifested in judgment."[83]

Arendt's attraction to the life of the spectator shines in statements such as the one Bernstein quotes. She clearly had much sympathy for spectators who could see the whole by achieving a certain distance, for they are in the best position to discover exemplars and appreciate the meaning of events.[84] However, we need to be somewhat careful here because we do not want to conflate the situation of the spectator who judges events with that of the philosopher. Both require distance from social and political events but not in exactly the same fashion. The spectator who judges, unlike the philosopher or thinker, is part of an audience for Arendt.

> The withdrawal of judgment is obviously very different from the withdrawal of the philosopher. It does not leave the world of appearances but retires from active involvement in it to a privileged position in order to contemplate the whole. Moreover, and perhaps more significantly, Pythagoras' spectators are members of an audience and therefore quite unlike the philosopher. . . . Hence the spectator's verdict, while impartial and freed from the interests of gain or fame, is not independent of the views of others—on the contrary, according to Kant, an "enlarged mentality" has to take them into account. The spectators, although disengaged from the particularity characteristic of the actor, are not solitary.[85]

So Arendt was of the conviction that the position of the judging spectator is not quite like that of the philosopher: Although both clearly require distance from the actors and the seeing of the whole, the judging spectator is part of an audience. "The advantage the spectator has is that he sees the play as a whole, while each of the actors knows only his part or, if he should judge from the perspective of acting, only the part of the whole that concerns him. The actor is partial by definition."[86]

If we were to carry the analogy to the theater a bit further, we might say that although Arendt recognizes that judging spectators are in an audience, she would not want to view the members of the audience as having a stake in the play. To do so would be to deny the spectator his or her critical edge by making him or her an interested party, an actor (of sorts). The problem from the pragmatist's perspective is that Arendt not only wants to be critical, she wants to be distant enough to see the whole—the whole play, that is—and is convinced that she can find a position to do so. No doubt Mead would be uncomfortable with the manner in which Arendt appears at times to erect a divide between the spectator and actor.

Placing Arendt's views on the positions of those who judge on a continuum may help reveal why this is the case. At one extreme we would find the political actor who judges, at the other the philosopher. Between these two poles of involvement in practical affairs we would find the spectator in an audience. Now Mead would be comfortable with the notion of the actor as judge, as an engaged spectator, and would even find elements of Arendt's audience of spectators congenial. However, there would be a suspicion that the latter individuals may ultimately have a greater kinship to the philosopher than to the actor. This conclusion would be reinforced, for example, by the manner in which Arendt talks of seeing the whole. There is a real danger here of introducing a divorce from the world and a kind of contemplative orientation toward knowledge and judgment that the pragmatic method sought to break. Interests are not to be forgotten but grappled with, balanced, circumscribed, challenged, and realized. To put this in terms of the generalized other, as opposed to navigating the whole from within a generalized other or evaluating one generalized other from the position of another overlapping (perhaps more encompassing) one, the spectator in the audience appears to be a member of a disengaged plurality and thus leaves one concerned about the nature and source of his or her critique.[87] Arendt does suggest that audiences observe from different locations in history. The latter is appealed to because it provides distance. But distance of this sort can place individuals closer to contemplative philosophers than to thoughtful actors. Meaning then becomes lodged in an audience (or thinker), and impartiality is remanded to the mountaintop. And if this comes to pass we may be inclined to ask, "What kind of respect for the particular remains if wholes viewed by spectators are the objects of judgment?" Too much distance, too much "impartiality," and we may not be able to appreciate the viewpoint of those who act. (Impartiality does not have to be understood in terms of a Kantian notion of disinterestedness, a Habermasian counterfactual communication community, the other in Levinas's thought, or even Arendt's privileged spectators.)

For the purpose of illuminating their differences, I have been demarcating Mead's and Arendt's positions in rather dramatic terms. So I should reiterate that Arendt was not simply a contemplative in disguise when it came to the political world, for so much of her thought contradicts this; for example, in addition to speaking at times as if it is the political actor who is in a position to judge, her whole model of judging through communication points to interaction as crucial to political life.[88] Yet there is clearly a pull in her thought that leads her at times to seek a kind of high ground that pragmatists doubt exists, and I have sought to highlight this in the last few paragraphs.

Setting aside the issue of the source of our ability to make critical assessments, we can approach what is at stake between Arendt and Mead in terms of questions that revolve around the dignity of the particular and unique. Arendt would have been irritated by the manner in which Mead appears to violate the particular by emphasizing systemic connections and class inclusion and by conflating meaning and knowledge. In response, Mead would not only question the epistemological basis of Arendt's criticisms but would suggest that she overestimates the danger the systemic and universal pose to the unique and particular. (Regarding the latter point, as we shall see, he would have a similar objection to Levinas.) One can have a unique and dignified place in a (social) system, given that no two parts of it are quite the same. We can call this, following Mead, the Leibnizian monad approach to particularity. However, Mead has another avenue for respecting the particular, and it parallels the role of natality in Arendt's thought. I refer here to Mead's metaphysics, which is attuned to the manner in which creative events and acts, particulars, regularly transform the seemingly fixed.

For Mead, the novel and the emergent arise because systems are not completely isolated and because natural and organic forms undergo modification. Rather surprisingly, the emergent, a particular, can transform not only the present and future but also the past. How so? The so-called past, whether viewed metaphysically or epistemologically, is actually richer than any of our assumptions about it. When a novel event occurs and survives aspects of the past that may never have seen the light of day suddenly appear on center stage. To use the example of the ecosystem once again, if a mutation had not arisen and interacted with a previously existing system, the potentials latent in the system may never have been realized. When they are actualized, a new present is born and along with it a new past, for the past only exists in the present, and the present is now seen to be connected to the past in different ways than if the emergent had never arisen.[89]

The pasts that we are involved in are both irrevocable and revocable. It is idle, at least for the purposes of experience, to have recourse to a "real" past within which we are making constant discoveries; for that past must be set over against a present within which the emergent appears, and the past, which must then be looked at from the standpoint of the emergent, becomes a different past. The emergent when it appears is always found to follow from the past, but before it appears it does not, by definition, follow from the past.[90]

Of course, such a position suggests numerous metaphysical conundrums. If we so choose, we can treat Mead's claims as epistemological rather than metaphysical; that is, the knowledge of the past is in the present, not its "reality." For Mead, however, this division would be somewhat misleading. There is no spectator's position from which one could ever have access to a past in itself, metaphysically speaking, apart from the meaning that it has in the present. Its meaning and reality lie in the present. They are inextricably bound together. Arendt would respond that this sort of claim reveals just what is wrong with Mead's position: The past is seemingly remade in light of the present, and reality lies in the present. (The defeated cause is forgotten, perhaps even by Cato.) Mead would reply that he is not suggesting that the past has no integrity; rather, he is suggesting that the past is not inscribed on some scroll, for in possessing unrealized possibilities, it is actually richer than our present understanding of it. We are humbled by the fact that the past is not fixed and that our meanings are never the final ones, a claim in which Arendt would find some merit because of her respect for natality.[91]

Perhaps these speculations and counterclaims have already begun to take us too far afield. What is at issue, however, is pertinent to a central concern of this work. Can Mead's framework respect and find a place for the particular, either in cultural or individual terms, even as it recognizes the particular's involvement in relationships that support its existence and make it intelligible? We return to this question a number of times, especially in chapter 5.

Arendt, as we have seen, would have us believe that claims to truth have no place in the political arena for the simple reason that they destroy political life by ending debate. It is on just this point that Habermas criticizes Arendt. From his perspective, Arendt holds dated views on the relationship of theory to praxis and, quite mistakenly, excludes truth from the latter because she has an "outmoded concept of theoretical knowledge that builds upon ultimate evidence." And this in turn holds her back "from conceiving the coming to agreement about political questions as a rational formation of consensus."[92]

Habermas's discomfort with Arendt's position would not have gone unnoticed by Mead. The latter would have agreed with her that plurality and debate, taking the perspective of the other, and an enlarged mentality are crucial to political life. But like Habermas he would not have wanted to draw a fixed divide between theoretical knowledge and the political world. His views on the modern world's potential to cultivate and educate citizens who can judge would also have been markedly different from Arendt's, in part because of his belief in the potential of the sciences to inform political life. Mead appealed to science to help explain how the capacity for taking the place of the other arises, why this skill is so fundamentally important for our political and social life, and how we might promote it. Yet Mead would *not* have found Habermas's notion of rationality entirely congenial, as we shall see in chapter 3.

Excursus

Before moving on to Habermas, I would like to develop some of the issues at stake in Arendt's reading of Kant by turning to a piece, "Economimesis," which Derrida first published in the 1970s.[93] The article is germane because it takes up specific disagreements Derrida has with Kant on the issue of communication and does so in the context of a discussion of the third *Critique*. It also iterates a number of typical Derridean themes, such as the dangers of presence and logocentrism. Although Derrida is at times being playful, it is play with a serious intent: to show just how wrong Kant's approach to communication was and remains. His remarks are worthy of consideration here because his criticisms of Kant might just as well be directed against Mead or Habermas (especially as he draws on Mead). Derrida's attack would also apply to other modernists (and quasimodernists) in the pragmatic tradition, particularly Dewey, who shared Mead's conception of language.[94] In addition, aspects of Derrida's concerns will serve as a harbinger for issues that are given far more concentrated treatment in the chapter on Levinas. This excursus focuses on the claims of Derrida's article. I have no intention of dismissing Derrida's corpus, containing as it does some intriguing challenges to modernist sensibilities, in a few short pages.

In "Economimesis" Derrida seeks to uproot a perennial source of the belief in presence, namely, the sense of self-grounding and completion that comes from being both the speaker and the hearer of one's own words. As we give birth to our own words we can immediately capture them through our own instrument, the ear, so as to complete a circuit and ourselves. Autoaffection, Derrida would have us believe, is a consequence of being able to speak and hear, a process of production and closure, which makes reflection and closed systems second nature to us. He proceeds in "Economimesis" by taking to task the notion of the mimetic. But the mimetic he criticizes is not a notion of mere imitation, as when one speaks of a work of art imitating life. What concerns him is the activity of imitating the (self) productive power of nature itself, a power our noblest souls, our genii, claim as their own. According to Derrida, it is this sort of mimesis that inspired Kant.

> We have recognized the fold of *mimesis* at the origin of pure productivity, a sort of gift for itself [*pour soi*] of God who makes a present of himself to himself, even prior to the re-productive or imitative structures (that is foreign and inferior to the Fine-Arts): genius imitates nothing, it identifies itself with the productive freedom of God who identifies himself in himself, at the origin of the origin, with the production of production. . . . The analogy between the free productivity of nature and the free productivity of genius, between God and the Poet, is not only a relation of proportionality or a relation between two—two subjects, two origins, two productions. The analogical process is also a refluence towards the *logos*. The origin is the *logos*. The origin of analogy, that from which analogy proceeds and towards which it returns, is the *logos*, reason and word, source as a mouth and as an outlet [*embouchure*].[95]

Kant not only privileges the speaking arts in general, Derrida tells us, but he privileges certain forms of the spoken word over others, poetry over rhetoric. Why? Poetic speech is truthful speech, and it can be truthful because it allows full presence. And presence is guaranteed by the word that issues from the mouth and can be captured immediately by the ear. "The value of full presence guarantees both the truth and the morality of the poetic. The plenitude can only be achieved within the interiority of hearing oneself-speak [*du s'entendre-parler*] and poetic formalisation favors the process of interiorization by doing without the aid of any external sensible content."[96]

This is a sin of sorts for Derrida. It is a sin against the absent, that which is excluded, the other that cannot and should not be fully (re)appropriated. The autoaffection of speech resounds in the chord that blends mouth–speech–logos–idealization–mastery. Commenting on Kant, Derrida tells us, "If hearing-oneself-speak, in so far as it also passes through a certain mouth, transforms everything into auto-affection, assimilates everything to itself by idealizing it within interiority, masters everything by mourning its passing, refusing to touch it, to digest it naturally, but digests it ideally, consumes what it does not consume and *vice versa*, produces disinterestedness in the possibility of pronouncing judgments, . . . what is the border or the absolute overboard [*le bord ou le débord absolu*] of this problematic?"[97]

Is there an excluded that frames and gives contour to this closed system? If there is it cannot be the negative, for even negation can be included and disarmed within a logophonocentric system. The excluded must be the indigestible, "an irreducible heterogeneity," that which does not allow itself to be "transformed into oral auto-affection,"[98] that which by definition resists system. And Derrida tells us the answer to this puzzle with tongue somewhat in cheek: "Vomit lends its form to this whole system,"[99] for it is the thoroughly indigestible.

It appears that Derrida hopes to undermine the power of speech to master through presence by appealing to "an irreducible heterogeneity" or an unrepentant excess. (The return of *de trop*, as the Sartreans might have it.) What is at stake, however, is not whether we can pay the unsystematizable its due, live with heterogeneity and excess, and hence avoid the totality of system, but whether Derrida does justice to the various possibilities for understanding the role of language and speech in Kant. Does Kant's understanding of the connection between speech, communication, and universality necessarily promote the hegemonic, as Derrida clearly suggests? Derrida quotes Kant from paragraph 18 of his *Anthropology from a Pragmatic Point of View:* "It is precisely by this element, moved by the organ of voice, the mouth, that men, more easily and more completely, enter with others in a community of thought and sensations, especially if the sounds that each gives the other to hear are articulated and if, linked together by understanding according to laws, they constitute a language."[100] Derrida replies,

> "More easily and more completely": no exterior means is necessary, nothing exterior poses an obstacle. Communication here is closer to freedom and spontaneity. It is also more complete, since interiority expresses itself here directly. It is more universal for these reasons. Speaking now of tone and modulation, the third *Critique* discovers in hearing a sort of "universal tongue." And once sounds no longer have any relation of natural representation with external sensible things, they are more easily linked to the spontaneity of the understanding.[101]

It is worth noting that the passage Derrida quotes is from Kant's *Anthropology*, whereas his comments refer to the third *Critique*. But this is not to deny that there is a special place for hearing among the five senses for Kant. The question is whether Derrida is correct about the implications of Kant's claims. To examine Derrida's remarks, I return to Arendt's reading of the third *Critique*. Recall that for Arendt the Western philosophical tradition can be seen as emphasizing the Socratic quest for self-consistency. Yet, as I have noted, she tells us that in the *Critique of Judgement* "Kant insisted upon a different way of thinking, for which it would not be enough to be in agreement with one's own self, but which consisted of being able to 'think in the place of everybody else' and which he therefore called an 'enlarged mentality' (*eine erweiterte Denkungsart*)."[102]

Arendt is not only interested in suggesting that there is an irreducible intersubjective element in judgments of taste and that one cannot escape an appeal to *sensus communis* in such judgments. She also wants to emphasize that intersubjective relations entail a genuine plurality of actors, a plurality that is a necessary condition for the meaningfulness of speech. "And this enlarged way of thinking, which as judgment knows how to transcend its own individual limitations . . . cannot function in strict isolation or solitude; it needs the presence of others 'in whose place' it must think, whose perspectives it must take into consideration, and without whom it never has the opportunity to operate at all."[103]

And the connection here to freedom of thought is significant. Arendt quotes Kant as claiming,

> It is said: the freedom to speak or to write can be taken away from us by the powers-that-be, but the freedom to think cannot be taken from us through them at all. However, how much and how correctly would we think if we did not think in community with others to whom we communicate our thoughts and who communicate theirs to us! Hence, we may safely state that the external power which deprives man of the freedom to communicate his thoughts *publicly* also takes away his freedom to *think*, the only treasure left to us in our civic life and through which alone there may be a remedy against all evils of the present state of affairs.[104]

Now Derrida appears concerned that otherness is readily appropriated through the reflected word. But there is a real issue here of how one understands this appropriation. Must we understand the word as an always already (re)appropriated moment—a done deal—or are we dealing with a recouping that often fails itself? The accusation appears to be that with the vocal one always has at one's disposal the pleasure of consensus with oneself and by extension with one's community of interlocutors, who also accept the self-grounding of the vocal. Furthermore, we cannot seem to stop ourselves from being seduced by the word's pretense of presence.

But does speech always rest assured in the immediacy of an autoaffective moment, or doesn't the anticipatory nature of communication often humble this mode of (self) presentation? Political speech, in having to meet the words of others for confirmation, appears to involve ever-renewed negotiations for Arendt, and Mead would extend this to speech in general. When Dewey and Mead look to consensus, they see it not as an event but as an ongoing process, so that "permanent consensus" would be an oxymoron. Perhaps Derrida merely exaggerates the degree to which speech breeds the autoaffective. However, if Derrida exaggerates to make a point about the hegemonic character of the autoaffective word or to score one against Kant, he allows his voice to dismiss actual practices in the pursuit of the grand statement. As the pragmatists would say, we are dealing with differences that make a difference here. To adequately and fairly address them entails (in part) a turn to the empirical, to concrete practices and competencies.

Would Derrida deny the slippage in meaning that presses us to negotiate? Hardly. It is clearly woven into the fabric of language for him. How, then, is one to react to his aperçus? A Deweyesque response to the Derridean machine has a certain appeal: Perhaps what stands behind his suspicions of the word is his suspicion that ordinary folk and philosophers have not recognized how their speech deforms the different and denies the absent, overwhelmed as they are by the presence of the word. Strategy: Bypass the word, and write about the written. Possible consequence: A lack of respect for actual social intercourse and the very real accomplishments of the bearers of speech.

A model of universality that does not overwhelm and dismiss the particular would be of assistance in meeting some features of Derrida's concerns. Mead has such a model to offer. His model of functional universality—which would be too empirical for Kant's taste and yet has a definite kinship to Arendt's reading of the third *Critique*—was addressed earlier in this chapter. For Mead, as noted, significant symbols—that is, words—which are heard as they are spoken (and are apt to leave us mired in autoaffection for Derrida), arise and must be maintained in and through the interactions of agents. They are universal only in a restricted sense, for they are born in particularity and remain tied to distinct communities, even if the communities are understood as abstract communities, such as a scientific community that uses a particular symbolic system. However, the use of significant symbols implies an irreducible moment of universality. "But signification is not confined to the particular situation within which an indication is given. It acquires universal meaning. Even if the two [individuals] are the only ones involved [in using a symbol], the form in which it is given is universal—it would have the same meaning to any other *who might find himself in the same position.*"[105]

The emphasis in the last sentence should fall on "might," that is, on the possibility of finding oneself in the same (or similar) position as another and thereby understanding a symbol in the same fashion. Because of this "might," no position is permanently enthroned for Mead. We are not dealing with a guarantee of universality here but of its possibility, and it is the possibility of shared positions that makes our plural world potentially one world. To attempt to locate and share (in some sense) in the positions of others is required for Kant's enlarged mentality, as we have seen. It is also required for what Mead calls international-mindedness. And Mead doesn't doubt that sharing is at times possible, despite all the intricacies and false starts that the use of language entails. After all, language does not exist in a hermetically sealed universe.

Consider how Derrida uses a quote from Kant's *Anthropology*. Kant says about the deaf person,

> One can evoke by gestures the usual speech from a deaf person, granted that he has once been able to hear. In this, the eyes serve [in place of ears]. The same thing may happen through observing the movements of his teacher's lips, indeed by feeling the movements of the lips of the other person, and this [of course] can occur in darkness [where not sight, but touch, is the substitute for hearing]. If the person is born deaf, however, the sense of seeing the movements of another's organs of speech must convert the sounds, which his teacher has coaxed from him, into a feeling of the movement of his own speech muscles. But he will never attain real concepts [*wirklichen Begriffen*], since the signs necessary to him are not capable of universality. . . . Which deficiency [*Mangel*] or loss of sense is more serious, that of hearing or sight? When it is inborn, deficiency of hearing is the least reparable [*ersetzlich*].[106]

To this Derrida replies, "Hence hearing, by its unique position, by its allergy to prosthesis, by the auto-affective structure that distinguishes it from sight, by its proximity to the inside and to the concept, by the constitutive process of hearing-oneself-speak is not merely one of the senses among others." He continues, as quoted earlier, "If hearing-oneself-speak, in so far as it also passes through a certain mouth, transforms everything into auto-affection, assimilates everything to itself by idealizing it within interiority, masters everything by mourning its passing, refusing to touch it, to digest it naturally, but digests it ideally, consumes what it does not consume and *vice versa*, produces disinterestedness in the possibility of pronouncing judgments, . . . what is the border or the absolute overboard [*le bord ou le débord absolu*] of this problematic?"[107]

What is most striking here is that Derrida's machine for reducing the speaking–hearing circuit to autoaffection, to a moment of idealization, has bypassed what is compelling and follows from Kant's account: the role of the other in the self-education (of the senses).[108] One does not learn language without hearing the other speak. If I could not hear the other, I could not learn to hear myself. Derrida has punctuated the process at the point of seeming completion in the autoaffection of the language-bearing adult, but the genesis of this capacity must be addressed to understand the nature of the capacity, and this is just what Mead attempts to do. And when we do so we discover the obvious; that is, we are not only confirmed in the usage of terms by others but challenged and led into negotiation by them. Nor is the genesis of speech something one can dismiss when, as an adult, one has autoaffective language at one's disposal, for as Kant noted in his passage about free speech quoted earlier, I continue to need the other in order to think. I need the other so that my own language does not lose its capacity to reveal and to judge. This, I take it, Arendt saw as a crucial aspect of the unique kind of thinking that Kant put forth in the third *Critique*. Monological consistency in not enough, and truth out of its proper sphere can even be pernicious, at least for the political and social worlds of human beings.

According to Arendt, truth and opinion are very different things and are addressed in separate spheres of human interest. Arendt is telling us that Kant perceived something of this when he acknowledged that our route of access to the tasteful is very different from our path to science. Yet Kant's disciplinary sensibilities—which allowed him to divide the world so conveniently into moral, scientific, and aesthetic realms (that is, into spheres of practical reason, understanding, and feeling)—did not carry him to the shores of Arendt's extreme bifurcation of truth and opinion.[109] Nevertheless, Arendt's pressing of this distinction can be understood (to some degree) as stemming from a Kantian imperative to avoid the dangers that flow from conflating distinct spheres.

But of course, Derrida would press on. It isn't the micro-autoaffective system (of the person) that he worries most about; it is a macro-autoaffective system, that is, a civilization, our Western logocentric civilization, that vaporizes the past (and all that is marginal) by having as its only horizon the living presence of its word. The narcissism of the vocal has no real challengers on the macro level, for all of our negotiations take place within the horizons of its words, its culture. Isn't what is at stake here whether our speech can honor not only the marginalized living but also the dead, or at least respect their footprints? In Arendt's reading Kant had his parallel dilemma: If I believe in progress, how do I not violate the worth of our ancestors, who seem to have become a means for acculturation of the species? Despite his transcendental musings and dreams of universal progress, the question of the sanctity of the other, even the other who no longer lives, did not go unnoticed by the sage of Königsberg. It remains to be seen whether modern-day (neo-)Kantians (namely, Habermas) and pragmatists can speak of and to the dead.

3 Universality and Individuality: Habermas and Mead

Contemporary social theorists often must confront the question of how a social conception of the self can explain existential freedom and the integrity of the individual. This is not a new issue. A century and a half ago Kierkegaard challenged a modern social conception of the self by waging a dramatic war against Hegel, his system, and his notion of universality. Kierkegaard would have found Mead's position wanting, no doubt because he would have read Mead as a systems theorist, despite the latter's claim that the individual must be understood in terms of the "I" and "me," that is, in terms of spontaneity and system. Habermas probably would have fared no better at Kierkegaard's hands.

Habermas has had to confront a seemingly endless string of criticisms of his various appeals to the notion of universality. And the challenges have come not only from friendly critics who argue that he has failed to justify a quasitranscendental approach to universality in his discourse ethics but also from those who feel that any appeal to universality is bound to an Enlightenment project that can only deny difference. There are those—rear-guard existentialists, phenomenologists, the followers of Levinas or Buber—who would argue that his approach simply cannot grasp the irreducible otherness and uniqueness of the individual.

This last criticism appears to be the motivating factor behind Habermas's significant and extended article on Mead: "Individuation through Socialization: On George Herbert Mead's Theory of Subjectivity." In this piece Habermas asserts that the Western sociological tradition has failed to account for individuation. Sociologists have continually confused processes of differentiation with those of individualization. Habermas states that Hegel could still appeal to "the concept of the 'individual totality' in order to explain why the mere diversity of predicative determinations does not exhaust the essence of individuality. But the sociologist, who finds himself faced with similar problems on his own terrain, lacks an equivalent concept; he lacks the reference point that could prevent him from confusing processes of individualization with processes of differentiation." Habermas then goes on to claim, "The only promising attempt to grasp the entire significance of social individualization in concepts is, I believe, initiated in the social psychology of George Herbert Mead."[1]

The stakes are suitably high. Habermas has tied his hopes for redressing social theory's failure to understand individuation to Mead's approach. Furthermore, the ante is raised because Habermas argues that modern experiences of individuation, in terms of both autonomy and life history, are inextricably linked to a notion of universality that he believes he shares with Mead. In this chapter I examine just how far Habermas has succeeded in correctly interpreting Mead's project and suggest some of the implications of his reading. What is ultimately at stake, however, is not merely the accuracy of an interpretation of an important historical figure but possible avenues for approaching some of the most trenchant issues in contemporary philosophy and social theory. What makes the task difficult is that Habermas is quite close to Mead on many critical points; what makes it necessary is that a failure to untangle their thought leaves the impression that Mead's position suffers from some of the same difficulties that plague Habermas's thought, thereby masking the potentially unique contributions Mead and the pragmatic tradition have to offer contemporary social theory and philosophy. I also develop further Mead's positions on universality, pluralism, and the individual. After an account of Levinas's position in chapter 4, chapter 5 returns to the question of individuality in Mead's thought in the context of addressing Levinas's critique of Western philosophy's failure to appreciate the true nature of impartiality and the uniqueness of the other.

I turn first to Mead and passages from a letter he wrote to his wife's parents at the end of his second semester as an instructor at the University of Michigan. As a young teacher at the University of Michigan, Mead fell under the influence of the chair of his department, John Dewey. Mead, in turn, came to influence his lifelong friend in the years ahead. Just how fully he shared Dewey's democratized Hegelianism at this time can be seen in this intriguing letter. Mead—who grew up in a deeply religious Congregationalist household, studied philosophy with Josiah Royce at Harvard and with Dilthey and Wundt in Germany, studied physiology in Germany, and in his later years was the quintessential secular humanist—writes under Dewey's influence,

> I have been able in the year that I have passed here to make a synthesis of the abstract thinking that I have done, have studied and listened to ever since I became interested in philosophy, and [the] meaning of American life—have been able to follow the connection that has gradually been established between abstract philosophy and daily life.
>
> I have learned to see that society advances, men get closer and closer to each other and the kingdom of heaven is established on the earth, so far as man becomes more and more organically connected with nature. This has generally been laid up against America as materialism—and she has been scouted as sunk in money getting and as letting go [the] spiritual side of life. But it seems to me clearer every day that the telegraph and locomotive are the great spiritualizers of society because they bind man and man so close together that the interest of the individual must be more completely the interest of all day by day. And America in pushing this spiritualizing of nature is doing more than all in bringing the day when every man will be my neighbor and all life shall be saturated with the divine life.[2]

And in the same letter he goes on to talk about physiology. "For me in Physiological Psychology the especial problem is to recognize that our psychical life can all be read in the functions of our bodies—that it is not the brain that thinks but . . . our organs so far as they act together in processes of life. This is quite a new standpoint for the science and has a good many important consequences—especially does it offer new methods of experiment which must be worked out."[3] Less than a year later he enthusiastically wrote to a close friend, "I have at last reached a position I used to dream of in Harvard—where it is possible to apply good straight phys. psy. to Hegel, and I don't know what more a mortal can want on earth."[4]

My purpose in quoting these passages—besides the sheer desire to confirm suspicions that the present obsession in the United States with the information superhighway has its roots in an American salvation tradition—is to suggest that much of Habermas's misreading of Mead can be accounted for by a lack of appreciation of Mead's lifelong quasi-Hegelian commitment to reconciling the local and concrete with the universal. As a matter of fact, were it not for its oxymoronic ring, the phrase "contextual universalist" might be a suitable label for Mead. The mature Mead would have found Habermas's universalist vision too dependent on a thin, linguistified, procedural domain, and this despite clear sympathies he would have had for a nontranscendental interpretation and application of the principles of Habermas's discourse ethics. In terms of the thinness of Habermas's universalism, one of the themes that stands out in Mead's letters is the overcoming of divisions—for example, of mind and body—through an experimental study of physiology, a concern that is reflected in the importance the attitudinal and bodily in his mature thought. The issue of divisions, of alienation, is addressed in chapter 5. I return to Mead shortly.

For Habermas, we no longer live in a time when "social types" or roles are the only source of individuation. In a postconventional context the individual must see herself as responsible for her own story and her own morality. This encounter with one's postconventional self requires a universalistic vantage point from which to judge and view the self, a vantage point that has become a live option in the modern world. The following passage brings together nicely a number of the critical themes of Habermas's article while clearly revealing the influences of Kant and Mead, as well as Peirce and Hegel.

> The idealizing supposition of a universalistic form of life, in which everyone can take up the perspective of everyone else and can count on reciprocal recognition by everybody, makes it possible for individuated beings to exist within a community—individualism as the flip side of universalism. Taking up a relationship to a projected form of society is what first makes it possible for me to take my own life history seriously as a principle of individuation—to regard it *as if it were* the product of decisions for which I am responsible. The self-critical appropriation and reflexive continuation of my life history would have to remain a nonbinding or even an indeterminate idea as long as I could not encounter myself before the eyes of all, i.e., before the forum of an unlimited communication community.[5]

In a paragraph Habermas has managed to suggest a notion of self-fashioning that brings together Mead's claims about the necessity of social interaction for the genesis of a self, Hegel's dialectic of recognition (which is related to Mead's model), and Kant's quest for the universal, but in the form of communication community that Habermas views as being rooted in the work of Peirce. He has also managed to make the remarkable claim that one cannot ultimately take one's own life history seriously—that is, one cannot become fully individuated—unless one can ground one's uniqueness through a relationship to an unlimited communication community.[6]

Habermas argues that if we presume that the self arises through a process of affirmation and recognition, then we must look to something more than immediately or mediately given roles to explain postconventional morality and selfhood. Why? Premodern selves tended to be defined in terms of specific networks of interaction that should be thought of in terms of social types. To deal with the challenges of increasing societal differentiation in the modern world, individuals have been pressed to "reconstruct conventional identity." These processes of societal differentiation "have set in motion a generalization of values and, especially in the system of rights, a universalization of norms, and these processes demand a specific kind of independent accomplishment from the socialized individual. The onus of these decisions requires a nonconventional ego-identity."[7]

Habermas's borrows Mead's well-known "I–me" distinction to suggest that the "I" "*projects* the context of interaction that first makes the reconstruction of a shattered conventional identity possible on a higher level."[8] This "higher level" makes irreducible individuality possible. Because so much of Habermas's argument hinges on an interpretation of Mead's terms, it may be helpful to return briefly to some of the latter's key ideas.

As noted in chapter 1, Mead's role theory should be approached in light of his understanding of symbolic interaction, which in turn was indebted to Wundt's work on gestures. For Mead, although many animals have the capacity to gesture to each other, human beings are capable of reflexively responding to symbols, which most often occurs through vocal gestures. I can hear my words as I speak, and as I speak I can also see your response. A capacity for responding to one's own gestures as the other responds to them emerges, and with it there develops a consciousness of meaning based on a functional identity of responses. One learns to anticipate the responses of others and thereby also learns to respond to oneself as if one were the other. Constellations of responses arise that call out other constellations, and these can be thought of as roles. It is worth noting here that an ability to reverse positions or perspectives is built into the fabric of our symbolic interaction.[9]

As we have seen, not only do we take roles in relation to specific others, but roles become systematically organized in terms of generalized others. This occurs when I take the perspective of a social group and see myself as a self, as a "me," in relationship to a group. Groups that give rise to generalized others can be thought of as systems, which have implicit or explicit behavioral rules. The term *system* here is open ended—a ball team, an institution, or a family can be conceived of as a system—whereas the term *rule* can be understood as a pattern of interaction. Each system can also be called a perspective. One can be said to take the perspective of the other both when one takes roles and when one takes more complex networks of responses that are understood in terms of generalized others. There is an intimate link between Mead's notion of universals and his concept of the generalized other.

As we shall see, Habermas is quite convinced that he is operating with notions of universality and rationality that are comparable to Mead's, and in many respects they indeed are. Nevertheless, there are crucial differences, and these differences when fleshed out have repercussions for a number of controversies in contemporary ethical and social theory. Perhaps the easiest way to frame the discussion is by suggesting that Habermas is ultimately a Kantian who knows that one cannot be a full-fledged Kantian in a post-Hegelian and pragmatic world. Mead, on the other hand, can be viewed as developing an empiricized and pluralized Hegelianism that is also in line with implications and aspects of Kant's third *Critique*. Habermas, though bowing to the historical and empirical, finds his transcendental aspirations driving him to locate a suitably respectable sociological substitute for the *a priori* of the second *Critique*. Or, to be more specific, Habermas's reading of Mead is systematically misleading because he takes Mead's genuine cosmopolitanism, which is clearly in the Kantian spirit of the enlarged mentality, and combines it with a distorted account of Mead's understanding of the "me" and the "I," as we will see later. This leads the reader to believe that Mead would have endorsed the notion of an unlimited communication community, not as a guiding ideal of interaction—which Mead would have endorsed—but as the condition for the possibility of autonomy *and* individuated life history. Among the repercussions of such an approach is that it undercuts the importance of the attitudinal and habitual in Mead.

Before turning to Habermas's text, a word on the "I" in Mead's thought is in order. In chapter 1 we saw that if the "me" were thought of as the socially constituted "object" of which we are aware, then the "I" could be viewed as that which allows us be aware of this object. The "I" can be understood as the "consciousness of" that allows this social object to appear, and when one is conscious of this "me," one can be said to be self-conscious in the sense of being aware of an identity. Although the "me" presupposes the existence of an "I," the latter is never directly presented in conscious experience.[10] Mead tells us that "if you ask, then, where directly in your own experience the 'I' comes in, the answer is that it comes in as a historical figure."[11] And therefore it has become a "me." The "I" is also the "locus" of novel responses.

With these elements of Mead's orientation in mind, we can turn once again to Habermas's claim that it is the "I" itself that "*projects* the context of interaction that first makes the reconstruction of a shattered conventional identity possible on a higher level."[12] How does the "I" accomplish this? By anticipating a universalistic community, that is, a projected communication community from which it can return to itself to define itself in postconventional terms. Habermas tells us that "a post conventional ego-identity can only stabilize itself in the anticipation of symmetrical relations of unforced reciprocal recognition."[13] Because of this idealized community I can define myself as having a life history that is not circumscribed by any particular role. I can determine and define myself because of the possible affirmations of this community. Modernity has prepared the way for such an anticipatory dialogue through its future directedness, a future directedness that views the present in terms of anticipated future-presents.

Habermas distinguishes two sides of a postconventional ego-identity: moral autonomy and individuated life history. One does not relate to oneself as the alter ego of a member of a concrete group (that is, as a "me") to achieve a postconventional ego-identity, but "as the alter ego of *all* others in every community—specifically, as a free will in moral self-reflection and as a fully individuated being in existential self-reflection."[14] Although no doubt Habermas would want us to remain open for a dialogue with specific others—one must avoid the ethereality of the purely transcendental—the fact is that the stabilization of a postconventional ego identity depends on our relationship to an anticipated unlimited communication community. It is the "I" that has the task of anticipating this community. Habermas claims that "the anticipatory establishment of interactive relations to a circle of addressees is imputed to the 'I' itself; for it is from their perspective that the 'I' is able to return to itself and assure itself of itself as an autonomous will and an individuated being."[15]

In other words, we now have a postconventional ego-identity, the result of seeing oneself "as the alter ego of *all* others in every community." This is a very clever move. If Nietzsche could call Kant an underhanded Christian, then at least in this context we can call Habermas a quasi-Kantian in Mead's clothing. But something must be seriously amiss here if Habermas believes that Mead's position has led to this result. The notion of an "I" that can return to itself and assure itself of its autonomy and individuality clearly departs from Mead's understanding of the functions of the "I." Habermas's position is especially curious given that Mead was willing to refer to the "I" as a "fictitious 'I' always out of sight of himself."[16] Mead would insist that no return is "pure," and it is possible only by way of the mediation of a "me."[17]

Mead emphasizes that the "I" should be viewed in terms of novel responses; its freedom, so to speak, needs no reassurance because in a sense it is spontaneity even if it is a spontaneity whose responses are contextualized by and addressed to prior conditions. One must take quite seriously the moment of spontaneity, novelty, that the "I" represents and not ground it too quickly in an autonomous reflexivity. From Mead's vantage point one can only conclude that Habermas is sneaking in some sort of a quasitranscendental ego that threatens the *existential* spontaneity of the "I."

Even more problematic is the manner in which Habermas connects the notions of autonomy and individuation.[18] By appealing to an unlimited communication community he believes that he has found a moment of liberation from the conventional that allows one to be autonomous. But even if we set aside the difficulties of establishing an autonomous ego in this fashion (and the tendency on Habermas's part to conflate the voluntary in the pragmatic tradition with the autonomous in the Kantian tradition[19]), and even if we agree that the conditions for the possibility of autonomy could best be met by considering the role of an unlimited communication community, it wouldn't follow that a postconventional sense of individuation should be grounded in the same fashion or, more accurately, that it needs to be grounded in this fashion at all. The major challenge a postconventional identity must meet is the integration and maintenance of a multitude of selves in some sort of coherent whole, whereas the challenge facing the ego who wants to become autonomous is the constraints of the conventional. Habermas uses the same mechanism to ground both, however, and in so doing fails to articulate the conditions for a full-bodied individuality. He fails to do so because he too closely affiliates the idea of "the continuity of [one's] life history" with the idea of being responsible for oneself.[20] Note his language here: "Taking up a relationship to a projected form of society is what first makes it possible for me to take my own life history seriously as a principle of individuation—to regard it *as if it were* the product of decisions for which I am responsible."[21]

Habermas has simply transformed the problem of individuality into a species of the problem of autonomy. Having warned us in the past against conflating the moral and the ethical, Habermas appears to be doing just that through the manner in which he frames the question of individuality. And, I might add, his appeal to the logic of the use of first- and second-person pronouns to support his orientation cannot go very far in resolving certain difficulties he faces. The use of a grammatical "I" might reinforce or assist one in remaining individuated, but it can do very little to help supply the continuity a so-called postconventional self requires. Why? Because the issue here is how one can achieve continuity or unity in the face of having to face so many different others, so many different mirrors through which we examine and, in part, come to be who we are.[22] It is precisely the multiplicity of others that is so challenging in this regard, a challenge that requires a heightened sensitivity to how we contribute to the shaping of our own narratives as we negotiate our relationships with these others. (Mead did not speak in terms of narrative, but I believe that his approach can accommodate the notion of it presented here.)

For Mead, we do not seek to be assured simply that we are unique, but that we are unique in some specific manner, in relation to a vital community.[23] Although Habermas would view such an emphasis on the interactional as jeopardizing both autonomy and irreducible individuality, he is pressing for an abstract approach to individuality that Mead would find inadequate to the task at hand. Unfortunately, in his quest Habermas may appear to be giving the "I" and "me" their due, but in fact he is transforming the nature of Mead's concepts. Habermas accomplishes this in part by viewing the "me" as so purely conventional that a post-conventional "I" must come to its rescue to help ground identity and autonomy. By making this move Habermas manages to undercut the whole dialectic of social and political transformation that is made possible by the relationship of the "me" to the "I" in Mead's thought and to undercut the notion that one can be a critical contextualist. Note how Habermas characterizes the "me." "The 'me' characterizes an identity formation that makes responsible action possible only at the price of blind subjugation to external social controls, which remain external in spite of the internalizing effect of role-taking."[24]

Habermas confines the universalizing potential of the individual to the "I" precisely to avoid the dangers of the conventional. Yet his clear-cut division between conventional and postconventional can be viewed as turning on a parochial understanding of the "me."[25] He is in fact conflating his own notion of a hyperconventional "me" with Mead's concept. The "me" is indeed conventional, but its conventionality is given a wide berth in Mead and includes sensibilities Habermas might even think of as postconventional. For example, one could define a "me" in terms of an international agency—an organization of the United Nations, for instance—in which the conventional is actually universalistic, at least in a sense that Mead would accept. And certain "me's" can oblige an "I" to act or try to act in a universalistic fashion. Leaving to one side the "I" and "me" jargon for a moment, what is at stake here is whether, in what manner, and to what degree the sphere of the substantive must be kept apart from the procedural to guarantee criticality and individuality. For Habermas both self-determination and self-realization require being saved from the stifling grip of the "me's" conventionality. Mead simply does not have to view the "me" in this fashion.

Because one cannot step outside one's social skin, Habermas is clear that the solution to the conventionality of the "me" will entail an appeal to a self capable of defining itself in terms of a community that transcends the given. The question is how we are to understand such an larger self. For Mead, the answer takes us to some extent back to Hegel. For although the "I" is the initiator of the novel, it can also be viewed as actualizing principles that are implicit in a given historical epoch or society. Its creative activity is at times a discovery of implicit possibilities. The following example, in which Mead discusses the connection between the "I" and genius, reveals something of this:

> An individual of the type to which we are referring arises always with reference to a form of society or social order which is implied but not adequately expressed. Take the religious genius, such as a Jesus or Buddha, or the reflective type, such as Socrates. What has given them their unique importance is that they have taken the attitude of living with reference to *a* larger society. That larger state was one which was already more or less implied in the institutions of the community in which they lived. Such an individual is divergent from the point of view of what we would call the prejudices of the community; but in another sense he expresses the principles of the community more completely than any other.[26]

And it is the individual who is attuned to the possibilities of a given social structure who is in the best position to help effect such a transformation.[27] "It is this feel for a social structure which is implicit in what is present that haunts the generous nature, and carries a sense of obligation which transcends any claim that his actual social order fastens upon him. It is an ideal world that lays the claim upon him, but it is an ideal world which grows out of this world and its undeniable implications."[28]

Of course, we can be critical for Mead. The critical edge arises from our capacity to engage in reflection, which is grounded in the activity of taking alternative perspectives. We can at times step outside the community in which we find ourselves by appealing, as Mead tells us, to a "higher sort of community which in a certain sense out-votes the one we find."[29] And sometimes the communities into which we step can be defined in highly abstract terms, such as a community of logical discourse. We are drawn to step out of a given community by conflicts that are part of our world. "The ethical problem," Mead says, "is always a specific one, and belongs only to those habits and values which have come into conflict with each other."[30]

This last quotation is from Mead's article "Philanthropy from the Point of View of Ethics" and is found in a paragraph that Habermas leans on rather heavily in his interpretation of Mead. He does so not only in his article on individuation but also in *The Theory of Communicative Action*. It is arguably the paragraph in Mead that most closely supports Habermas's reading of Mead. So we shall take the case to Habermas's doorstep by first reproducing the passage as it appears in the English version of *The Theory of Communicative Action*.

> In logical terms there is established a *universe of discourse which transcends the specific order* within which the members of the community ["may" in Mead], in a specific conflict, place themselves outside of the community order as it exists, and agree upon changed habits of action and a restatement of values. *Rational procedure*, therefore, sets up an order within which thought operates, that abstracts in varying degrees from the actual structure of society. . . . It is *a social order that includes any rational being who is or may be in any way implicated in the situation with which thought deals.* It sets up an ideal world, not of substantive things, but of proper method. Its claim is that all the conditions of conduct and all the values which are involved in the conflict must be taken into account in abstraction from the fixed forms of habits and goods which have clashed with each other. It is evident that a man cannot act as a rational member of society, except as he constitutes himself as ["as" added in *TCA2*] a member of this wider common world ["commonwealth" in Mead] of rational beings.[31]

In "Individuation through Socialization" Habermas uses the same passage but breaks it up with his own commentary, whereas in the German version of the latter he replaces Mead's "a universe of discourse" in the first sentence with the German phrase for "unbounded communication community" so that there is little question that an equation between the two has been and should be made.[32] There are good reasons for questioning this correspondence. A "universe of discourse," for Mead, is not solely, or even essentially, a projected or ideal community. Mead claims that "this universe of discourse is constituted by a group of individuals carrying on and participating in a common social process of experience and behavior."[33] Furthermore, one can speak in the plural of universes of discourse.

This brings up again the problem of the universal. In so far as the individual takes the attitude of the other that symbol is universal, but is it a true universal when it is so limited? Can we ever get beyond that limitation? The logicians' universe of discourse lays plain the extent of universality. In an earlier stage that universality was supposed to be represented in a set of logical axioms, but the supposed axioms have been found to be not universal. So that, in fact, "universal" discourse to be universal has had to be continually revised. It may represent those rational beings with whom we are in contact, and there is potential universality in such a world as that. . . . There are, of course, different universes of discourse, but back of all, to the extent that they are potentially comprehensible to each other, lies the logicians' universe of discourse.[34]

For Mead, universes of discourse are actual communities. There are varying degrees of universality in Mead's model, with the abstractions of the logician's universe serving as an exemplar because its symbols are potentially available to the widest possible range of individuals. This potential for transparency can be spoken of as counterfactually ideal, but the emphasis always comes back to actual communities, actual universes of discourse. The logician's universe is an actual community, one that has the potential to become ever larger because of the availability of its symbols. It is also a community whose symbols may need revision. Note the connections in the following passage between the universe of discourse, common meanings, and the generalized other, as well as the idea that universality brings with it a certain "impersonality of thought," which we can read as impartiality.

> The significant gesture or symbol always presupposes for its significance the social process of experience and behavior in which it arises; or, as the logicians say, a universe of discourse is always implied as the context in terms of which, or as the field within which, significant gestures or symbols do in fact have significance. This universe of discourse is constituted by a group of individuals carrying on and participating in a common social process of experience and behavior, within which these gestures or symbols have the same or common meanings for all members of that group. . . . A universe of discourse is simply a system of common or social meanings.
>
> The very universality and impersonality of thought and reason is from the behavioristic standpoint the result of the given individual taking the attitudes of others toward himself, and of his finally crystallizing all these particular attitudes into a single attitude or standpoint which may be called that of the "generalized other."[35]

Mead's vision appears to entail a universalism of shared experience, which can lead to a kind of impartiality akin to Smith's impartial spectator, as opposed to a Habermasian one of procedures.[36] As a matter of fact, the danger lurking in the preceding quotation is that it may lead the reader to believe that Mead is a pure contextualist or relativist. For Mead, however, certain procedures, or perhaps I should say certain types of interaction, clearly have a more universalistic ring to them than others and therefore can better help us to share experience. With regard to the notion of "rational procedures," Mead is a minimalist compared to Habermas. I address this issue, and additional questions raised by Habermas's reading of the passage from "Philanthropy," later. But first we should take a further look at elements of Mead's position on universalism.

How can we best understand the connection between universalism and perspectivism in Mead's thought? A sensitivity to perspectives can bring with it a parochialism of the contextual and so end the possibility of impartiality, as Habermas fears. Universalism, on the other hand, runs the danger of riding roughshod over differences. What does Mead have to offer regarding this dilemma? As we have seen, Mead stresses that universals are best described in functional terms. As mentioned in chapters 1 and 2, Mead is willing to call a gesture shared by two interlocutors a universal, in that it is responded to in a similar manner and is sufficiently internalized so that either of them can call out this response in the absence of the other, as when they talk to themselves. "But signification is not confined to the particular situation within which an indication is given. It acquires universal meaning. Even if the two are the only ones involved, the form in which it is given is universal—it would have the same meaning to any other who might find himself in the same position."[37]

As noted in earlier in this work, what makes the symbol a universal for Mead is not merely its actually being shared but its potential to be understood by anyone who "might find himself in the same position." Mead believed that it is indeed possible to stand linguistically in the position of the other, in part because language is itself tied to attitudes. For the purposes at hand, *attitudes* can be described as physiologically based preparations for activity, and they arise through involvement in shared contexts or environments.[38] Furthermore, Mead tells us that "the development of communication is not simply a matter of abstract ideas, but is a process of putting one's self in the place of the other person's attitude, communicating through significant symbols."[39]

With these insights we can begin to specify further Mead's understanding of the place of universality in our personal, political, and moral lives. On a purely descriptive level, universality is the sharing of symbols and attitudes between two or more interlocutors, with the proviso that in Mead's words, "any other who might find himself in the same position" could do the same. But this descriptive take on universality is closely connected with a prescriptive one. For Mead, while it is true that modern forces of interdependence are pressing us in the direction of enlarging our frames of reference, we have a compelling moral obligation to actually find ways to share perspectives. "We all belong to small cliques, and we may remain simply inside of them. The 'organized other' present in ourselves is then a community of a narrow diameter. We are struggling now to get a certain amount of international-mindedness. We are realizing ourselves as members of a larger community. The vivid nationalism of the present period *should*, in the end, call out an international attitude of the larger community."[40] The *should* here appears to be descriptive, but there is also a prescriptive ring to these sentiments. And the prescription should not be viewed solely in terms of the institutional, for it extends to our daily interactions with others.

It might be very tempting to equate Mead's references to a "larger" self and community with Habermas's communication community, especially because Mead himself argues for the importance of impartiality and universality in matters of morality. And there are indeed strong affinities. However, Mead would have been wary of divorcing such a community from actual communities and too zealously separating the political and the moral. Habermas is certainly aware of the fact that in practice one cannot readily separate the moral and political, but he insists on their conceptual separation because he believes that without it discourse ethics will lose even its limited transcendental ground. Mead's position is different. His words on how differentiation should operate in a democracy are revelatory in this regard. A democratic community strives to enhance differences, in terms of both groups and individuals, and it can do so because it is held together in part by the presence of universals, which must be understood in terms of the activity of taking the attitudes of others. Attitudes are not purely cognitive, if we mean by cognitive that which is currently undergoing reflective appraisal.

> It is often assumed that democracy is an order of society in which those personalities which are sharply differentiated will be eliminated, that everything will be ironed down to a situation where everyone will be, as far as possible, like everyone else. But of course that is not the implication of democracy: the implication of democracy is rather that the individual can be as highly developed as lies within the possibilities of his own inheritance, and *still can enter into the attitudes of the others whom he affects.*[41]

For Mead, an attitude is not to be understood as taking place solely at a linguistic or cognitive level, for it must also be understood in terms of the habitual and biological.[42] The formal *a priori* togetherness that we find in Kant, or even the improved dialogical one of the communication community in Habermas, tends to set aside the attitudinal and the kind of existential confirmation that comes in the wake of the sharing of attitudes.[43] Although it is no doubt true that the larger selves that Mead hopes and expects to come into being are objects of cognition, there is a sense in which one can be said to have universalistic attitudes, which, for example, may be inferred from a receptivity to new responses.[44] And these attitudes can be understood in both moral and political terms. Emphasizing this aspect of Mead's position has definite repercussions for the kinds of activities we take as politically and morally transformative. In this regard it is not a trivial matter that neither Kant nor Habermas would have much use for interpreting popular culture as a possible source of universality. Mead, on the other hand, would find such a path congenial or at least plausible.

It is worth noting here that Mead's position allows for, even necessitates, a notion of rationality that at times comes close to Pierre Bourdieu's position on the nonreflective reasonableness of practices.[45] The role of habit and the reasonableness of everyday practices are continuing themes among pragmatists, and Bourdieu shares a good deal of this sensibility. However, it may appear peculiar to saddle Mead with a notion of reasonableness of this sort, given his emphasis on the importance of reflection in problem-solving behavior. But one has to keep in mind that for Mead much of the world is actually nonproblematic, and the way in which we deal with it is based on our collective experience, which appears before us in the form of *a world that is there*. Furthermore, Mead is well aware that changes that take place in our social worlds often are nonreflective. "Take a person's attitude toward a new fashion. It may at first be one of objection. After a while he gets to the point of thinking of himself in this changed fashion, noticing the clothes in the window and seeing himself in them. The change has taken place in him without him being aware of it. There is, then, a process by means of which the individual in interaction with others inevitably becomes like others in doing the same thing, without that process appearing in what we term consciousness."[46]

I mention this not because Habermas would disagree about the existence of non-(self)-conscious processes (his formal–pragmatic orientation depends on a notion of the implicit) but to suggest that the temper of Mead's thought often comes closer to that of present-day communitarians than that of Habermas. Yet by appealing to the reasonableness of nonreflective practices are we not in danger of losing the ground—reason, that is—on which we can rest critique and morality? We began this section with a concern that Mead's perspectivism might lead to a parochialism, one that might leave us mired in partiality. Without reason supplying a sphere of insight that is separate from our daily practices, will we not be led down the slippery slope of parochialism? Obviously Mead does not think so, for as we have seen, the conventional, the "me," can itself be a source of universality; we can be disposed to view the status quo with the eyes of a "larger" community.[47] Furthermore, we are never completely mired in the day-to-day because the day-to-day presents us with problems that require reflection, and the latter can begin to move us to an enlarged mentality. But perhaps it would be helpful to directly address one of Habermas's greatest concerns in this area, the conflation of strategic and communicative rationality, for without such a distinction we lose the possibility of moral high ground. Habermas distinguishes strategic rationality from communicative rationality in part to help clarify our capacity to critique the status quo. As his analysis of speech directed at mutual understanding attempts to show, certain conditions built into our exchanges guarantee the presence of a nonstrategic form of communicative rationality, which allows us to achieve moral high ground.

However, before we can address the merits of this distinction, a bit more legwork is necessary. We must first consider how Mead might respond to the division between the procedural and ethical in Habermas. It is safe to say that Mead would not have felt the latter's need to sunder the two. As a matter of fact, Mead's words from his article "Philanthropy from the Point of View of Ethics," the same article that Habermas leans on to support his interpretation of Mead, can be used to help show this. Mead's article is intended to show how we must distinguish mere impulses to assist others, which are based on the sympathetic assumption of the place of the other, from more sophisticated responses that entail a sense of obligation, a sense of the effort we must expend to alleviate distress. We move from feeling the other's distress, which incorporates a reaction to assist, to "a judgment upon that situation" that created the pain. Furthermore, "one cannot assume the role of the wretched without considering under what conditions the wretchedness can or may be avoided."[48] We come to resent the individuals or institutions that may be causing such distress. "The step from this attitude to the idea of social conditions under which this evil would not exist is inevitable. Out of these ideas arise plans, possibly practical, for remedying at the source the misfortunes of those in distress."[49]

Mead tells us that such is the path from impulse to social reconstruction. The thrust of his article is to alert us to the fact that real charity should not be confused with merely impulsive sympathetic responses; rather, it entails a responsibility to engage in social reconstruction and reform. The true appeal of charity is not to be found in the mere alleviation of suffering but in the realization of potentials that society has not thus far helped to realize. Those of us who are better off, who have more access to the wealth of society to realize ourselves, "feel the adventitious nature of our advantages, and still more do we feel that the intelligence which makes society possible carries within itself the demand for further development in order that the implications of life may be realized." Mead immediately goes on to say,

> It is this feel for a social structure which is implicit in what is present that haunts the generous nature, and carries a sense of obligation which transcends any claim that his actual social order fastens upon him. It is an ideal world that lays the claim upon him, but it is an ideal world which grows out of this world and its undeniable implications.
> *It is possible to specify the claims of this ideal world in certain respects.*[50]

The last line of this quotation is the first line of the paragraph Habermas leans on in his interpretation of Mead, referred to earlier in this chapter and to which I promised to return.[51] Habermas does *not* quote this line, nor does he reproduce the entirety of Mead's lengthy paragraph. When Habermas's citation from Mead is placed in its original context, and in the context of Mead's references to universes of discourse, it is clear that Mead had no intention of setting up any sort of separate realm of procedural rationality of the Habermasian sort, of separating self-actualization and self-determination, or severing questions of justice from those of the good life. When Mead appeals to an ideal world he means one in which we are not embedded in the impulsive, one in which we allow ourselves to take various perspectives, and by so doing abstract from the sides of a given conflict. Listening to reason here means putting oneself in the place of a social group that can move beyond the partiality of the perspectives or the immediacy of certain impulses that particular actors bring to a specific situation. Given Mead's wording in the paragraph, specifically that he uses the phrase "commonwealth of rational beings," it is understandable that Habermas might read the passage as a reflection of his own ideas. But if Mead were more careful here, and consistent with his own formulations, he would have said that there are actually many commonwealths of reason, and what they share in common is the willingness of their members to judge from an enlarged perspective of another social group or a social group that is implicit in the present one.

Of course, we may still want to know whether Mead's contextual universalism provides any advantages over Habermas's approach. To address this question we turn first to Habermas's own words regarding the steps necessary to show the value of the communicative action for social theory.

> First, it would have to be shown in detailed analyses that all non-strategic interactions are derivates of action oriented to reaching understanding. Then it would have to be demonstrated through conceptual analysis that the rational potential of language can be put into effect only in communicative action, because linguistic communication is, so to speak, by nature aimed at building consensus and not at influencing. And finally, we would have to show, conceptually as well as empirically, that the symbolic structures of the life-world can be reproduced only through the medium of action oriented to understanding.[52]

This is an exceedingly difficult agenda, and many will worry that the upshot of his approach will be to leave our moral intuitions skating on rather thin ice. Habermas must find a (quasi) transcendental ground for the postconventional stage of moral development, a stage that will allow us to realize the implicit universality present in speech geared to understanding, at least with regard to normative rightness. Mead is under no such pressure. If one were to ask him about universal conditions for the possibility of moral insight, not just about universal symbols, he would offer a more modest list than Habermas's. There is the exchange of gestures and the exchange of roles, there is the more complex network of roles that we find in groups that give rise to generalized others. Thus, reciprocity and mutuality are built into the belly of the beast, so to speak, and therefore these conditions can be spoken of as transhistorical, at least for as long as human beings have been language-bearing and role-taking creatures. When one does not simply heed impulse, when one gains some distance on one's activities by internalizing the perspectives of one's fellows, when one anticipates their actions and considers them in one's response, when one uses this ability to see the nonhuman natural world from alternative vantage points—in other words, when one's actions are mediated by the perspectives of others—a moment of rational reflection has arisen. Mead tells us,

> What I have attempted to do is to bring rationality back to a certain type of conduct, the type of conduct in which the individual puts himself in

the attitude of the whole group to which he belongs. This implies that the whole group is involved in some organized activity and that in this organized activity the action of one calls for the action of all the others. What we term "reason" arises when one of the organisms takes into its own response the attitude of the other organisms involved. It is possible for the organism so to assume the attitudes of the group that are involved in its own act within this whole co-operative process. When it does so, it is what we term "a rational being." If its conduct has such universality, it has also necessity, that is, the sort of necessity involved in the whole act—if one acts in one way the others must act in another way.[53]

There are degrees of rationality in Mead's model; the greater the range and extent of specific symbols, the greater the universality and the greater the rationality. This is an equation that clearly will not end debates about the nature of reason. Needless to say, Habermas would find it a bit thin and filled with the danger of leaving reason, the guardian and the ground of morality, at the mercy of the crowd. There is simply insufficient attention to procedure.[54] Mead could live with a minimalist conception of reason because he did not need a more extravagant model to promote social justice (or science for that matter). He trusted that the multiplying of perspectives provides a critical check. He also trusted the world. He seemed to have a faith (an animal faith, perhaps) that the world would push back if we tried to push it too far off its moorings. Given that the Occident has seen everything from the Logos to merely "successful" behavior labeled rational, I will not attempt to defend Mead's approach to rationality as an all-encompassing one. Its best defense would entail restricting its claims to the realm of practical reason. When saturated with the impetus to an enlarged mentality, this form of reason would be adequate for ensuring a good enough form of impartiality in moral and political decisions, or so the argument would go.

Actually, this is not quite right. Given all the baggage that the term *reason* is expected to carry, perhaps (contra Habermas) it would be best if we did not place too much weight on a notion of reason for our present purposes. What we have been most interested in locating are the conditions or circumstances that lead to *good judgment,* and much of the language we have just used to describe Mead's position on reason is well suited to this task. On this reading, Mead appears to be laying down the conditions that allow political (and moral) actors to judge and to judge well.

What Mead gains with his approach are more easily defensible conditions for the possibility of "rationality" (or judgment) and universality. This gain would come at a terrible price for Habermas: the conflation of strategic and communicative rationality, a topic we put off addressing a few pages back. For Habermas, Mead's formulation is not one that can be used to assert the superiority of mutual understanding over strategic influence. Such an approach makes a mockery of the distinction between strategic rationality and communicative rationality, between manipulation and understanding, and between struggle and consensus. If this is in fact Mead's position, Habermas would argue, it offers us very little turf to assert ourselves against the distortions of the life-world we find on the contemporary scene. At the level of conditions for the possibility of communication, Mead could not claim that one form of rationality (communicative or strategic) is more "rational" or basic than the other.

However, what Mead loses by refusing to make this distinction at the level that Habermas does may have its rewards. There may be a closer tie between so-called strategic and communicative rationality than Habermas is willing to admit. In fact Habermas's distinction may call on us to push the world a bit too far off its moorings. For Habermas, the strategic can at best lead only to a balancing of interests; it cannot provide consensus, generalized interests. "To the extent that strategic interactions are linguistically mediated, language serves as a *means of influencing*," Habermas says.[55] And when it does so we fall into at least one of Dante's peripheral circles, as the following striking passage suggests.

> Under conditions of strategic action, the self of self-determination and self-realization slips out of intersubjective relations. The strategic actor no longer draws from an intersubjectively shared lifeworld; having himself become worldless, as it were, he stands over and against the objective world and makes decisions solely according to standards of subjective preference. He does not rely therein upon recognition by others. Autonomy is then transformed into freedom of choice (*Willkürfreiheit*), and the individuation of the socialized subject is transformed into the isolation of a liberated subject who possesses himself.[56]

No doubt Mead would be critical of certain features of strategic action in certain contexts, but he would not be willing to deprecate it so thoroughly. Consider the exchange between two individuals who share a cultural horizon in which haggling over a piece of merchandise is part of a way of life. Clearly these two individuals appear to be behaving in a strategic fashion. They are both seeking to get the best deal possible by influencing the other's behavior. And they appear to be willing to use skills gained through linguistic interaction, even ones geared to mutual understanding, to anticipate and manipulate the responses of the other. But because there are established "rules" guiding their interpersonal conduct, the exchange actually has the potential for bringing the participants together, based on shared understandings of the activity and the experience of having engaged in it. Attitudes are reinforced, created, and taken home. There is a subtext. The point here is not that they must compromise, which Habermas agrees may be necessary in situations in which consensus cannot be achieved. Nor is it to claim that modern systems of money and power can do without the strategic for Habermas. He knows that they cannot. Nor is it to argue that Habermas does not have a place for self-interested behavior in his approach, for surely he does; it is behavior that modern law helps to circumscribe, thereby allowing some positive repercussions to flow from self-interest. Nor is it to suggest that Habermas is unaware of the importance of the habitual and nonreflective in our social life. Rather, it is to suggest that there can be a mutuality that lies beneath or in the midst of an apparent agon, one that can even be extended by a struggle. In other terms, there is no prima facie reason why we must assume that communicative action always trumps other forms of action in producing interpersonal and personal goods. Habermas's reliance on communicative action is a throwback to Kant's categorical imperative—that is, one should never treat the other solely as a means to one's ends—and to Kant's desire to privilege the transcendental, in this case by viewing the strategic as parasitical on the more basic communicative. But under certain conditions communicative action may not be as productive in producing goods as strategic interventions might be, and this should not be construed as a claim simply about the market. For example, often in psychotherapy it is found that by *not* engaging in communicative action one can be more helpful than by engaging in it. Sometimes the strategic path is the more therapeutic route. The point here is that a pragmatist such as Mead, although he would not be ill-disposed to singing the praises of communication geared to understanding, would presume that different contexts can call for very different kinds of responses. Of course, Habermas knows this too—he should not be viewed as a simple stand-in for dyed-in-the-wool moralists of old— but there is little question that there is a different sensibility at play here. Mead is a pragmatist. Habermas is not.

In general it is safe to say that Mead appears more comfortable than Habermas with the notion that moral and political conflicts can have positive results. (This is not to suggest that Habermas has no place for conflict in his approach.) Certain types of conflict may resolve themselves into or produce a greater unity, whereas others are important because they help prevent totality and ensure plurality. The former theme would make sense if we have read Mead's Hegelian sympathies correctly. The latter

may in part be attributable to Mead's firsthand experience with the ago-
nistic organization of the government and economy of the United States,
a nation toward which Mead was positively disposed, despite all its problems.[57]

Of course there may be times when strategic action destroys community or feeds forms of "community" that are destructive of the self-
development of their members. How can we protect ourselves against a
conflation of strategic with communicative action? From Mead's vantage
point this Habermasian question may be framed improperly. The question for Mead is how we are to create a social order that will satisfy interests that help individuals actualize their potentialities, that help them
to achieve well-being. Habermas is also favorably disposed to this end,
but his orientation may leave him too concerned with finding "structur-
al" and legal guarantees and with consensus, thereby cutting off alternative paths. I will not belabor this point here, as it has been addressed else-
where on many occasions, but I will offer an observation in passing. In a
sense Habermas would like us to recognize that we agree before we actually agree, and the mechanisms that support communicative action are
there to show us our always already agreement. Perhaps this "forced"
agreement, this "forced" rationality, even if it is merely formal or struc-
tural, is what irks so many pluralists of the pragmatic or postmodern
stripe about Habermas's position, smacking as it does of a finality born
of transcendental conditions. I say this knowing that in Habermas's own
view the quasitranscendental helps guarantee that different forms of life
can flourish.

Community is a good for Mead, but not all communities are equally
good, and some that go by the name do not deserve the appellation. And
not all are "rational" in the same manner. For Mead, "The very existence . . . in human experience of universal meanings sets up the demand
for a society in which the common meanings shall become means that
embody common ends. But, as Hegel has insisted, universals may be either abstract or concrete."[58] Thus we can conceive of societies in which
people are unified—that is, rational—in one of two ways. On one hand,
we have societies of abstract universals, such as ascetic societies in which
wants should disappear, that have Nirvana as an ideal, that seek to rid
the world of strife in a New Jerusalem.

> The other conceivable type of a rational society is one of concrete uni-
> versals, that in which the common ends may be so embodied in highly
> organized means that to procure food for one's self is to take part in pro-
> curing it for everyone else. Adam Smith enunciated the ideal when he
> maintained that every sound economic bargain was good for both of those

who were involved in the exchange. This is the ideal of a rational society which has been gradually taking form in men's minds since the time of the Renaissance. This ideal implies, then, something more than the abstract universality of its meanings. It implies that if the society in which these meanings obtain universally were sufficiently developed, the values which these meanings embody would be at the disposal of all its members.[59]

The last lines clearly reveal Mead's egalitarian sympathies. And he doesn't hesitate to use Adam Smith and the market to support his vision of ever-increasing circles of universals that would tie peoples together. (This is not to suggest that Mead uncritically accepted the market. He was a progressive, after all.) So-called strategic uses of language in certain circumstances may actually serve a greater unity, which Mead takes to be a good thing, if it is not a totalizing unity. Strategic actions can also obviate totality and guarantee plurality. And plurality, as we have seen, is a condition for the political in Arendt's view. The function of strategic action, then, seems to depend on circumstance and context. In the wrong place, at the wrong time, the strategic would surely disrupt Mead's desire to view the other as a neighbor. (With these remarks we have introduced the question of the role of alterity in the body politic, that is, the role of the other in realizing or displacing consensus. These are concerns of the coming chapters.)

Mead shares something more with Smith than the hope that the market can be a source of cosmopolitanism. Mead is committed to a notion of impartiality that resembles Smith's notion of the empirically minded impartial spectator.[60] For Mead, removing ourselves from the context in which we are embedded requires that we achieve a degree of impartiality. In other words, when Mead speaks of challenging the status quo, it is from the perspective of more extensive or less parochial communities, ones that allow us to see the properties of things from more "abstract," less localized perspectives, which nevertheless remain context bound in a manner that the unlimited communication community does not.

The themes of community, interest, and impartiality are addressed in the chapters ahead. I want to close this chapter with a much more general claim about Mead and Habermas, one that I cannot hope to prove outside an extended study of Habermas but one that I believe illuminates the differences between them. It also sets the stage for the concerns of chapter 5. The claim is as follows: One of the fundamental differences between these thinkers has to do with their sensitivity to the notion of creative activity. As pointed out in chapter 1, the notion of emergence in Mead's work is tied to a model of the natural world in which novelty is par for the course. Mead is so smitten with the importance of the novel that he is even willing to bank our sense of the flow of time on the occurrence of novel events. In terms of the "I" and "me," it was pointed out that the "I" is the "source" of spontaneity in the individual; one is never quite sure how one is going to respond until one actually does respond. And this is not merely a result of a lack of epistemological insight; it is part and parcel of the nature of things that varying degrees of novelty slip in among the patterns.

There is a passage in his article on individuation in which Habermas alludes to the spontaneity of the "I," but the manner in which he describes it says more about his own views than Mead's. For Mead, the "I" can be thought of as the base of self-assertion, for it allows us to challenge the fixed habits of the "me."[61] Although Habermas mentions the creative power of the "I" in an earlier passage, what I believe really captures his fancy is how the "I" helps us to remain who we are by avoiding the entrapments of social givens. "Thus, the communicative actor is encouraged by the bare structure of linguistic intersubjectivity to remain *himself*, even in behavior conforming to norms," Habermas says. "In action guided by norms, the initiative to realize oneself cannot in principle be taken away from any one—and no one can give up this initiative. For this reason, Mead never tires of emphasizing the moment of unpredictability and spontaneity in the *manner* in which the actor interactively plays his roles."[62]

What Habermas is concerned with here is the perpetuation of the identity of the person over time. For example, we act from the position of a grammatical pronoun, the "I," which reinforces our sense of irreplaceability. And there is indeed a sense in which the "I" as the source of novel and spontaneous actions helps us to assert ourselves against the status quo, thereby acting as a source of self-affirmation for Mead. However, to focus on this attribute of the "I" leaves something crucial out of the picture: the novel itself. Aside from its repercussions for the individual, spontaneity is worthy of consideration. Nature is itself filled with novel occurrences for Mead. From this vantage point the "I" would be viewed as merely a (descriptive) marker for the upsurge of novel (re)actions in the human being. As noted in chapter 2, the cosmopolitan, who is in fact Mead's universalist, is one who can grapple with the novel and flourish in sociality. I will go out on a limb here. If we think of theorists as having guiding threads or principles that inform much if not all of their work, then Habermas's and Mead's are not the same, and the difference revolves around their attitudes toward creativity and novelty.

In chapter 1 I appealed to the work of systematic pluralists, and I do so once again for the sake of interpretive insight. I noted that according these thinkers, we can approach texts according to their authorial voice, method, ontological focus, and governing focus or principle. We examined the authorial voice in Mead and found him to have a disciplinary one. Habermas shares the same sort of voice. Here I want to take up what is called the governing focus. These principles can be divided into creative, elemental, comprehensive, and reflexive. I want to concentrate here on the first and last. When a creative principle is operative it shows up in an author's emphasis on that which differentiates by transcending the given. "The creative principle emphasizes making a difference . . . in which the new replaces the old. It generally functions as an assumption of volitional efficacy or agency . . . however, it can take the form of some generative cosmic process."[63] Some thinkers who use creative principles are Saint Augustine, Kierkegaard, William James, Sartre, and Derrida. The reflexive principle, on the other hand, "may be described as Aristotle's principle of the essential variety of goods and functions, or as the principle of self-sufficiency, autonomy, and self-completion of a specific nature or of a thing's intrinsic form or function."[64]

Philosophers such as Anaxagoras, Descartes, Kant, Spinoza, and Peirce use reflexive principles. Obviously, from a cursory account such as this the reader cannot be expected to take much home, and of course there are limitations to such metaphilosophical models, but perhaps one can see that Mead and Habermas are actually on two sides of a divide: Mead appeals to creative principles and Habermas to reflexive ones. Mead is driven to explore spontaneity and novelty and Habermas to the self-completing grounds of autonomy. (Derrida, picking up on the reflexivity theme, might view Habermas's idealized communication community as entailing a quest for reflexivity that produces autoaffectivity.)

Actually, the story is somewhat more complicated. Habermas appeals to reflexive principles and to creative principles, the latter being rather difficult to avoid in a cultural climate that so often bows to historicism. Therefore, what I earlier described as Habermas's collapse of the voluntary (creative) into the autonomous (reflexive) in his reading of Mead's work is far from accidental. Here we should have some sympathy for the burden Habermas must carry, for even Hegel could not reconcile the historical (creative) with the reflexive; ultimately the reflexivity of the Idea devours a historicity driven by difference, by negativity. The negative must continually wind back on itself in the negation of the negation, which is the reflexive moment. Mead may not be as comprehensive or as distinction conscious as Habermas, but he is more consistent in this regard. Universality, read as an ongoing process of creating and realizing potentialities for universality, simply does not require the closure that a reflexive sensibility brings with it, although it can afford an appeal to moments of reflection. There can be both universality and creation in Mead's world because of the manner in which he understands universality. Yet even Mead's limited universalism would offend Levinas, for the latter is a thinker for whom only the other is able to defeat the reflexivity of systems and the imperial ego. Anything less is deception. For Levinas, as we shall see, there must be moments of "absolute" creation, "absolute" transcendence, if there is to be morality.

4   Levinas and the Other Side

As we have seen, Mead is a pluralist and a universalist, a thinker who does not imagine that we need to depend on the transcendental to realize universality. Nor would he suggest that we must take a transcendental turn to grasp the kind of impartiality needed for good judgment in a democratic context. For pragmatists, impartiality can never be absolute; one's interests must be acknowledged, although these interests can be extended, redefined, and even transcended to a degree.[1] This is what Mead's cosmopolitan actor can accomplish, an actor who bears a striking resemblance to those who possess what Arendt and Kant would call an enlarged mentality.

Thus far my line of argumentation has been leading in the direction of the "reasonable," as opposed to the transcendentally inspired, as the ground for grappling with diversity, universality, and impartiality. In the process I have bowed to the context-bound, perspectivist sensibilities that seem to be our lot in the early twenty-first century while also acknowledging that features of the self's development can conspire with certain historical conditions to promote a healthy reception to diversity. In Rorty's terms, it appears that we have the capacity to become liberal ironists, and something more and less, to be liberal at times without the irony. We can develop an awareness or set of skills—call it an enlarged mentality or a metaperspective—that lends itself to a certain capacity for impartiality, which if not the disinterestedness of the Good is at least good enough for dealing with our fellow humans. We are relativists enough to know that we do not have the final word. We are social enough to be able to appreciate the words of others. (No doubt this is an optimistic projection of where our increasingly culturally entwined planet is heading.) The debate between Habermas and Mead rests in part on how best to develop respect for other peoples and oneself. Habermas thinks we need a quasitranscendental apparatus to help defend us against the parochial. Mead would place more weight on the realm of ethical life, on attitudes that promote universalistic sensibilities. Arendt bows to conflict but calls on us to enlarge our mentalities and seek exemplars. If not siblings, then, these thinkers are at least cousins.

Levinas will have none of it. And because he will have none of it, he can help sharpen the focus of this study. From Levinas's vantage point the earlier chapters of this book would have lacked a certain seriousness. They dance around the question of impartiality, disinterestedness, by promulgating the possibility of a reconciliation between self-interest and the interests of others. One can never achieve genuine impartiality through any form of universalism for Levinas. Furthermore, the thinkers addressed in these chapters often sought to privilege their own approaches by refuting the thematized claims of their adversaries. Dialectic and argumentation will not do. Traditional philosophical discourse will never allow us to arrive at a telling impartiality.

So I will use Levinas to help crystallize what is at stake if we attach ourselves to one set of contemporary assumptions, rather than another, with regard to notions of universality and our relationship to others. In thinking about how Levinas might react to Mead and company, I am reminded of a remark Charles Taylor made about Habermas in his *Sources of the Self*. Although Taylor is clearly not a Levinasian, a sense of loss is reflected in this passage that Levinas might recognize.

> What gets lost from view here is not the demands of expressive fulfillment, because Habermas does take account of these—they have their own different sphere of modern rationality, alongside the moral–practical and the cognitive–instrumentalist. Rather, what cannot be fitted into his grid is what the last two chapters have been mainly occupied with, the search for moral sources *outside* the subject through languages which resonate *within* him or her, the grasping of an order which is inseparably indexed to a personal vision. . . . But there is no coherent place left for an exploration of the order in which we are set as a locus of moral sources, what Rilke, Pound, Lawrence, and Mann were doing in their radically different ways. . . . It falls between the holes in the grid.[2]

Taylor and Levinas are guided by religiously informed moral compasses; Taylor is a Christian whose work rings with Hegelian and Heideggerian overtones, and Levinas is an Orthodox Jew who has his own idiosyncratic reading of the tradition. Taylor feels the absence of something irreducibly valuable in the work of a Habermas. Levinas, I believe, would be drawn to Taylor's line about the "holes in the grid." We can always argue about grids and their adequacy for the task at hand, but what if the truly important must fall through any grid? Structures and procedures, it seems, will always obscure what stands before us: the face of the other. By the way, this is not to suggest that Levinas is unphilosophical, only that there are sensibilities present in his work that seemingly draw their inspiration from a place other than the aesthetic, scientific, or political value spheres of modernity.

Levinas has a story to tell, although it is unlikely that he would feel comfortable calling it such. It is a story that seeks to disrupt modernist tales and all other stories, be they metanarratives or narratives, that desire to privilege: being, the ego, strife, logos, arche, totality, presence, the dialectic, self-interest, and almost any of the other notions that Western thinkers have taken kindly to over last two millennia or so. It is a story that includes an account of a tradition bound to ontology, bound to violence, violence against the other, who provides the condition for morality. It is a story that must overcome itself as a story, for to tell a story one must deal with the thematic, which falls into the realm of what Levinas calls "the said." Levinas wants to point us to what he calls "saying," that is, the nonthematic, nonviolent approach or response to the other. But our tradition, our ontologically inspired logocentric tradition, has us focus on themes, being, and presence in a manner that dissipates "saying" and leaves us only with the thematic "said."[3] The story as thematic cannot provide us with saying, and yet if told properly it can inspire us to turn to saying. (In any case, we cannot avoid the said, for we are told that saying and the said are intimately linked.)

One cannot hope to do justice to the complexities of a serious thinker in the confines of a chapter. This goes without saying, and most readers would take it for granted. But curiously, Levinas manages to make one feel somewhat guilty about even trying. One must apologize in advance for presenting his thought thematically, even though he acknowledges that he himself must do the same. Levinas seeks to have us move beyond the thematic, which he at times strives to transcend through the use of evocative language. Although his language is not my language, I will try to provide the reader with some access to his thought. One of the ways I will attempt to do so is by concentrating primarily, although not exclusively, on his later publications, which use a language that is, in part, meant to address the criticism that his earlier work had not escaped the language of ontology. In particular, I draw on *Otherwise Than Being or Beyond Essence*, his most important later work.[4] Recognizing the impossibility of doing full justice to the evocative character of his work, I often turn to his own words to give the reader a taste of Levinas's language, recognizing that the act of extraction here must to some degree be one of deformation or at least reformulation. After the initial exposition of his thought, I raise some preliminary objections. The latter will serve as a bridge to a more sustained critique in chapter 5.

How to approach the thought of Levinas? Because we are dealing thematically with his work, I suggest that we begin by locating one of the chords that resounds throughout his work: War and violence are everywhere, yet there is a way of peace. On the very first page of the Preface of *Totality and Infinity*, the first of his two major philosophical works, he writes, "Does not lucidity, the mind's openness upon the true, consist in catching sight of the permanent possibility of war? The state of war suspends morality; it divests the eternal institutions and obligations of their eternity and rescinds ad interim the unconditional imperatives. In advance its shadow falls over the actions of men. . . . The visage of being that shows itself in war is fixed in the concept of totality, which dominates Western philosophy."[5]

Violence is endemic. It pervades our thinking. It is in our history. It is in our relations with one another. It is in our attempt to provide a history of our relations with one another. We want to draw within our own sphere everything that presents a semblance of otherness, and histories can serve just such an end. In doing so, we do violence. Hegel's system is paradigmatic in this regard. For Hegel, we are looking to return home, to end the odyssey that spirit has had to take to come to know itself. The odyssey has required diremptions of the self, but the lacerations in spirit's being are overcome through the power of self-consciousness. Through reflection we can bring the differences that constitute the world into unity, into totality. But Hegel's system is merely the paradigmatic offender.

We typically use representations to bring the past into the present, to give ourselves an identity in the present, to give ourselves a gift of the present. Philosophers have time and again promised us that through the active efforts of our intellect and the work of our will we can overcome alterity. Perhaps we can even transform the planet into our own garden. Even thinkers who seek to escape promises of this nature, such as Heidegger, do not realize that they are committed to an ontological mode of thought that fosters the dismissal of alterity. And if alterity is dismissed, then violence will follow, for there will be little or nothing to prevent the ego from privileging its own needs. As Pascal says, it will seek to find its place in the sun, and it will feel entitled to do so. And "that is how the usurpation of the whole world began."[6] "My being-in-the-world or my 'place in the sun,' my being at home, have these not also been the usurpation of spaces belonging to the other man whom I have already oppressed or starved, or driven out into a third world; are they not acts of repulsing, excluding, exiling, stripping, killing? Pascal's 'my place in the sun' marks the beginning of the image of the usurpation of the whole earth. A fear for all the violence and murder my existing might generate, in spite of its conscious and intentional innocence."[7]

That we can be responsible, that we are in fact responsible, even when we do not consciously choose to be so, is another of Levinas's themes. The ego that actively and self-consciously engages the world through its choices is not the self, not the deeply responsible subject, not the unique individual Levinas wants to bring to our attention. If violence in its multiple forms is an ongoing theme in Levinas, so is his concern with uniqueness of the individual. And we do not find true individuality in the ego, although we often believe that we do. Uniqueness cannot be found in qualities or characteristics of the individual. Nor can it be found in a recollected personal past. Nor can it be found in relations of mutual respect. Nor can it be found in commitments or self-interested behaviors. Paradoxical as it may seem, the uniqueness of a subject can be found only in its responsibility for the other, in its subjecting itself to the other to the point of being willing to substitute itself for the other. But this willingness to be for the other is not something one consciously chooses. I am commanded, and I heed the command to be for the other even before I self-consciously know that I heed it. In one of the more accessible summaries of his thought in *Otherwise Than Being* Levinas tells us,

> The I approached in responsibility is for-the-other, is a denuding, an exposure to being affected, a pure susceptiveness. It does not posit itself, possessing itself and recognizing itself; it is consumed and delivered over, dis-locates itself, loses its place, is exiled, relegates itself into itself, but as though its very skin were still a way to shelter itself in being, exposed to wounds and outrage, emptying itself in a no-grounds, to the point of substituting itself for the other, holding on to itself only as it were in the trace of its exile. What verbs like "to deliver itself," "consume itself," "exile itself" (*se* livrer, *se* consumer, s'exiler), suggest by their pronominal form is not an act of reflection on oneself, of concern for oneself, it is not an act at all, but a modality of passivity which in substitution is beyond even passivity. . . . This inwardness without secrets is a pure witness to the inordinateness which already commands me, to give to the other taking the bread out of my own mouth, and making a gift of my own skin.[8]

Are these words literature, philosophy, prayer? They are clearly not words that would appeal to the enlightened self-interest of Adam Smith or the secularized sensibilities of Mead. But perhaps they would appeal to Kierkegaard, the thinker of inwardness, especially to Kierkegaard of the *Philosophical Fragments*. In the *Fragments* Kierkegaard asks us to engage in a thought experiment. What if truth is not something we can recollect, call out of ourselves with the assistance of a teacher, Socrates. "In the Socratic view each individual is his own center, and the entire world centers in him, because his self-knowledge is a knowledge of God. It was thus Socrates understood himself, and thus he thought that everyone must understand himself."[9] This understanding leads us to pay little heed to the teacher. For once we have attained eternal truth, the moment in which we attained it is of little consequence. "My relation to Socrates or Prodicus cannot concern me with respect to my eternal happiness, for this is given me retrogressively through my possession of the Truth, which I had from the beginning without knowing it."[10]

But what if this were not the case? What if the moment is of decisive significance because the condition for truth comes to us from the outside, as a gift, and is given to us by a very different kind of teacher, a teacher who is a savior, a redeemer, but also a judge? "This Teacher is thus not so much teacher as *Judge*," Kierkegaard says. "Even when the learner has most completely appropriated the condition, and most profoundly apprehended the Truth, he cannot forget this Teacher, or let him vanish Socratically."[11]

Presumably Kierkegaard is a less remote thinker than Levinas, and following the principle of using the less obscure to help explain the more obscure I have introduced his voice at this juncture. As is well known, Kierkegaard condemns systems, sytematizers, and concept mongers of all stripes. Kierkegaard and Levinas, as it happens, share a distaste for many of the same things. They are both engaged in a campaign to convince us that "salvation" is not to be had through conceptual schemes, through the thematic or the said (in Levinas's terms). They have a passion for pursuing the source of the uniqueness of the individual. They distrust not only systematizers but all forms of mediation, for they believe that mediation cannot but lead to system, that it is a cover for system. And as Kierkegaard suggests in his thought experiment, it is the meeting with an (infinite) Other that shakes my confidence in my own capacity to find "salvation" by withdrawing myself into the eternal via knowledge. The Other who should not (or cannot) be incorporated into my system, my world, is the "catalyst" who allows me to become me, that is, a self, a subject. For Kierkegaard, we cannot forget the Teacher who brings us the condition for the Truth; for Levinas we cannot forget the other who brings to us a veracity more urgent than conceptual truth. Levinas tells us in *Totality and Infinity,* "The relation with the Other, or Conversation, is a non-allergic relation, an ethical relation; but inasmuch as it is welcomed this conversation is a teaching [*enseignement*]. Teaching is not reducible to maieutics; it comes from the exterior and brings me more than I contain."[12]

Make no mistake: There are striking differences. The other is not God for Levinas, at least not in anything like the sense in which the Teacher is God for Kierkegaard. As a matter of fact, for Levinas God has never appeared in a moment that can be called the present. And it is our quest to harbor the world in the present that turns us away from the trace of God revealed in the approach of the other. "The Infinite then has glory only through subjectivity, in the human adventure of the approach of the other, through the substitution for the other, by the expiation for the other. The subject is inspired by the Infinite, which, as *illeity,* does not appear, is not present, has always already past, is neither theme, telos, nor interlocutor."[13]

I am moving a bit too quickly here. For before we speak of God we must have a more finely grained understanding of what is entailed in our relationship to the other. How should we approach the other? If we are to have an ethical relationship to the other, we must leave behind the notion of reciprocity. Reciprocity exists for Levinas, but it is not to be found in the face to face, the realm of ethics. It is to be found when third parties are introduced and thematization must enter the scene to deal with the complexities of multiple claims. The ethical relationship to the other is one of asymmetry. It is not a matter of reciprocity or recognition. For example, Hegel's dialectic of recognition leaves individuals in the world of "the same," a world in which true alterity cannot show itself, where the other is simply another me, a world of mirrors (and smoke). Levinas says,

> But communication would be impossible if it should have to begin in the ego, a free subject, to whom every other would be only a limitation that invites war, domination, precaution and information. To communicate is indeed to open oneself, but the openness is not complete if it is on the watch for recognition. It is complete not in opening to the spectacle of or the recognition of the other, but in becoming a responsibility for him. The overemphasis of openness is responsibility for the other to the point of substitution, where the for-the-other proper to disclosure, to monstration to the other, turns into the for-the-other proper to responsibility. This is the thesis of the present work.[14]

From Levinas's vantage point there is little difference between Hegel's dialectic of recognition and Sartre's account of the Look.[15] Neither account has the resources to understand how violence is ended. For Sartre, if I am looked at by another I lose my subjectivity because I become an object with an outside that is defined by the other. I maintain the integrity of my subjectivity, my freedom, by turning the other into an object, into stone, through my look. I strive to maintain my own freedom at the price of the other's in Sartre's model. This is, no doubt, a vision of endless war. But Hegel's dialectic is perhaps even more insidious because although it seeks to overcome violence through recognition, it actually leads to entwinement in a system that has no room for genuine alterity. And although it is only alterity that can truly halt war, Hegel argues that the overcoming of alterity through mutual recognition not only is possible but is the fundamental goal of spirit. "What still lies ahead for consciousness is the experience of what Spirit is—this absolute substance which is the unity of the different independent self-consciousnesses which, in their opposition, enjoy perfect freedom and independence: 'I' that is 'We' and 'We' that is 'I.'"[16]

Levinas is not concerned with the reconciliation of oppositions in and by spirit. If such were to come to pass, radical alterity and the uniqueness of the subject that it makes possible would vanish. The alterity of the other is the key to the ethical. It is also the key to peace. What we want is a social order of real plurality, not one given to the unity of differences. This order must start from the subject, not from political activity. For Levinas, "The unity of plurality is peace, and not the coherence of the elements that constitute plurality. Peace therefore cannot be identified with the end of combats that cease for want of combatants, by the defeat of some and the victory of the others, that is, with cemeteries or future universal empires. Peace must be my peace, in a relation that starts from an I and goes to the other, in desire and goodness, where the I both maintains itself and exists without egoism."[17]

If I am to contribute to the creation of a truly plural order, I must meet my obligations to the other, I must allow myself to be exposed to the other, but in a passive manner, even a hyperpassive manner. There must be no mediation here, no intervening activity that allows me to keep my distance from the other while simultaneously gathering the other into some larger whole, a whole in which the present subsumes the past. I must come close to the other, but my proximity to the other should not be seen as a joining in spirit. No, this proximity should be a paradoxical one. The closer I come to the other, the greater should be the alterity of the other. If there is no greater alterity, then the other becomes ripe for inclusion within my narcissistic horizons. Levinas's translator, Alphonso Lingis, speaks of exposure and proximity as follows:

> The Subject is exposed to alterity before it can gather itself up and take a stand. This closeness without distance, this immediacy of an approach which remains approach without what approaches being circumscribable, locatable *there,* Levinas calls proximity. The other, my neighbor (*le prochain*) concerns, afflicts me with a closeness (*proximité*) closer than the closeness of entities (*prae-ens*). The relationship with alterity, which is what escapes apprehension, exceeds all comprehension, is infinitely remote, is, paradoxically enough, the most extreme immediacy, proximity closer than presence, obsessive contact.[18]

Notice that proximity avoids presence: Whereas presence overcomes alterity, proximity nurtures it. Presence is suspect. This latter theme clearly drifts through the work of numerous writers who have been labeled postmodernists. We saw it addressed in chapter 2 in Derrida's concern with autoaffection (a term we find in Levinas's text and to which we will return).[19] Privileging presence is a way of circumscribing the other for Levinas, and thereby hangs a tale because if we are to respect the alterity of the other we must find a way out of the present. Like certain postmodernists, Levinas sees a connection between our fondness for privileging presence and a predilection for an intellectual imperialism that overwhelms the other. "In the realm of truth, being, as the *other* of thought becomes the characteristic *property* of thought as knowledge. The ideal of rationality or of sense (*sens*) begins already to appear as the immanence of the real to reason; just as, in being, a privilege is granted to the *present*, which is presence to thought, of which the future and the past are modalities or modifications: re-presentations. . . . Knowledge is re-presentation, a return to presence, and nothing may remain *other* to it."[20]

How do we avoid the omnipresence of the present? There must be a time that is available to us that we cannot circumscribe. An understanding of time in terms of protentions or retentions will not do, for they merely service the present by rendering past, present, and future synchronous, that is, present. We must be affected by the other in a way in which we cannot recoup his or her alterity in our own present. Not to be so moved allows the worst of modernity to triumph. "Modern Man persists in his being as a sovereign who is merely concerned to maintain the *powers of his sovereignty.* Everything that is possible is permitted," Levinas says. "In this way the experience of Nature and Society would gradually get the better of any exteriority. A miracle of modern Western freedom unhindered by any memory or remorse, and opening onto a 'glittering future' where everything can be rectified."[21]

Perhaps memory can provide the opportunity to escape from our penchant for absorbing everything into our present, that is, a memory powerful enough not be encapsulated by my present (and my present visions of the future). But for a memory to accomplish this we would need a past that can avoid being captured by our retentions, which can slip by the present even as it "presents" itself to us. Lingis comments,

> The present instant is extended by a past which it cannot catch up with or coincide with or represent, render present. It exists in this internal distension. . . . Levinas's bold thesis is that the relationship with alterity is the original case of this affliction of the present of consciousness with a past that it cannot render present, represent. The present is afflicted with a bond with something that comes to pass without being convertible into an initiative of the present, and that holds on, and in this hold distends one.[22]

In this sort of time, Levinas tells us, "this duration remains free from the sway of the will, absolutely outside all activity of the ego, and exactly like the aging process which is probably the perfect model of passive synthesis, a lapse of time no act of remembrance, reconstructing the past, could possibly reverse."[23] What we need to defeat the present is a memory of an immemorial past, that is, a memory of a time that cannot be trapped by the present. We find that the other's past presents itself in this manner. It is a past that I cannot possess. It eludes my present and yet it has a presence, a presence in absence, which appears as a trace.[24] Furthermore, it is the other who confronts me with a responsibility that comes from a time immemorial, a responsibility that I did not choose, that I cannot encompass, but that claims me nevertheless. "A responsibility stemming from a time before my freedom—before my (*moi*) beginning, before any present. A fraternity existing in extreme separation. *Before,* but in what past? Not in the time preceding the present, in which I might have contracted any commitments. Responsibility for my neighbor dates from before my freedom in an immemorial past, an unrepresentable past that was never present and is more ancient than consciousness of."[25]

It is out of my responsibility for the other that the me is born, the unique subject that I am. It is not in what I say but in the saying itself that I approach the other. In saying I leave myself vulnerable before the other.[26] My concern is not to be heard but to stand before the other, open to other in my "willingness" before there is a will to substitute myself for him. Yet I cannot insist that the other do the same for me, for to ask the other to substitute herself or himself for me would be criminal. Reciprocity is not to be had on the ethical level. Reciprocity brings with it the general and the universal. Only through asymmetry can we hope to avoid a move to the level where the thematic rules. Only through saying that is prior to reflection, prior to knowledge, do we avoid the ego, the generic, and the violence that stems from the generic. Fabio Ciaramelli comments,

> The subject of this Saying says himself not by offering information, but simply by exposing himself, by announcing himself, that is, by *expressing* himself in his Saying. Far from being the tale of a private adventure such as may befall a reflective consciousness, expression is a disinterested bearing witness. It is the response of the one for the Other, and since the Saying responds even before hearing the appeal of the Other, Levinas calls it anachronistic and diachronic. There is a paradoxical immediacy to the Saying, a sort of unthinkable immediacy which escapes the present. . . . *Saying offers and obeys before any order has been given. It is, therefore, inspired. It is prophetic. Indeed, prophecy belongs to the essence of human language.*[27]

But if saying is prophetic, then individuality is under siege, as Fabio Ciaramelli points out. How so? The uniqueness of the individual evaporates into a vocation that belongs to humanity at large. We are all called, and through this general call anyone can substitute for the other. Yet this is precisely what Levinas wants to avoid, that is, the reduction of the individual to a cipher, to just another self, to a universal ego. Ciaramelli comments, "The radicality of Levinas's point of view demands that we conceive proximity to exclude the possibility of theater: 'le rôle du moi' is mine alone and no one can play this part except me."[28]

How do I avoid burial in the universal? I live the uniqueness of my position in relationship to the other, for I am the one who actually substitutes myself for the other. I am persecuted by the other. I am responsible and not humanity at large. I take a stand that no one else can take, for it is me and not another who responds, "Here I am." And with this we have arrived back at the place of God in Levinas's thought:

> "Here I am," just that! The word God is still absent from the phrase in which God is for the first time involved in words. It does not at all state "I believe in God." To bear witness [to] God is precisely not to state this extraordinary word, as though glory would be lodged in a theme and be posited as a thesis, or become being's essence. As a sign given to the other of this very signification, the "here I am" signifies me in the name of God, at the service of men that look at me, without having anything to identify myself with, but the sound of my voice or the figure of my gesture— the saying itself.[29]

What are the thematic, the systematic, being, and so on, but idols? Idols seek to capture the evanescence of God, to make God present, circumscribable. God cannot appear for those who heed the voice of God, a voice that says, "You shall have no other gods before Me." Levinas's thought can be read as a meditation on the proscription in Judaism against any representation of God. Carrying this proscription to its logical conclusion teaches us that God is converted into an idol by those who seek to make the Infinite present through themes, or concepts, or in any other manner. Kierkegaard also caught sight of the false idols of thematization and systematization. His answer was to move deeper into subjectivity. He did not understand that it is the other, the face of the other, who frees me from the systemic by providing a glimpse of the Infinite.[30] As Levinas tells us, "The Infinite then has glory only through subjectivity, in the human adventure of the approach of the other, through the substitution for the other, by the expiation for the other. The subject is inspired by the Infinite, which, as *illeity,* does not appear, is not present, has always already past, is neither theme, telos nor interlocutor. . . . Glorification is saying, that is, a sign given to the other, peace announced to the other, responsibility for the other, to the extent of substitution."[31]

And through this invocation of the Infinite we have returned to our original theme: peace. For peace precedes humanity's idolatries. It is found on the hither side of mutuality, reciprocity, equality, presence. It is found before reflection takes place. It is found on the other side of being, in the Good that is beyond being. It is what refuses the presence of being. The spoken word is autoaffective for Derrida, and as we saw in chapter 2 it produces a false sense of closure and presence.[32] The autoaffective is also unacceptable to Levinas because it leaves one mired in autonomy, resting on oneself, without an approach of the other.[33] But Levinas does not see his work leading to a dismissal of the human because it tries to move us from privileging autonomy. It is meant to speak more fully to our humanity because it allows us to remain open to transcendence, a transcendence that is found only through a human relationship. "Goodness in the subject is anarchy itself," Levinas says. "As a responsibility for the freedom of the other, it is prior to any freedom in me, but it also precedes violence in me, which would be the contrary of freedom. For if no one is good voluntarily, no one is a slave of the Good. . . . Peace with the other is first of all my business. The non-indifference, the saying, the responsibility, the approach, is the disengaging of the unique one responsible, me. The way I appear is a summons."[34]

Goodness is to be found in the anarchic, in a time that avoids privileging the present. However, we have seen that there is a fall into the said, the realm of the present, into violence and war. We find that besides the neighbor facing me there are others, third parties, whom we must also take into consideration. "If proximity ordered to me only the other alone, there would have not been any problem, in even the most general sense of the term," Levinas says. "A question would not have been born, nor consciousness, nor self-consciousness. The responsibility for the other is an immediacy antecedent to questions, it is proximity. It is troubled and becomes a problem when a third party enters."[35]

What troubles does the existence of the third and the multitude bring us? We can no longer deal in the face to face alone. We must consider that the other is another to someone else, as am I. We must consider how we are to justly judge claims that are made by these others on each other. Symmetry, reciprocity, must enter the scene. "Justice is necessary, that is, comparison, coexistence, contemporaneousness, assembling, order, thematization, the visibility of faces, and thus intentionality and the intellect, and in intentionality and the intellect, the intelligibility of a system, and thence also a copresence on an equal footing as before a court of justice," Levinas says.[36]

The apparently negative spin given to the realm of the third when it was introduced earlier is misleading, for without such an order, I could not be who I am. Levinas has told us that although I must be willing to substitute myself for the other, to ask the other to substitute him or herself for me would be criminal. So the existence of the third raises a new possibility, that I can see myself from a different vantage point as one who can make claims on others, as one whose lot can be viewed as important. Levinas says, "There is betrayal of my anarchic relation with *illeity*, but also a new relationship with it: it is only thanks to God that, as a subject incomparable with the other, I am approached as an other by the others, that is, 'for myself.' 'Thanks to God' I am another for the others."[37] As one among others I am entitled to ask for justice, for equal treatment, which I could not do in the asymmetrical situation of the face to face. Levinas continues,

> Synchronization is the act of consciousness which, through representation and the said, institutes "with the help of God," the original locus of justice, a terrain common to me and the others where I am counted among them, that is, where subjectivity is a citizen with all the duties and rights measured and measurable which the equilibrated ego involves. . . . Is not the Infinite which enigmatically commands me, commanding and not commanding, from the other, also the turning of the I into "like the others," for which it is important to concern oneself and take care? My lot is important.[38]

But let us make no mistake about it. My lot is *not* important because I have interests, such as the interest in keeping death at bay.[39] It is important because I have a responsibility for myself (and not just for the other), which my relationship to more than one individual brings to light. I am responsible for my neighbor and for my neighbors who are at a distance, and they are responsible for each other and for me. Now I know that I am one among many, one who also deserves justice.[40] Symmetry is required in a world inhabited by third parties. However, symmetry is not the guardian of justice. Authentic disinterestedness is grounded in my asymmetrical relationship with the other who faces me. If the capacity for saying that exists on this ethical level does not permeate society, then symmetry will not lead to justice but to totality and tyranny. "My relationship with the other as neighbor gives meaning to my relations with all the others. All human relations as human proceed from disinterestedness," Levinas says.[41] So despite all that the level of the said can do for us, without our willingness to substitute ourselves for the other, justice cannot maintain itself.

> But the contemporaneousness of the multiple is tied about the diachrony of two: justice remains justice only, in a society where there is no distinction between those close and those far off, but in which there also remains the impossibility of passing by the closest. The equality of all is borne by my inequality, the surplus of my duties over my rights. The forgetting of self moves justice. It is then not without importance to know if the egalitarian and just State in which man is fulfilled (and which is to be set up, and especially to be maintained) proceeds from a war of all against all, or from the irreducible responsibility of the one for all, and if it can do without friendships and faces.[42]

The face to face is the condition for the possibility of justice. It is not accidental, then, that Levinas dedicates only a few pages to the justice of the symmetrical in *Otherwise Than Being or Beyond Essence*.[43] But is the choice actually between founding the state in the war of all against all or in the proximity of the other? Are there not other options? Is enlightened self-interest truly a myth? There are indeed many either–ors in Levinas's work, many bifurcations of complex issues. My goal in the next section is to raise questions about Levinas's position, and it is a position, not to refute his experience, an experience that makes certain claims on us, even if we cannot accept the philosophy it generates.

The cards have been stacked. I have approached Levinas's work as a thematizer and therefore will be able to find tensions and knots in the themes, contradictions that might make less sense if saying could be given equal weight to the said. And additional offenses are at hand. I want to show the inadequacies of his thought, but this requires a form of self-assertion, and self-assertion is a form of violence.

Levinas wants to claim that there is a human drive toward self-assertion, toward finding one's place in the sun. In self-interest, in self-involvement, one is led to violence, and the most primal violence is Cain's act against Abel: murder. We are violent before we even recognize our violence.[44] However, violence can be stemmed by the face of the other. "The true essence of man is presented in his face, in which he is infinitely other than a violence like unto mine, opposed to mine and hostile, already at grips with mine in a historical world where we participate in the same system," Levinas says. "He arrests and paralyzes my violence by his call, which does not do violence, and comes from on high."[45]

For Levinas, it is not just that we happen to be violent from time to time, but that something in the vulnerability of the other calls us to commit acts of violence, and something within responds with violence if not halted by the face of the other.

> True *self*-expression stresses the nakedness and defencelessness that encourages and directs the violence of the first crime: the goal of a murderous uprightness is especially well-suited to exposing or expressing the face. The first murderer probably does not realize the result of the blow he is about to deliver, but his violent design helps him to find the line with which death may give an air of unimpeachable rectitude to the face of the neighbor; the line is traced like the trajectory of the blow that is dealt and the arrow that kills.[46]

The mortality of the other, the exposedness of other, incites me to violence. It can also summon me to morality. "But, in its expression, in its mortality, the face before me summons me, calls for me, begs for me. . . . The other man's death calls me into question, as if, by my possible future indifference, I had become the accomplice of the death to which the other, who cannot see it, is exposed," Levinas says.[47] Contra Heidegger and a host of other thinkers, it is not my own death but the other's death that must ultimately concern me. I must not cause it. I must do what I can to prevent it. And given the violence of Levinas's world, a world in which he witnessed the Holocaust, one can understand the urgency of this demand.

Levinas is indeed proposing solutions, and we must ask whether they speak to our understanding of the human condition, a condition that extends beyond the horizons of our woeful last century. Where do Levinas's claims about vulnerability leave us? Should we not be concerned that our "goodness" is being linked in a rather mysterious way to a phenomenon—exposure, vulnerability—that is also the instigator of evil actions? Why is it or how is it that I avoid the temptation to violence and the next person cannot? Why am I summoned when he who should be my neighbor kills? How am I different from those who murder and maim? Why does exposure call out such different responses in different individuals? We cannot even appeal to choice here, for not only do I not choose to be commanded by the face of the other, but I respond before self-consciousness enters the scene.

If I actively strive to prevent evil by reshaping the social order, I am presumably involving myself in the systemic. Now Levinas does not want to dismiss the need for the thematic and systemic; after all, there are thirds and a world of thirds. However, we should see to it that society is organized in such a way that we do not forget our responsibility to the neighbor. But does preventing violence require a willingness to give myself completely over to the other, the other who also tempts me? "All the transfers of feeling, with which the theorists of original war and egoism explain the birth of generosity (it is, however, not certain that war was at the beginning, before the altars), would not succeed in being fixed in the ego if it were not with its whole being, or rather with its whole disinterestedness, subjected not, like matter, to a category, but to the unlimited accusative of persecution. The self, a hostage, is already substituted for the others," Levinas says.[48]

And is it really true, as the preceding passage suggests, that "transfers of feeling"—which I take to be sympathy and empathy—play a role in moral life only because we are first subjected to "the unlimited accusative of persecution," that is, to the nonnegotiable claim of the other? Must actions performed out of sympathy, empathy, or even love be inherently amoral? Note Levinas's words: "The recurrence of the self in responsibility for others, a persecuting obsession, goes against intentionality, such that responsibility for others could never mean altruistic will, instinct of 'natural benevolence,' or love. It is in the passivity of obsession, or incarnated passivity, that an identity individuates itself as unique, without recourse to any system of references, in the impossibility of evading the assignation of the other without blame."[49]

I must respond to the persecution of the other or I will not be good. This is a hard doctrine. It is in part hard because it appears to leave little room for explaining other moral imperatives, such as an imperative to treat animals, creatures that do not have a human face, with kindness. I do not want to belabor the issue of our relationship to animals here, for this theme has often been raised by those interested in Levinas's thought.[50] I raise it here because it seems to go hand in hand with the second-class status that Levinas gives to the realm of empathy and sympathy. In short, it does not seem possible to generate obligations to other life forms directly from the face to face. Sympathy-minded empiricists, on the other hand, manage to give a consistent reason for why it is wrong to mistreat living things, at least ones that can suffer. Whether it suffers is the question, not whether there is a face before us.

There is a striking issue on the horizon, one I return to in chapter 5. Levinas wants a world that thrives on alterity. I suggest that this is one of the reasons for his growing attraction. Many multiculturalists and postmodernists share a common cause: They want to rupture the hegemony of West and its logocentric traditions, a rupture that is necessary to do justice to individuals and different cultures. They hope to succeed by wielding the wedge of alterity. And Levinas is arguably without peer as a thinker of alterity. However, Levinas distrusts the political and condemns all the violence that follows in its wake. He wants pluralism but, as noted earlier in the chapter, a pluralism of peace that starts with the I: "Peace must be my peace, in a relation that starts from an I and goes to the other, in desire and goodness, where the I both maintains itself and exists without egoism."[51]

Presumably the question of how we are to bring about a world that tolerates and even thrives on difference is as much a political question as an ethical one. Can one organize political activities around pure disinterestedness? Levinas would be skeptical. He is well aware that the realm of the third, the realm of justice, must include an appeal to and an acceptance of competing interests. Yet, as we have seen, disinterestedness must inform this realm for Levinas. But is the kind of impartiality that Levinas sees informing the just social order the one on which we want to place our bets? Even as a vision of ideal human conduct, does it not amount to a call to a form of martyrdom that might prove counterproductive? As a preview of chapter 5, I mention Adam Smith's response to those he felt were excessively disposed to regarding benevolence as the only virtue. As we have seen, Levinas does not view his own project in terms of benevolence.[52] Nevertheless, the tenor of Smith's response does have something to say to Levinas's claims about one's "obligation" to substitute oneself for the other:

> Benevolence may, perhaps, be the sole principle of action in the Deity, and there are several, not improbable, arguments which tend to persuade us that it is so. It is not easy to conceive what other motive an independent and all-perfect Being, who stands in need of nothing external, and

whose happiness is complete in himself, can act from. But whatever may be the case with the Deity, so imperfect a creature as man, the support of whose existence requires so many things external to him, must often act from many other motives. The condition of human nature were peculiarly hard, if those affections, which, by the very nature of our being, ought frequently to influence our conduct, could upon no occasion appear virtuous, or deserve esteem and commendation from any body.[53]

Does this refute Levinas? Of course not. It does introduce a sensibility that I want to explore in chapter 5, a different voice. No doubt Levinas's voice is a distinctive one, one that appears to be finding an evergrowing audience, drawn to it for many reasons, perhaps for the mystery of the other that it invokes. Of course, there are reasons other than mystery for being intrigued and moved by Levinas. He promises to find ethical ground where few have been looking, and it turns out to be right before our eyes. Some will ask whether immersion in the ethical substance of a community—in "ethical life," as Hegel called it—could guarantee the moral high ground that Levinas insists can be found only in relation to the other. We know that Habermas would reject this course, for ethical life is too susceptible to context and community. Transcendental ground must be found to guarantee justice. And if we were to ask Levinas whether ethical life of a Hegelian sort could perform the same function as the command of the face, we know what his answer would be: Without the approach of the other we will be mired in egoism, and autoaffection will rule the day. Relativism, self-interest, egoism, presence, logocentrism, mediation, and system are all in some sense manifestations of the absence of the approach. We also know something more.[54] Both Habermas and Levinas had to face the Holocaust in a way that is all but impossible for Americans of my generation to understand, and their thought is troubled by a responsibility too heavy to contemplate: Never again.

5   *Pluralism, Radical Pluralism, and the Perspectives of Others*

Levinas poses a unique challenge to the nontranscendental approach to universalism that I have been recommending in this work, and he does so by offering an approach to plurality that is at odds with the understanding of pluralism found in Mead and Dewey. For these pragmatists pluralism is possible because we can appreciate both the differences and the common humanity of persons in various cultural contexts and walks of life. This sort of pluralism would strike Levinas as resting on a fundamental error. Yes, in the political realm, the realm of justice and thirds, such an approach makes sense, but not in the domain of ethics, for in the latter domain asymmetry rules. Plurality, for Levinas, is not a social and cultural phenomenon. It is found in the transcendence we encounter in the face of the other. This is the realm in which the deepest respect for the other is to be encountered. And without it the domain of justice and symmetry would ultimately have nothing to sustain it, and totality would have nothing to counter its seductions.

It may seem that the discussion should end at this point. From Levinas's position the romanticized enlightenment sensibilities of Mead and company simply do not reflect the importance of the face of the other. They see only reciprocity and symmetry, and these are only one step removed from narcissism and egoism. From Mead's vantage point Levinas would be a religious thinker whose claims are beyond any sort of scientific analysis, no matter how generously science is construed, and they threaten the sort of cosmopolitanism that he thinks is practically realizable, one in which interest and self-interest are woven into the fabric of social and ethical life. Yet we should not avoid having these thinkers address one another, for what is at stake is whether difference and alterity can be acknowledged in a framework that is universalistic and political (for example, Mead's) or whether we must develop a very different type of thinking and experience to fully engage the other (for example, one we find in Levinas). A version of this question, if I am not mistaken, has been at the heart of much recent debate between thinkers of alterity, often the postmodernly inclined, and those who actively adhere to some version of the modernist agenda, such as Habermas. Can pragmatists speak to the concerns of those who follow Levinas, call them radical pluralists, or must they too be dismissed by the latter in the same manner as more traditionally inclined transcendental or quasitranscendental modernists?

One of the ways to address the divide between Levinas and Mead is through the question of sympathy. Despite the importance of Hegel and the romantics for Mead, he is in some sense an heir of the British sympathy theorists, and their notions of sympathy can be interpreted as precursors of his own ideas about taking the perspective of others, as can Smith's notion of coming to judge ourselves through the looking-glass others present. Levinas, on the other hand, views his own approach as actively trying to move away from this British tradition. Sympathy and empathy are ways of dismissing and ultimately overcoming the alterity of the other.

There is much elasticity in Smith's use of the term *sympathy*, and teasing out the tensions in his use of the term should provide a good opening for this chapter, in which I intend address how Mead's ideas—ideas that are the not-so-distant kin of Smith's—might stack up against those of Levinas. When combined with chapter 3, on Habermas, this should provide a more detailed picture of where Mead and those who share his vision, such as Dewey, might stand in relation to Levinas and other radical pluralists. I hope to show that Mead's pragmatic approach to universalism and pluralism through taking the perspectives of others can support the uniqueness of the individual and can do so without leading to the disjunction between the political and ethical that we find in Levinas.

We have seen that Levinas confronts the Western tradition with a severe critique. To grossly but not unjustly simplify, we are selfish, we have always been so, and we have built elaborate castles in the air to defend and excuse our selfishness. Morality can never be grounded on self-interest, and although there have been thinkers who have argued this case, they have missed the extent to which their own ontologizing was just another form of a primal placing of the self before the other. Without alterity there is no morality. Sympathetic attachments will not do, for they saturate the alterity of the other with our own presence. Perhaps it is only fair, then, to hear what Smith thinks sympathy can and cannot accomplish. I should add a note of caution here. What follows is not intended as a close textual analysis of *The Theory of Moral Sentiments*. Such an analysis would require that we highlight the differences between the various editions of his work, which were published over more than a thirty-year period. My goal is more modest: to propose an alternative to Levinas's vision, one that has affinities to Mead and other pragmatists, as well as to Arendt.

First it must be said that Smith did not intend sympathy simply to be equated with pity and compassion. The latter "are words appropriated to signify our fellow-feeling with the sorrow of others. Sympathy, though its meaning was, perhaps, originally the same, may now, however, without much impropriety, be made use of to denote our fellow-feeling with any passion whatever."[1] Imagination plays a key role in the process of sympathetic attachments to others for Smith, so much so that we might ask whether one is merely projecting one's own (imagined) feelings when one appears to be sympathizing with the other. If so, this would be grist for Levinas's mill, for then sympathy would be little more than narcissistic projection. And there are occasions when Smith appears to speak this way. One interesting example of the latter is when we are moved by the dead:

> The idea of that dreary and endless melancholy, which the fancy naturally ascribes to their condition, arises altogether from our joining to the change which has been produced upon them, our own consciousness of that change, from our putting ourselves in their situation, and from our lodging, if I may be allowed to say so, our own living souls in their inanimated bodies, and thence conceiving what would be our emotions in this case. It is from this very illusion of the imagination, that the foresight of our own dissolution is so terrible to us . . . makes us miserable while we are alive.[2]

Smith goes on to note that this dread of death, which is so painful to the individual, has the positive impact of protecting society from injustices that individuals might commit if they did not fear death. Surely these are just the sort of claims Levinas would expect from Smith, that is, sympathy as projection and goodness as a function of self-interest.

Yet this is not the whole story. For Smith has another understanding of how sympathy operates, one that will still leave Levinas unsatisfied but will open the door to a set of sensibilities that are congenial to Mead and his compatriots. Although sympathy can be viewed as a mere narcissistic unfolding of one's own projections—in which I can only imagine what it would feel like for me if I were in the other person's shoes—Smith also claims that we are not mired in self-interest:[3]

> Sympathy, however, cannot, in any sense, be regarded as a selfish principle. When I sympathize with your sorrow or your indignation, it may be pretended, indeed, that my emotion is founded in self-love, because it arises from bringing your case home to myself, from putting myself in your situation, and thence conceiving what I should feel in the like circumstances. But though sympathy is very properly said to arise from an imaginary change of situations with the person principally concerned, yet this imaginary change is not supposed to happen to me in my own person and character, but in that of the person with whom I sympathize. When I condole with you for the loss of your only son, in order to enter into your grief I do not consider what I, a person of such a character and profession, should suffer, if I had a son, and if that son were unfortunately to die: but I consider what I should suffer if I was really you, and I not only change circumstances with you, but I change persons and characters. My grief, therefore, is entirely upon your account, and not in the least upon my own. It is not, therefore, in the least selfish. How can that be regarded as a selfish passion, which does not arise even from the imagination of any thing that has befallen, or that relates to myself, in my own proper person and character, but which is entirely occupied about what relates to you?[4]

One can find competing statements in Smith's *Theory of Moral Sentiments* about the degree to which we can experience the experience of another. Sometimes the accent is placed on our capacity to genuinely share experiences. At other times he hedges, for example, suggesting that we are closed off from the full intensity of what others may feel. This occurs because imagination fails us—that is, we cannot sense what the other senses—or self-interest comes into play and we remove ourselves from the other's influence.[5] In light of these tensions in Smith's thought it is important to note that for Smith an experience of sympathy is by no means restricted to directly imagining the passions that another feels; rather, it is more accurate to say that sympathy "does *not* arise so much from the view of the passion, *as from that of the situation which excites it.* We sometimes feel for another, a passion of which he himself seems to be altogether incapable; because, when we put ourselves in his case, that passion arises in our breast from the imagination, though it does not in his from the reality."[6] Context is king here. It is also important to note that Smith believes that the other wants us to sympathize with him or her. We recognize that sympathy cannot last indefinitely, that it is fleeting, but the individual "passionately desires a more complete sympathy."[7] The desire to be close to the other, to overcome alterity, appears to be a human need for Smith. We can gain pleasure from feeling what the other feels, even if what the other feels is unpleasant.

Although sympathy is pivotal in overcoming crass self-interest for Smith, it is not enough to guarantee that I consider the needs and wants of others. What is called for is an impartial spectator, a figure who arises in our interactions with others and moves us to do the right thing.[8] "According to Smith, conscience is a product of social relationship. Our first moral sentiments are concerned with the actions of other people. Each of us judges as a spectator and finds himself judged by spectators. Reflection upon our own conduct begins later in time and is inevitably affected by the more rudimentary experience. 'Reflection' is here a live metaphor, for the thought process mirrors the judgement of a hypothetical observer."[9]

Once developed, the impartial spectator is *not* to be thought of as an external observer who judges my actions from the mountaintop, praising or blaming as it sees fit, but as oneself in the role of a judicious observer. In evaluating my actions an *external* observer may be thought to be more impartial than I am—in the sense of having more distance, of being less invested in my situation—but I may know more about my case and therefore can actually do a superior job at judging. It is possible, then, to improve on the evaluations of external spectators by imagining ourselves in their roles, drawing on their views, in the context of our knowledge of specific circumstances.[10] Appealing to such an imagined (impartial) spectator also provides the distance needed to avoid simply accepting what a given public demands. (One is reminded here of the importance of imagination and common sense for judicious evaluation in Arendt's formulations. For Arendt, the actor must become a spectator who turns over and inspects in her mind, away from the immediacy of the crowd but imbued with common sense, that which is in need of evaluation. Yet Arendt at times appears to be more committed than Smith or Mead to distancing the spectator from the concerns of the actor.)

So if my actions are to be judged, I am—in the role of the impartial spectator—at times in the best position to judge because I have more information than others, for example, regarding my motives. This doctrine will not sit well in the early twenty-first century, geared as we are to suspect ourselves of self-deception. However, it may be time to sus-

pect our suspicions and suggest that we can (at times) know our own motives at least as well as the best-informed observers. Insight may be an
overplayed therapeutic tool, but it still may be of some value in formu-
lating judicious evaluations, especially if we can count on a little help from
our friends in these matters. In any case, Levinas and Habermas would
be suspicious of Smith's line of thought, for there appears to be no ground
from which to evaluate the propriety of the impartial spectator's analysis. Despite some of Smith's august language describing the impartial
spectator and his own attempts in later editions of *The Theory of Moral
Sentiments* to distinguish praiseworthiness from mere praise—that is, the
impartial spectator's views from popular opinion—they would argue that
the danger of a descent into the conventional cannot be avoided.[11]

Smith, like Mead, is not as troubled by the possibility of a descent
into the conventional. Both are social theorists of the self, and both are
convinced that one cannot talk of morality without addressing the sorts
of reactions that others have to us. Both are confident that out of the
interplay between self and other a creature capable of moral judgment is
born.[12] According to Smith, "Were it possible that a human creature could
grow up to manhood in some solitary place, without any communication
with his own species, he could no more think of his own character, of
the propriety or demerit of his own sentiments and conduct, of the beauty
or deformity of his own mind, than of the beauty or deformity of his own
face. . . . Bring him into society, and he is immediately provided with the
mirror which he wanted before."[13]

One of the great differences between Mead and Smith on one hand
and Levinas on the other is that ultimately for the latter morality is located in the individual. I become a unique self through my encounter with
the other, and it is my response to the other, my responsibility for the
other, that gives rise to this uniqueness. There is no social constitution
of morality, for morality cannot be left to the vagaries of social commerce.
The social conception of the self would be condemned by Levinas as a
harbinger of war, leading as it does to the overcoming of the other by the
same and to the dismissal of the infinite in favor of totality. And strangely
enough, Levinas would have something of an ally in Habermas. Although
Habermas takes his stand with a social conception of the self and is clearly much closer to Mead as a thinker than he is to Levinas, his urgency
and drive to find a ground that can guarantee removal from the conventional, at least with regard to his discourse ethics, is something he shares
with Levinas. This urgency is not present in Mead. For him the absence
of the transcendental does not make moral behavior any less possible. Nor
does it reduce morality to the merely conventional. It just makes us work

in a different ways to achieve it. This is precisely why for Mead the political task of organizing the right sort of society is so imperative.

Subtleties aside, despite Levinas's claims about the possibility that peace preceded war, he has basically accepted the egoist's rendition of human nature. This is to say that we are indeed fundamentally egocentric creatures. Like the egoist, Levinas thinks that even altruistic behavior is suspect, for when we scratch the surface we find not altruism but crass self-interest. His is a picture of an imperialistic ego, the ego that knows no bounds, that will not stop, that cannot be stopped by anything that is like it, for that which is like it can be absorbed by it. It is a desiring ego of the Hobbesian variety. It can be stopped only by the other, by an alterity that it does not or cannot encompass. The other is sovereign, must be sovereign. Of course, Levinas is not advocating the egoist's position, but his formulations seem to entail the continuing presence of the desiring ego. Without the latter, what would mark any act of substitution as an act for the other? That is, there must be sacrifice for the other, and sacrifice here entails a stepping away from the ego's desires.

My general claim is quite straightforward: Persecution and being held hostage by the other makes sense only if we believe that without being so held we are truly doomed to a war of all against all (in its multitude of forms) because war and violence are, if not the natural course of things, a course that we cannot shake. Recall that for Levinas sympathy and empathy, transfers of feeling, can never be the ground of morality. They can never truly end war. We must trust that which commands from on high, not feelings. Without the challenge of the other, the "persecution" of the other, sympathy could never explain generosity: "All the transfers of feeling, with which the theorists of original war and egoism explain the birth of generosity (it is, however, not certain that war was at the beginning, before the altars), would not succeed in being fixed in the ego if it were not with its whole being, or rather with its whole disinterestedness, subjected not, like matter, to a category, but to the unlimited accusative of persecution. The self, a hostage, is already substituted for the others."[14]

Note the parenthetical comment, "it is, however, not certain that war was at the beginning, before the altars." Just who is the audience for this aside? Are these not the words of one who is trying to convince himself that peace is really possible? Violence appears to be omnipresent. What we need to avoid violence is *not* the disinterestedness of an impartial spectator, who presumably does not lose touch with the interests of others and himself, but the disinterestedness of a hostage. Only the latter can prevent the egotism of the ego from lending itself to violence. Levinas could retort that we are confusing levels. He too is aware of the need for interests to be considered, and he does so on the level of justice. Yet such a retort will not do, for what is at stake here is whether morality itself requires absolute disinterestedness, and whether the realm of justice could be sustained without a realm of absolute disinterestedness.

Smith would not have accepted the disinterestedness of the hostage that we find in Levinas. Yet there is clearly some tension in his thought regarding self-interest, and I have already alluded to it. On one hand, he seems to suggest that we can transcend our self-interest. "My grief, therefore, is entirely upon your account, and not in the least upon my own. It is not, therefore, in the least selfish." On the other hand, he appears to suggest that self-interest is always present. We can read this as a contradiction. Or we can be charitable. Perhaps what the tension in Smith's thought reveals is the impossibility of escaping the mixing or intertwining of motives, that self-interest is bound to wind its way through our moments of disinterest. Is this a problem? It is a problem if one believes that an either–or is called for here, that to be self-interested is to be infected by a primal disregard for the other, that in any rearing of its head self-interest is to be viewed as evidence of a lack of moral rectitude, that we cannot help but be overcome by self-interest once it shows itself on the scene.[15] It is not a problem if we do *not* accept the sort of bifurcation Levinas wants to foist on us, that is, either self-interest or being for the other.

Levinas may not be able to avoid the reality of mixed motives on the subject of self-interest, and this is problematic for him in a way that it is not for Smith or Mead. Consider the significance of being a unique individual. For Levinas, one becomes a unique "me" through substitution, through responsibility for the other, which is intimately intertwined in Levinas's thought with the overcoming of violence. "Has not the Good chosen the subject with an election recognizable in the responsibility of being hostage, to which the subject is destined, which he cannot evade without denying himself, and by virtue of which he is unique? . . . But this desire for the non-desirable, this responsibility for the neighbor, this substitution as a hostage, is the subjectivity and uniqueness of a subject."[16] This appeal to uniqueness is not an afterthought. If one reads the chapter on "Substitution," the heart of *Otherwise Than Being or Beyond Essence*, one cannot help but be struck by the number of references to uniqueness and the notion of irreplaceableness. "In the exposure to wounds and outrages, in the feeling proper to responsibility, the oneself is provoked as irreplaceable, as devoted to the others, without being able to resign, and thus as incarnated in order to offer itself, to suffer and to give. It is thus one and unique, in passivity from the start, having nothing at its disposal that would enable it to not yield to the provocation."[17]

It goes without saying that one cannot easily avoid the attraction that uniqueness presents in our culture, and Levinas has managed to tie it to another totem, responsibility. This is a heady rhetorical brew. Isn't it possible that Levinas's followers are moved as much by their own self-interested desire to become unique and responsible as they are by the "force" of the other? Levinas's formulations are so immersed in a language of sensitivity toward the other, so filled with the pain of the violence he has seen, that one almost feels sacrilegious in challenging his formulations. But here is my concern: Is it really the other that one worries most about while reading some of his texts, or is it the unique "me" of the reader? Is it the other's difference that compels me, or is it my longing for difference from the other that seduces me? In the latter case Levinas could blame the reader for not hearing the message, for being too involved with self-assertion, for not appreciating true subjectivity, for failure to understand what is really at stake. Nevertheless, are we not dealing with an unavoidable subtext here, the carrot of pristine uniqueness?[18]

Something appears to be amiss that such a challenge should even be raised. Certainly the concern is for the other; that is the whole point. However, even if Levinas's motives are pure, his language seems to beckon in different directions—to a fixation on uniqueness and to the other's claim on me—while arguing that these different directions are part of the same package, a package that cannot include what is usually thought of as self-interest, for an interest in becoming a "me" would subvert my being for the other. Yet one may wonder just what role the promise of uniqueness, the desire for uniqueness, plays in the economy of his thought or his attraction for certain readers, specifically for readers drawn to a path that tells them that one can truly become a "me" only by forgoing a selfish interest in becoming one. Perhaps the real challenge would be if my responsibility for the other entailed *a loss of any sort of genuine selfhood,* including Levinas's nonempirical sort, not the promise of uniqueness. (Of course, if motives can be mixed and self-interest not dismissed, it is much easier to accept how an interest in uniqueness can be present without notably damaging my responsibility to the other. Service to the other has it rewards, uniqueness being one of them. With this, consequentialism has truly reared its unruly head, and Levinas can only shake his head in wonder at how confused people can become on these matters.)[19]

My interest here has not been to explore in detail the manner in which Smith negotiates his way around the issue of our sympathetic attachments to others. It is to introduce a different moral universe from Levinas's, one that is at least as plausible as his, and one that can lead to a less dramatic rift between the ethical and political, a rift I address shortly. In this world not only is moral behavior dependent on sympathy, but a different conception of the self is operative. It is a universe that shares much with Mead's, yet it should not be conflated with it. Mead's conception of the self is richer than Smith's, for in addition to the British empiricists, Mead (like Dewey) was influenced by Hegel, the romantics, and the Darwinian turn. Having raised the issue of self-interest in Levinas by contrasting his views with Smith's, I would now like to compare more directly Levinas and Mead, and through Mead the tradition that emphasizes the importance of recognition and mutuality, namely, Hegel and his descendants.

––––––––––

In Levinas's quest for the ultimate pluralism of alterity, it appears that points of view about ethics and moral problems other than his own must be viewed as suspect. (Of course, this penchant is not uncommon to philosophers.) Leaving aside the whole question of means, what are we to make of the fact that Levinas would have us believe that the problems that he addresses are *the* problems?[20] Given my location in history, I am clearly sympathetic to his concerns. However, one can readily think of political and ethical problems that seem to have little hope of solution if we follow Levinas's teachings.

One particular issue comes to mind, one that moved Mead and Dewey as well as other pragmatists and nonpragmatists alike. It even moved Hegel. And for Mead and Dewey it is affiliated with a crucial good: self-actualization. The problem is alienation, the deep dislocation of the self, of spirit, caused by the lack of ties with one's fellows and nature. The answer is community. And this end-in-view was eloquently expressed by James Hayden Tufts, a colleague of both Dewey's and Mead's, when the cornerstone of the chapel was laid at the University of Chicago. "It is, then, our hope that in our chapel the spirit of service to mankind in its special forms will find reinforcement in common purpose and feeling; that our partial interests and sympathies will be broadened and deepened by contacts with those of like minds and hearts; and that the common purpose will find renewed vitality and ampler range as the ties which bind mankind are felt to be but manifestations of the larger life in which we share."[21]

Compare these words with Dewey's own autobiographical statement of the problem:

There were, however, also "subjective" reasons for the appeal that Hegel's thought made to me; it supplied a demand for unification that was doubtless an intense emotional craving, and yet was a hunger that only an intellectualized subject-matter could satisfy. It is more than difficult, it is impossible, to recover that early mood. But the sense of division and separations that were, I suppose, borne in upon me as a consequence of a heritage of New England culture, divisions by way of isolation of self from the world, of soul from body, of nature from God, brought a painful oppression—or, rather, they were an inward laceration.[22]

And recall once again young Mead's words:

I have learned to see that society advances, men get closer and closer to each other and the kingdom of heaven is established on the earth, so far as man becomes more and more organically connected with nature. This has generally been laid up against America as materialism—and she has been scouted as sunk in money getting and as letting go [the] spiritual side of life. But it seems to me clearer every day that the telegraph and locomotive are the great spiritualizers of society because they bind man and man so close together that the interest of the individual must be more completely the interest of all day by day. And America in pushing this spiritualizing of nature is doing more than all in bringing the day when every man will be my neighbor and all life shall be saturated with the divine life.[23]

Levinas would have us believe that Mead and Dewey's problem is one that can be framed only in terms of self-interest, thereby falling outside the range of the ethical. (*I* feel alienated. *I* feel the lacerations. I am concerned for myself in being concerned about others who share this pain.) This is not to say that Levinas has no concern for community but that communities tied together by sympathetic attachments—without a deeper grounding in the face to face—must be suspect, ethically speaking. Furthermore, if the problem Mead and Dewey point to is itself grounded in an egoism that cannot escape its own purview, then pursuing any answer would be misguided. Their concern with alienation already presupposes a particular image of human interaction, entailing an ethic of goods, that is itself questionable. So we cannot avoid certain questions. Isn't the very conception of the self that Mead puts forward built on displacing the other? Isn't taking the perspective of the other a form of hubris, and, in fact, a violation of the alterity of the other? And would not the overcoming of alienation through the development of community lead to the absorption of the other by the same? Is not Mead's paradigm itself the problem?

We are not just dealing with Mead here, for we are using him as a stand-in for a whole set of sensibilities, ones that we can find in other pragmatists and ones that we can (to a degree) locate in Hegel and other so-called modernists. So let us go right to what is arguably at the heart of the matter: the dialectic of recognition or the paradigm of mutuality, the position that argues that symmetry and community are at the heart of our ethical and political lives. Hegel declares, "What still lies ahead for consciousness is the experience of what Spirit is—this absolute substance which is the unity of the different independent self-consciousnesses which, in their opposition, enjoy perfect freedom and independence: 'I' that is 'We' and 'We' that is 'I.'"[24]

Mutuality has been the model for ethical dealings with our fellows time and again in modernist programs, and of course versions of it can be found throughout history. However, we know what Levinas's reaction to the whole set of categories that surround this model would be.

> But communication would be impossible if it should have to begin in the ego, a free subject, to whom every other would be only a limitation that invites war, domination, precaution and information. To communicate is indeed to open oneself, but the openness is not complete if it is on the watch for recognition. It is complete not in opening to the spectacle of or the recognition of the other, but in becoming a responsibility for him. The overemphasis of openness is responsibility for the other to the point of substitution, where the for-the-other proper to disclosure, to monstration to the other, turns into the for-the-other proper to responsibility. *This is the thesis of the present work.*[25]

Note that Levinas juxtaposes the thesis of his work, *Otherwise Than Being*, against the backdrop of dismissing the centrality of recognition. This dialectic is at center of what he wants to overcome, for it promises that the self can find itself in the other and that the other can retain its integrity in the process. The self, it tells us, can find its place in the sun, can be at home, and can do so by being at home with others who remain other. Selves and others can be independent, in opposition, and yet in unity.

If Hegel's thesis is correct, if through mutual recognition one can recognize the otherness of the other while also joining together with that other, then we have a path that may not require persecution and substitution. But in a sense Levinas has an easy target here, for he can point to Hegel's system and say something along the following lines: "You see where this leads, it leads to a self (ego) that is saturated with spirit and history, that cannot see itself (or the other) as anything but a part of a larger whole. The self cannot see the responsibility it has for the other. The other has disappeared and the self has failed to be born. Pluralism becomes impossible."

Surely I have not done full justice to Levinas or Hegel in the preceding paragraphs, but in light of the earlier chapter on Levinas they can serve as an adequate refresher regarding his concerns. So let us leave Hegel and ask the following questions. Can Mead's framework provide an alternative reading of the dialectic of recognition that can meet some of Levinas's concerns? Must a program of mutuality lead us to deny the uniqueness of the other, to deny the sanctity of the other?

One answer is that mutuality is never mutual; it is always a form of narcissism of the ontological or psychological variety. We do not see the other. We see only ourselves. (Furthermore, if it were thoroughly mutual, then the otherness that is present would evaporate in a mirror play of egos.) At first glance Mead's account of the development of the self appears to support this view. I internalize specific roles and generalized others, and they shape who I am and how I see myself, which in turn shapes how I see others. I become my social roles and see others through them. I recognize others in recognizing something about myself in the other. The notion of a generalized other should be especially suspect in this regard, for the other is not seen as a person but a set of relationships, a set of relationships that became "me."

From Levinas's vantage point Mead has simply reduced the self to sets of behaviors that can be correlated with generalized social behaviors. We do not then have a self but a composition of themes incapable of saying, of approaching the other. Levinas might also point out that we are confused about alienation. We are not alienated, if you want to call it that, because we are disconnected from a community. We are alienated because we have not become who we always should have been: a self in responsibility for the other. Furthermore, if you look at Mead's sense of time you will see a thinker who cherishes the present, who even defends the notion that the present trumps the past by redefining it, by subsuming it in its own territory. There is no place for the Infinite to pass in the face of the other, for its passing would be absorbed by the present. Mead wishes to overcome separation to such a degree that he is blinded to true alterity and cannot welcome the other. And this is to be expected. Mead is a modernist, and modernism, as we have seen, lends itself to imperialism. "Modern Man persists in his being as a sovereign who is merely concerned to maintain the *powers of his sovereignty*. Everything that is possible is permitted. In this way the experience of Nature and Society would gradually get the better of any exteriority. A miracle of modern Western freedom unhindered by any memory or remorse, and opening onto a 'glittering future' where everything can be rectified," Levinas says.[26]

This is one of Mead's sins, for he was an optimist, a rectifier, a believer in the possibilities of science, a believer in political action that is intimately linked to morality. What can be done to redeem a figure who turns the unique self, the one who is capable of saying, into the said? Given the intimate connection Levinas has established between alterity and the uniqueness of the self, taking up the question of uniqueness may help provide an answer.

What is it that justifies calling ourselves different from each other, calling oneself a unique individual? One possible answer is that each of us possess different socially generated characteristics or qualities. Even if we see ourselves as part of a larger whole or wholes we may reflect these social wholes from different vantage points. Call this the Leibnizian monad approach if you will. And Mead buys the latter to some degree, at least as we think about ourselves in terms of the "me" as opposed to the "I."[27] Of course this will not do for Levinas. We can also point to different biologically grounded dispositions and impulses, those that are not directly part of the structure of the self, that is, of the self that is primarily a cognitive object. And Mead also takes this into consideration. The person is not solely a self, as we have seen, but a nonreflective "biologic individual" who possesses impulses. We might call the combination of these two elements, self and biologic individual, a human organism. This also will not do for Levinas, for we are still in world of qualities and themes. We could also look to the unique life history of each individual and the narrative that one comes to call one's own, as we did in chapter 3.[28] (It is safe to say that Mead did not develop this path, but with modest modifications his approach could easily accommodate it. And it is necessary to augment Mead's approach in this manner.) We might even point to the unique stream of consciousness to which I am attuned, perhaps self-consciously so. Surely these avenues will not do for Levinas, especially because there is an appeal to self-consciousness as a source of the "me." We could say that all these elements—social, biological, historical, and self-reflexive—coalesce into a voice, an individual voice that others hear and that they recognize as me (and I also recognize as me). But this combination of elements will not do for Levinas, and surprisingly it will not do for Mead either, even though the latter would want to appeal to these elements in his approach to individuality, whereas Levinas would find their application to the individual ultimately misguided. (As a matter of fact, highlighting their disagreement over the value of this list of elements would be a good way to present the basic differences between these thinkers.) Nevertheless, there is some common ground here, for both thinkers would agree that this list appears to leave out the capacity of other human beings to exceed our expectations, to give rise to something new, to surprise us. Levinas is aware of the power or value of that which can surprise us. On the very first page of Levinas's chapter on substitution in *Otherwise Than Being*, we find him condemning the Western philosophical tradition in these terms:

> The detour of ideality leads to coinciding with oneself, that is, to certainty, which remains the guide and guarantee of the whole spiritual adventure of being. . . . Anything unknown that can occur to it is in advance disclosed, open, manifest, is cast in the mould of the known, and *cannot be a complete surprise.*
> For the philosophical tradition of the West, all spirituality lies in consciousness, thematic exposition of being, knowing.[29]

For Mead, as for many pragmatists, novelty is a crucial theme. And they clearly want to avoid the closure of ideality and the thematic exposition of being. But perhaps it is an ill-considered leap to move from Levinas's statement to Mead's concern with novelty, for from one vantage point the new is a modernist obsession. Yet there is a parallel that is worth considering here, and we can do so by juxtaposing Mead's position on novelty with claims Levinas makes about the notion of creation.

Although I do not want to suggest that Levinas's approach can be simply summed up as the march of Jerusalem against Athens, I am convinced that there is a deep-seated commitment to the importance of creation in Levinas, a notion that for him has biblical roots. The irony is that this notion for Levinas has been heisted by modernists who use it in a cavalier, imperial manner: We, who are children of the modern dawn, create the creations that allow us to own creation. For Levinas this is a perverse sense of creation. Creation is what foils totality, what separates creatures, what allows beings to avoid submersion in being. It is the absent that makes itself present in a manner that disrupts thematization and in the process prevents idolatry. Near the close of *Totality and Infinity* Levinas tells us,

> For the idea of totality, in which ontological philosophy veritably reunites—or comprehends—the multiple, must be substituted the idea of a separation resistant to synthesis. To affirm origin from nothing by creation is to contest the prior community of all thing [sic] within eternity, from which philosophical thought, guided by ontology, makes things arise from a common matrix. The absolute gap of separation which transcendence implies could not be better expressed than by the term creation, in which the kinship of beings among themselves is affirmed, but

at the same time their radical heterogeneity also, their reciprocal exteriority coming from nothingness. One may speak of creation to characterize entities situated in the transcendence that does not close over into a totality.[30]

And in *Otherwise Than Being* we are told,

> Western philosophy, which perhaps is reification itself, remains faithful to the order of things and does not know the absolute passivity, beneath the level of activity and passivity, which is contributed by the idea of creation.[31]

It is perhaps here, in this reference to a depth of anarchical passivity, that the thought that names creation differs from ontological thought. It is not here a question of justifying the theological context of ontological thought, for the word creation designates a signification older than the context woven about this name. In this context, this said, is already effaced the absolute diachrony of creation, refractory to assembling into a present and a representation.[32]

For Levinas, the Western tradition has not understood the importance of creation and has been captured by totalizing or thematizing thought.[33] And here is a link back to Mead. I suggested at the end of chapter 3 that one of the differences between Mead and Habermas is that the former uses what might be called a creative principle and the latter a reflexive one. One of the main characteristics of a creative principle is that it refuses closure by privileging the different, which is to be contrasted with the drive toward closure found in philosophers who emphasize the reflexive. In this scheme of things Levinas and Mead would actually fall into a similar camp in their resistance to totality. Framing the connection in this manner—that is, in terms of principles—in all likelihood will give Levinasians the shudders, for this is precisely the language they want to escape. And clearly there are serious limitations to painting the history of philosophy in such broad strokes. Yet it may have some heuristic value here, for despite the differences between Mead and Levinas as secular and religious thinkers, there is a sense in which novelty in Mead's approach can fruitfully be compared with the notion of creation in Levinas, even if, as we shall see, their positions are ultimately irreconcilable.

The question at hand is whether Mead's approach to novelty has any kinship to Levinas's notion of creation. Levinas would be highly skeptical, for Mead's approach is too closely aligned with the synthetic sensibilities of Hegel. In an earlier discussion of Mead it was suggested that the relationship between the "I" and the "me" is one in which the novel responses of one's "I" are either integrated into a new "me" or left by the wayside.[34] The analogy to be made here is with that of the mutation that is introduced into an ecosystem and either survives or doesn't. This may sound like a march of history, or being if you will, in which otherness is subverted by systemic ties. However, things turn out to be more complicated. Mead was clearly opposed to the ontology of being, a monism he associated with Parmenides. And his views on the present warrant further consideration in this light.

> For that which marks a present is its becoming and its disappearing. While the flash of the meteor is passing in our own specious present it is all there if only for a fraction of a minute. To extend this fraction of a minute into the whole process of which it is a fragment, giving to it the solidarity of existence which the flash possesses in experience, would be to wipe out its nature as an event. . . . For a Parmenidean reality does not exist. Existence involves non-existence; it does take place. The world is a world of events.[35]

The world of events is surely not the escape from an ontology of presence that Levinas would have hoped for, but neither is it the bowing before the idol of an enduring and encompassing present. It is important to note here that novelty is part and parcel of a world of events and not merely the result of the activity of an ego taken with its own creative powers. The world cannot be a totality because it is a world of nonexistence as well as existence, of events, and of events that are in principle novel. If events were not to some degree novel, that is, emergent, there would be no time—no past, present, and future—but the mere endless continuity of a continuum. Novelty for Mead is at the heart of diachrony. "A present then, as contrasted with the abstraction of mere passage, is not a piece cut out anywhere from the temporal dimension of uniformly passing reality. Its chief reference is to the emergent event, that is, to the occurrence of something which is more than the processes that have led up to it and which by its change, continuance, or disappearance, adds to later passages a content they would not otherwise have possessed."[36]

Novelty, difference, is itself the source of time for Mead. But doesn't this once again trivialize the novel, the truly new, the truly other? Doesn't it run the danger of seeing a continuity between the novelty of the physical world and the novelty that we find in human interactions, a continuity that would obviate any special claim that humanity has in the realm of morality? Surely such a world would not include true alterity for Levinas. However, Mead would not yield to the notion that the human world cannot be distinguished from that of rocks or amoebas because novelty plays a role in both. The human world emerges from the natural world, but it emerges as something dramatically unique though still natural.

For Mead, we are not only concerned with the novelty of our own responses, those that we cannot in principle predict in advance, but with a world in which the other and other things continually surprise us, in which new things are born. (Arendt would call this natality.) This opens Mead's approach to the sensibility that we find in Buber, namely, that the "thou" must be respected as the one who can exceed our grasp through an ability to surprise us, to present something new, to create. (The scintillating present of the "thou" must be contrasted with the finalized past of the "It.") Mead's approach to novelty might be viewed as complementary to Levinas's claims about creation, given the capacity of the other to surprise us, to move outside of our expectations, to avoid the embrace of the ego. The other is clearly not to be reduced to the same for Mead. However, Levinas would not be satisfied, for in large measure he sees variety and novelty as ways to sidestep the true alterity of the other.

> Nothing, in fact, is absolutely other in the Being served by knowing, in which variety turns into monotony. Is that not the thought of Proverbs 14:13 "Even in laughter the heart is sad, and the end of joy is grief." The contemporary world, scientific, technical, and sensual, is seen to be without issue, that is to say, without God, not because everything is permitted and is possible by means of technology, but because everything is the same. The unknown immediately becomes the familiar, the new, habitual. Nothing is new under the sun. The crisis described in Ecclesiastes is not of sin, but of boredom. Everything is absorbed, sunk, buried in sameness. . . . The notions of old and new, understood as qualities, are not adequate for the notion of the absolutely other. Absolute *difference* cannot itself delineate the plane common to those that are different. The other, absolutely other, is the Other (*L'autre, absolument autre, c'est Autrui*). The Other is not a particular case, a species of otherness, but the original exception to order. *It is not because the Other is novelty that it "gives room" for a relation of transcendence. It is because the responsibility for the Other is transcendence that there can be something new under the sun.*[37]

So the contrast is clear. Novelty is vital for Levinas not because it gives rise to transcendence but because in transcendence "there can be something new under the sun." The other must not be reduced to the same.

We are at an impasse. The attempt to draw Mead and Levinas closer together is finally shipwrecked on the shoals of the question, "Just how much transcendence is enough?" Even if we grant that Mead has a genuine notion of alterity in his world, it would not be sufficiently attached to transcendence for Levinas, for whom there must be a point of absolute discontinuity between self and other. Without such discontinuity the other inevitably will be reduced to the same. But Mead would have us ask, "How much alterity is actually necessary in order not to reduce the other to the same? Do we need the 'trace' of the divine to be confronted with the 'spark' of (we know not what) in the other?" For Mead, as we do not need absolute impartiality to judge well, so we do not need an absolute degree of discontinuity to avoid reducing the other to the same. Continuity and discontinuity can interpenetrate without the overcoming of the other. Novelty may not be creation in Levinas's sense, but if properly appreciated it can surely help us avoid reducing the other to the same. (Of course, that the other can surprise us, that we view the other as a source of novel responses, is obviously not enough in itself to make us respect the other. There are no doubt other factors involved.[38])

Levinas has reminded us of the obligations we owe to those who stand beside us, those who have been shaped by hands not our own. However, there is a limit to how far anyone can be persuaded by the writings of another to believe in God (or the Good) or of the need for "absolute" transcendence. And, when all is said and done, this is where Levinas wants to bring us, face to face with "absolute" transcendence. Levinas is no doubt correct: There is much sham novelty in the modern world, fashion without end, jejune otherness. However, this does not mean that one cannot find truly rich and novel happenings in the ordinary day to day. For Mead, we do not have to wait for the other to save us from boredom, to initiate a faith that the world is intrinsically wondrous and diverse, to convince us that it is a true plurality. The world does not need the other to salvage its richness. Nor does it need the other to have given birth to moral and political beings. Yet even in Mead's secularized words, we can still hear the echoes of a life, a spiritual life, that saturates his admonitions with something of the anxious passion of the elect. "We determine what the world has been by the anxious search for the means of making it better, and we are substituting the goal of a society aware of its own values and minded intelligently to pursue them, for the city not built with hands eternal in the heavens."[39]

Mead's neighbor is not the neighbor that Levinas has in mind, not the other, not the one for whom we must substitute ourselves to be moral, but the one who is like us, one with whom we can sympathize. Must we give up sympathy, attachment, to respond to the otherness of the neighbor? Levinas would view Mead's philosophy as a dream that self-interest uses to disguise itself. Mead, on the other hand, is convinced that doing or being good does not require treating sympathy as a form of imperial self-interest. "I would still maintain that back of these legalistic conceptions has lain the assumption of the parable of the Good Samaritan that we are neighbors of those in distress; back of the eschatology of the church has always lain the thesis of the Sermon on the Mount that men are all brethren in one family. In immediate sympathy with distress we have already identified ourselves with its victims."[40]

Although important, this immediate sympathy is inadequate for Mead, not because he is afraid that it is merely a cover for narcissistic projections—we really do have kindly impulses for him—but because it is still without reflection, that is, reflection on the situation that produces brethren in distress.

> We feel ourselves shrinking from or tending to push away the evil, and these attitudes stimulate our kindly impulse to relieve the sufferer. This is all, however, on the impulsive level. A sense of obligation has not yet arisen, for obligation arises only in the conflict of values. . . . This very attitude, however, of putting one's self in the other man's shoes brings with it not only the stimulus to assist him, but also a judgment upon that situation. Distress is conceivably remedial, or at the worst can be alleviated. . . . The bare impulse to help is on the same level with that of the dogs that licked the sores on Lazarus' body. The identification of ourselves with Lazarus puts in motion those immediate defensive reactions which give rise not only to efforts of amelioration but also to judgments of value and plans for social reform.[41]

We have already noted that Mead believes that impartiality is important in our dealings with one another. And we have also suggested that this impartiality comes not from total disinterest but from an expansion of one's interests, which can occur because the social self is not tied to immediate local concerns. This sensibility was linked to Kant or at least to Arendt's reading of Kant. However, the preceding passages have raised another issue. How are we to overcome the conditions that cause our brethren to starve, that create violence? One answer is that we sometimes must get angry, angry over their situation and pain. And here is the critical piece: It seems that this anger requires some degree of expanded self-interest. I become angry because I can take the position of the other and experience in some way what he or she is experiencing. Or I become angry because I can put myself in the situation of the other, as Smith suggests, even if the other is not in tune with the anger she could be experiencing. I feel her reactions (or potential reactions) as well as her pain. This happens through processes of identification and reflection, and identification here is mediated by reflection on the situation. I can become angry for the other in an abstract way, or I can experience his or her anger as my anger. In the latter case I am motivated to act. This is an overcoming of otherness to assist the other, which is not a problem for Mead because he does not view identification as necessarily a step in the direction of totality. And an appeal to interest is also not a problem for Mead, for like other pragmatists he is positively disposed to the virtue of interests as motivators, although of course not all interests are equally ennobling. This leads to a different take on politics than Levinas's. For the latter, politics and ethics *cannot* be branches of the same social philosophical tree.

No doubt for both Mead and Levinas politics and ethics can be viewed under certain circumstances as contradicting one another. "I think that there's a direct contradiction between ethics and politics, *if both these demands are taken to the extreme*," Levinas tells us. "It's a contradiction which is usually an abstract problem. Unfortunately for ethics, politics has its own justification. In mankind, there is a justification for politics."[42] But the real question is whether they must always be viewed in opposition. It is hard to see how this would not be true for Levinas, for the demands of ethics should be taken to an extreme. Is this not the whole point of Levinas's uncompromising ethics? Just how do we balance the sphere of the multiple with the face to face? Granted, the face to face should permeate this other world, the world of politics, but how do we get from asymmetry to symmetry (and back again)? The fact is that the boundary between the two must never be bridged, for it will leave the sanctity of the other exposed to the secular gyrations of power (or even justice).

Besides power and violence, we can also find negotiation and involvement in the political world, as well as the weighing of interests. The question is whether the weighing of interests is under certain circumstances an ethical activity. To separate the ethical and the just, asymmetry and symmetry, as Levinas does tends to place the weighing of interests on the underbelly of the ethical, condemning political solutions to a sort of netherworld. It is what we cannot escape because there are thirds. And even if the political could be seen as a possible avenue for self-realization, Levinas would remain uninspired. Self-actualization has nothing to do with ethics for him.

Let me draw an analogy here. Students of the law often debate the degree to which the law must be seen as separate from the claims of morality. Strict proceduralists, for example, want to keep what we might call disciplinary boundaries intact. Law is a field that must not be seen as circumscribed by the claims of morality, for to do so leaves the integrity of the law at the mercy of the moral whims of the populace. Habermas, though not a strict proceduralist, is also concerned to have the boundaries between law and morality properly fixed, even as he seeks to tie the legitimacy of the law to democracy.[43] I have no intention of pursuing this rather complex issue here, but I will make the following claim. Although law must not be conflated with morality, a law that has no concerns for the moral intuitions of the populace in a democratic society eventually loses its claim to legitimacy. Likewise, a morality that does not speak to the moral intuitions of the people in a democracy, and the processes of political engagement, eventually will not be viewed as legitimate. Disciplines must be respected and limits observed, but the spirit of the times must also be considered. Levinas has created such an insurmountable rift between the ethical and political, between morality and self-interest, a rift of such depth that if one actually tried to live by Levinas's ethical standards *and* remain politically engaged, authenticity would be impossible. And the integrity Levinas hopes to find through a relationship to the other would be compromised beyond repair. Who am I if my political and ethical lives cannot become part of one story? So, in a sense, I am accusing Levinas of a variant of what I accused Arendt's spectator of, namely, being inaccessible to political life, or at least democratic political life.

Perhaps this is a good place to link together two dimensions of this book: impartiality in the moral sphere and in the political world. There can be no morality without a degree of impartiality, for morality at a minimum entails not being so involved with one's own interests that one has no regard for the concerns and needs of others. Without regard there are no limits to oneself, for one would be everywhere in a sort of narcissistic stupor. And without a degree of impartiality, democracy would be impossible, for democracy depends on dialogue and debate, which involves some respect for the opinions of others, which entails a degree of respect for others, which entails not believing that the other is merely you in disguise. Both our moral and political lives, then, require some degree of impartiality. I have sought to provide a nontranscendental approach to impartiality through thinkers such as Smith and Mead.

That democracy is a good has been one of the underlying assumptions of this book. One of the reasons it is a good is that it allows the many to develop, to self-actualize, in ways that alternative political systems do not. So, contra Plato, by definition it is not a system that nurtures "sameness." Yet too much alterity, too much otherness, and the sense of community that allows actors to converse with one another begins to wane and genuine democracy becomes impossible. This is not to suggest that the path to democracy is one of cultural parochialism. For in addition to communal voices there must be critical ones, and the possibility of critique is intimately connected to the sort of cosmopolitanism favored by

Mead, that is, one entailing the capacity to take the perspective of others. In this framework sensitivity and respect for cultural and group differences are as vital as respect for individual differences. For Levinas, on the other hand, group differences reside and must be dealt with on the level of thirds, of justice. They do not exist on the same plane as the face of the other. This is a serious failing.

But if we follow Mead and his compatriots, does not morality become dependent on what we see as our own needs? Even if they are expanded ones, even if they are attached to the other, even if they are enlarged, they are still in some sense our needs. We do not respond with complete disinterest, which is at the heart of the ethical for Levinas. Becoming completely disinterested is not the issue, however. The issue is whether there is a problem and whether "x" will solve it. Put quite simply, does a pluralism of Mead's sort have a greater potential for lessening brutality and violence (while also diminishing alienation and fostering self-actualization) than does Levinas's approach? A good pragmatic answer would be that it depends on circumstance and situation, and we will have to test the waters continually to see. Levinas is looking for the Good beyond being, not goods that are good enough. For the pragmatist the latter must suffice.

Notes

Chapter 1: Mead and the Social Self

1. There are exceptions. Some contemporary commentators on Mead, such as Dmitri Shalin and Hans Joas, have highlighted this aspect of his work. See the bibliography at the end of this book. The relationship between the political and the ethical (or moral) is central to disagreements between Mead, Habermas, and Levinas.

2. Shalin, "G. H. Mead and the Progressive Agenda," 913–51.

3. Deegan, *Jane Addams and the Men of the Chicago School*, 118–21. See also Miller, *George Herbert Mead*, xxxi.

4. Deegan, *Jane Addams*, 120.

5. Ibid., 116, 210–11.

6. Diner, "George Herbert Mead's Ideas on Women and Careers," 408.

7. Ibid., 409.

8. Ibid., 408.

9. In *John Dewey and American Democracy*, Robert Westbrook argues that Dewey should be viewed as a radical progressive. He suggests that Mead, Jane Addams, and Robert Bourne should be placed in the same camp (189 n. 45). Mead was indeed a radical progressive.

10. Mead, "Philanthropy from the Point of View of Ethics," 406–7.

11. Shalin, "G. H. Mead and the Progressive Agenda," 919.

12. Ibid., 920–21.

13. Ibid., 923.

14. Mead, *Mind, Self and Society*, 132–33 (hereafter abbreviated *MSS*).

15. Ibid., 69.

16. Ibid., 134.

17. See Tugendhat, "Lecture 11," in *Self-Consciousness and Self-Determination*; Habermas, *Theory of Communicative Action*, vol. 2, 3–42 (hereafter abbreviated *TCA2*); and chapter 3.

18. Habermas, *TCA2*, 15–22.
19. Ibid., 23.
20. Halton, "Habermas and Rorty," 333–58.
21. Mead, *MSS*, 151.
22. Ibid., 154.
23. Ibid., 157.
24. Ibid., 194. The value of recognition and reciprocity is challenged by Levinas (see chapters 4 and 5).
25. Ibid., 156.
26. Mead, "The Social Self," 142.
27. Mead, *MSS*, 174.
28. Mead, "The Mechanism of Social Consciousness," 141.
29. Ibid. The manner in which Habermas interprets Mead's "I" is a key to the differences between them. See chapter 3, pp. 67–69.
30. James, "The Stream of Thought," 21–74. I cite this anthology because I believe it to be the most readily available and the best compendium of James's work.
31. Mead views instincts as malleable, and so prefers to call them impulses. He says in a supplementary essay in *Mind, Self, and Society*, "An impulse is a congenital tendency to react in a specific manner to a certain sort of stimulus, under certain organic conditions. Hunger and anger are illustrations of such impulses. They are best termed 'impulses,' and not 'instincts,' because they are subject to extensive modification in the life-history of individuals, and these modifications are so much more extensive than those to which the instincts of lower forms are subject that the use of the term 'instinct' in describing the behavior of normal adult human individuals is seriously inexact" (337).
32. Mead, *MSS*, 177–78.
33. Ibid., 352–53.
34. See Rosenthal and Bourgeois, *Mead and Merleau-Ponty*.
35. In chapter 5 I address how the role of novelty in Mead's work might be related to Levinas's thought.
36. Mead, *The Philosophy of the Present*, 47 (hereafter abbreviated *PP*).
37. For a discussion of these themes, see Mead, *The Philosophy of the Present*; and Aboulafia, *The Mediating Self*.
38. How this process works is a good question, especially considering the non-reflective nature of the "I," which requires the "me" for reflection and a consciousness of self, according to Mead. I try to address this issue in *The Mediating Self*.
39. See chapter 2, pp. 33–35.
40. Deegan, *Jane Addams*, 120, 196.
41. Deegan, *Jane Addams*, 194.
42. Diner, "George Herbert Mead's Ideas on Women and Careers," 409.
43. Mead, "Scientific Method and the Moral Sciences," 115.
44. Dewey, *Individualism Old and New*, 115.
45. Deegan, *Jane Addams*, 136 n. 22.
46. Mead, *MSS*, 265. Mead was not so oblivious to prevailing conditions that he thought such international-mindedness to be around the corner. In 1929 he even warned of the possibility that "another catastrophe may be necessary before we have cast off the cult of warfare, but we cannot any longer *think* our international

life in terms of warfare" ("National-Mindedness and International-Mindedness," 363). See note 69 in this chapter for an extended quotation on this matter.

47. Mead, *MSS*, 167–68.

48. Arendt, *Lectures*, 70–77.

49. Mead, *MSS*, 157.

50. Mead, *MSS*, 157–58. Habermas equates the phrase "universe of discourse" with the unlimited or unbounded communication community. In chapter 3 I try to differentiate these two notions.

51. Mead, *MSS*, 260–61.

52. "If, with George Herbert Mead, we understand the process of socialization itself as one of individuation, the sought-for mediation between individual and society is less 'puzzling.'" Habermas, *The Philosophical Discourse of Modernity*, 334. Also see Habermas, *TCA2*, 1–42, and chapter 3 of this book.

53. Mead, *MSS*, 326.

54. See Gould, *Marx's Social Ontology*.

55. It must be emphasized that an individual is not only a given social self, a "me," but an "I" that is future directed. The "I's" responses can modify a given social self. I am suggesting here that the "I" (in conjunction with a prior "me") has the capacity to be aware of privations and boundaries that mark off a given "me" and that this awareness can be viewed as transformative. See *The Mediating Self*, chapter 4, for a more detailed analysis of this process, and see chapter 3 of this book.

56. The theme of sympathy will return in chapter 5.

57. See McKeon, "Philosophic Semantics and Philosophic Inquiry."

58. Watson, *The Architectonics of Meaning*, and Dilworth, *Philosophy in World Perspective*.

59. Examples may be worth a thousand words here. The following figures have an affinity for the respective voices: Personal—Protagoras, Nietzsche, W. James, and Sartre; Objective—Democritus, Hume, Peirce, and Russell; Diaphanic—Plato, Augustine, Heidegger, and Levinas; Disciplinary—Aristotle, Aquinas, Kant, and Dewey. No doubt Mead's texts present certain problems if we are going to attempt to arrive at a common voice for the author behind the texts, in part because much of what we call his texts were not published by him; they were students' or unpublished notes. However, I argue that there is a preferred voice for Mead.

60. Dilworth, *Philosophy in World Perspective*, 27. In a private correspondence Dilworth suggested that Mead has a disciplinary perspective, and he gave as evidence the generalized other. I agree and appreciate the suggestion.

61. See Lewis and Smith, *American Sociology and Pragmatism*. Also see *Symbolic Interaction* 6 (Spring 1983) for an exchange on this book.

62. The issue is complicated by the fact that if one brings in other levels of analysis, other connections become apparent. Those familiar with this approach will find that Mead's method is very similar to that of James and Peirce, a problematic method, whereas his governing principle is that of James, not Peirce. All of this is further complicated by the fact that Mead often drew on a dialectical method, and this is apparent in the manner in which he discusses self and other; it is also related to certain Christian sensibilities that he never left behind.

63. Mead, *PP*, 35.

64. Mead, "The Teaching of Science in College," 62 (emphasis added).

65. Mead, "A Behavioristic Account of the Significant Symbol," 245 (emphasis and bracketed material added).

66. "And our disciplinary perspectives do not by their limitations limit the degree of truth we can attain, but rather it is through these limitations that it is possible to attain a truth appropriate to each perspective." Watson, *Architectonics of Meaning*, 34.

67. Just as there is no metaenvironment or system by which the reality of all other systems can be defined, there is no one scientific discipline that can act as the final arbiter for the rest. But this doesn't deny the knowledge that each can generate. Nor does it deny the potential oneness of the world if we view this oneness in terms of the capacity to exchange positions.

68. Perhaps it is worth mentioning that Kant, Habermas, and Mead share a bias toward the disciplinary. Arendt uses a disciplinary voice, but she also appears to be drawn to an objective one—to the objective voice of the thinker or philosophical spectator, that is, not to the objectivity of the scientist in the laboratory. In contrast, Levinas's voice is a diaphanic one, as we shall see.

69. Mead would have agreed with Kant that war will eventually become an unacceptable option in the modern world. However, this did not lead him to believe that warfare had already become impossible. In "National-Mindedness and International-Mindedness," published in 1929, he wrote, "The Great War has presented not a theory but a condition. . . . Every war if allowed to go the accustomed way of wars will become a world war, and every war pursued uncompromisingly and intelligently must take as its objective the destruction not of hostile forces but of enemy nations in their entirety. It has become unthinkable as a policy for adjudicating national differences. It has become logically impossible. This is not to say that it may not arise. Another catastrophe may be necessary before we have cast off the cult of warfare, but we cannot any longer *think* our international life in terms of warfare" (362–63).

70. Ibid., 355–70.

71. Ibid., 368–69.

Chapter 2: *Judgment and Universality in Arendt's Kant and Mead*

1. This is not to say that the strategic is without value for Mead and other pragmatists. Under certain circumstances strategic actions can help support communities. One of the differences between Mead and Habermas centers on the possible consequences of strategic action, with Mead taking a more "pragmatic" attitude toward the strategic than would be allowed by Habermas's quasitranscendentalism. See chapter 3, pp. 80–83.

2. Hannah Arendt, *Lectures*, 77. She begins this passage with the following discussion of the beautiful. "The beautiful is, in Kantian terms, an end in itself because all its possible meaning is contained within itself, without reference to others—without linkage, as it were, to other beautiful things" (77).

3. Bernstein, *Philosophical Profiles*, 222–23.

4. Habermas refers to the importance of spontaneity and initiative for Mead in

a passage in his *Theory of Communicative Action:* "In a very basic sense, the initiative cannot be taken from a person in communicative action however guided by norms; no one can relinquish the initiative. 'The I gives the sense of freedom, of initiative' [Mead declares]. To take the initiative means to begin something new, to be able to do something surprising" (*TCA2*, 59). Habermas follows this remark with a note (410 n. 53) in which he refers to the fact that Arendt developed just this insight in *The Human Condition*.

5. See, for example, Ronald Beiner's commentary in Arendt's *Lectures*.

6. Cassirer, *Kant's Life and Thought*, 273–74.

7. See Cassirer, *Kant's Life and Thought*.

8. Kant, *Critique of Judgement*, 18. Regarding Arendt's use of the term *general* instead of *universal*, see p. 42 and note 58 in chapter 2. In a seeming modification of Kant's position, Arendt hoped to emphasize that judgments are not valid for everyone by using the term *general*. Bowing to tradition, however, in most instances I use the term *universal*, but I clarify Arendt's position in the pages that follow.

9. On this point, once again, see p. 42 and note 58 in chapter 2.

10. Arendt would want to say, "beautiful for all *who judge*"; see p. 42.

11. Bernstein, *Philosophical Profiles*, 229 (emphasis added).

12. Kant, *Critique of Judgement*, Part I, 152–53.

13. Arendt, "Crisis in Culture," 220. Bernstein uses much of this quote in his piece "Judging" in *Philosophical Profiles*.

14. Arendt, "Crisis in Culture," 220–21. Of course, Arendt did not believe that the taking of perspectives was invented by Kant. What Kant contributed was a new way of thinking about perspectives that linked them to issues of taste. She is quite explicit about this in the "Crisis in Culture" (see pp. 221–22).

15. Arendt reminds us that as late as 1787 Kant still intended to call the *Critique of Judgement* a *Critique of Taste*. Arendt, *Lectures*, 66.

16. Levinas, as we will see in chapter 4, finds the powers of representation and recollection to be highly suspect and quite counterproductive in our quest for disinterestedness in ethics.

17. *Lectures*, 64.

18. Ibid., 66.

19. Ibid., 65.

20. Ibid., 67. These last few lines were written late in Arendt's career, and in interpreting them it is important to note that the role of the spectator, as opposed to the agent of historical change, was clearly central to much of her meditation in these years. (I plan to sidestep the rather complicated question of whether judgment for Arendt is ultimately best viewed in terms of the *vita activa* or the *vita contemplativa*. See chapter 2, pp. 48–51.) One should become the blind poet when judging. "By making what one's external senses perceived into an object for one's inner sense, one compresses and condenses the manifold of the sensually given; one is in a position to 'see' by the eyes of the mind, i.e., to see the whole that gives meaning to the particulars. The advantage the spectator has is that he sees the play as a whole, while each of the actors knows only his part or, if he should judge from the perspective of acting, only the part of the whole that concerns him. The actor is partial by definition" (*Lectures*, 68–69). The notion of the disinterested spectator is considered later in this chapter and in the chapters that follow.

21. Ibid., 69.

22. "The *beautiful* is that which, apart from a concept, pleases universally" (*Critique of Judgement*, Part I, 60). Kant, being Kant, is clearly concerned with showing the conditions for the possibility of universal claims in aesthetic judgments. However, the ground of universality should not be understood in the cognitive terms of the *Critique of Pure Reason*. His approach in the third *Critique* is to separate that which merely gratifies from the truly beautiful, explaining that the latter originates in the harmonious interplay of the imagination and the understanding and must inspire claims to universality. Kant tells in the third *Critique*, "For beauty is not a concept of the Object, and the judgement of taste not a cognitive judgement. All that it holds out for is that we are justified in presupposing that the same subjective conditions of judgement which we find in ourselves are universally present in every man, and further that we have rightly subsumed the given Object under these conditions. The latter, no doubt, has to face unavoidable difficulties which do not affect the logical judgement. (For there the subsumption is under concepts; whereas in aesthetic judgement it is under a mere sensible relation of the imagination and understanding mutually harmonizing with one another in the represented form of the Object, in which case the subsumption may easily prove fallacious)" (Part I, 147).

23. Arendt, *Lectures*, 69.

24. Ibid., 71. Arendt goes on to quote Kant as saying, "Now this operation of reflection seems perhaps too artificial to be attributed to the faculty called *common* sense, but it only appears so when expressed in abstract formulae. In itself there is nothing more natural than to abstract from charm or emotion if we are seeking a judgment that is to serve as a universal rule."

25. Arendt, *Lectures*, 71.

26. Ibid., 74–75.

27. Ibid., 42; Kant, Letter to Marcus Hertz, June 7, 1771.

28. Arendt, *Lectures*, 42.

29. Ibid. (emphasis mine); Letter to Marcus Hertz, February 21, 1772. This letter is also translated by Zweig in Kant, *Philosophical Correspondence*, 70–76. Zweig's translation of this passage reads as follows: "whereby it [the mind] is kept in readiness to view the subject matter from other sides all the time and to widen its horizon from a microscopic observation to a universal outlook in order that it may adopt all conceivable positions and that views from one may verify those from another" (73).

30. "Introduction," in Smith, *The Theory of Moral Sentiments*, 31 (hereafter abbreviated *TMS*). The editors note that Herz "goes on to compare the work of Smith with 'the first part' of 'Home, Kritik,' no doubt meaning *Elements of Criticism* by Henry Home, Lord Kames. As Eckstein points out, the date of 1771 . . . and the comparison with Kames show that the writer must have had *TMS* in mind. The passage also suggests that Hertz at least, like Lessing and Herder, was interested in the relevance of *TMS* to aesthetics."

31. John H. Zammito states categorically that Kant could not read English. See Zammito, *The Genesis of Kant's Critique of Judgment*, 24, 29.

32. "Editor's Introduction," *TMS*, 31. There were six authorized editions of *TMS*.

33. Fleischacker, "Philosophy in Moral Practice," 249–69. In this article Fleischacker suggests that the term *Liebling* in this quote refers to Kant's favorite "pre-

sumably among recent writers on the passions" (250). He also notes that if Friedländer is quoted accurately he must be referring to the Smith of *TMS* and not to *The Wealth of Nations* (250).

34. Zammito, *The Genesis of Kant's Critique of Judgment*, 23–24.

35. Smith, *TMS*, 112.

36. Ibid., 110, 110 h-h. Part of the last line follows the wording found in the first five editions.

37. Ibid., 129–30. This passage is found in the second to fifth editions of *TMS*.

38. "Introduction" to Smith, *TMS*, 31. This passage is cited in the editor's introduction to the German translation, *Theorie der ethischen Gefühle*, xxxiii–xxxiv. The complete text of the English editors reads as follows: "Eckstein goes on to note that there is a passage in Kant's "Reflections on Anthropology" where Kant writes of 'the man who goes to the root of things' and who looks at every subject 'not just from his own point of view but from that of the community' and then adds, in brackets, 'the Impartial Spectator' (*der Unpartheyische Zuschauer*)" (*TMS*, 31).

39. Zammito, *The Genesis of Kant's Critique of Judgment*, 29, 30.

40. "Editor's Introduction," *TMS*, 15. Determining where Hume's impact on Kant ends and Smith's begins would be a work unto itself.

41. Fleischacker, "Philosophy in Moral Practice." Although his article focuses on their connection as moral theorists, on more than one occasion he refers to the third *Critique* and Smith's book (see pp. 251 n. 11; 252; 252 n. 16; 267, 267 n. 61). Fleischacker recently published a work on Smith and Kant that discusses *The Wealth of Nations* and develops an account of judgment. See Fleischacker, *A Third Concept of Liberty*. Given its recent publication, I was able to make only limited use of this work.

42. Fleischacker, "Philosophy in Moral Practice," 267.

43. I was somewhat surprised, and delighted, to find that Fleischacker had suggested a connection between Arendt and Smith in his article. "I would like to add here that when Hannah Arendt was casting about for a source onto which to graft her theory of political judgment . . . she would have done much better to pick *TMS* than the third *Critique*. Kant seems quite deliberately to have kept judgment away from moral theory, while Smith reads as if he had consciously anticipated Arendt's views" (267 n. 62). I obviously agree regarding a connection but would qualify his claim and say "*certain* of Arendt's views."

44. Mead states, "Adam Smith makes moral judgment come back to the relation between the self and the community and emphasizes the social character of the judgement. The tendency of the child to play the part of another is simply that [the] child is in [the] early stages in our social consciousness in which the consciousness of the other is the dominant consciousness. The imagination of the child comes back to the necessary condition of thinking in terms of other persons. And in ourselves, if we think of a certain subject we indirectly think of it in terms of a friend and often think it out in terms of conversation with another person. Those processes are primitive processes and [the] beginnings of thought, and [it] arises out of images of other people's attitudes in terms of our own consciousness. [This is] so in conscience, ((this is what conscience means.)) And [it is] only through [the] construction of the other individual that we can construct

our own selves" (Unpublished Notes, Social Psychology Course, Lecture XVIII, July 20, 1910 [Wednesday]. The original of these notes is in the possession of Professor Harold Ohrbach of Kansas State).

45. "The Social Self," 143.

46. David Miller, a respected Mead scholar, writes in his work on Mead, "Although Cooley is known as a sociologist, he was definitely influenced by Adam Smith's looking-glass theory of the self. Adam Smith stressed that, in the economic world, the seller must look at himself from the point of view of the buyer, and vice versa: each must take the attitude of the other. Or as Cooley put it, in social behavior we can, through 'sympathetic imagination,' look at things as others in different situations do, and have the feelings others have in circumstances actually different from our own. Cooley's 'sympathetic imagination' became, with modifications, Mead's 'taking the role of the other'" (*George Herbert Mead*, xix–xx). As a young man, Miller studied with Mead. Although Miller cites an example from economics, the ideas he refers to were present in *The Theory of Moral Sentiments* years before Smith's famous economic work. It's worth noting that Mead was extremely fond of using the buyer/seller example to help explain his position. Harold Ohrbach, a Mead scholar at Kansas State University, has suggested to me that he doesn't believe that Cooley had much of a direct impact on Mead. However, I do not believe that there is any question that Mead was familiar with Cooley's work, even if the extent of his influence is open to question.

47. See Arendt, "Truth and Politics," 239 ff. Also, see Beiner in Arendt, *Lectures*, 106–9.

48. "At the very center of her being was the need to think but not necessarily to think in the way in which 'professional thinkers' think. It was thinking *particularity* that most intrigued her—judging. Throughout her writings she took herself to be a spectator of human affairs—seeking to understand them in their particularity and their 'exemplary validity.'" Bernstein, *Philosophical Profiles*, 235.

49. Arendt, *Lectures*, 76.

50. Ibid., 77.

51. "On Imagination," in *Lectures*, 80. Arendt also tells us that "in the *Critique of Pure Reason* imagination is at the service of the intellect; in the *Critique of Judgment* the intellect is 'at the service of imagination'" (84).

52. Arendt, *Lectures*, 84.

53. Arendt, "Postcriptum to Volume I," in *The Life of the Mind*, 216.

54. Arendt, *Lectures*, 84.

55. I am consciously avoiding the thorny epistemological issue of how one can recognize the sameness of two instances, that is, of the exemplar Achilles and the Tom, Dick, or Harry who is supposed to be like this example. As we will see later, there is a kind of essentialism in Arendt's thought that suggests an answer to how we originally recognize an exemplar and also suggests how instances of it come to light. However, this suggestion will not provide us with the details of the mechanisms by which the mind can perform the feat of recognition. Arendt was not an epistemologist or cognitive psychologist. Nevertheless, we do know in some detail how the results of these processes are validated for Arendt, that is, through intersubjective perspective taking.

56. Arendt, *Lectures*, 75–76.

57. Ibid., 73.

58. Arendt, "Crisis in Culture," 221. Beiner, the editor of Arendt's *Lectures,* suggests that this passage helps to explain why Arendt uses the term *general* instead of *universal* (*Lectures,* 163 n. 155).

59. Arendt, "Crisis in Culture," 210.

60. Beiner, in Arendt's *Lectures,* 110–11. The quotation in this passage is from Arendt's "The Concept of History," which is anthologized in the volume *Between Past and Future* (52).

61. Arendt, "Crisis in Culture," 210.

62. Mead summarizes his view on the genesis of romantic idealism as follows: "It was, perhaps, from these three different points that the new doctrine of Romantic idealism grew, or to which it attached itself: first was Kant's transcendental unity of apperception; second was the self, the free self which our moral attitude postulates; and third was the experience as depicted in the *Critique of Judgement* which sets up a sort of end or purpose as determining the life-process of living things, and which determines the structure of that which delights our aesthetic tastes." Mead, *Movements of Thought,* 68.

63. These lectures originally were given to undergraduates, so one must not presume that the often abbreviated formulations were Mead's last word on the issues. But we do find some interesting insights for our purposes.

64. "Man's intellect, in proportion as it is rational, is a lawgiving intellect. It can create society by being universal in character. In this sense, because he generalizes this principle of Rousseau's, Kant may be considered the philosopher of the Revolution." Mead, *Movements of Thought,* 27. Rousseau sought to answer the question of how the people can both be sovereign and subject. His answer, as is well known, turned on his analysis of the general will. How Mead presents Rousseau's general will is classic Mead. He says that "it presupposes that the very form of the will which man exercises is universal, that is, a man wills something only in so far as he puts himself in the place of everyone else in the community and in so far as he accepts the obligations which that act of will carries with it" (Ibid., 17). One might compare the wording in this passage to Arendt's interpretation of Section 40 of the third *Critique.* See pp. 35–36. Although one would not want to attribute to Mead claims made for the purpose of explicating the position of other thinkers, those familiar with Mead's work know that he often allows his own sentiments and language to slip into his discussions of other thinkers. And this is clearly the case here.

65. Ibid., 60.

66. Ibid., 63.

67. Miller, *George Herbert Mead,* xiv.

68. Shalin, "The Romantic Antecedents of Meadian Social Psychology," 43–65.

69. He asserts in *Movements of Thought,* for example, that "romanticism is a philosophy of evolution, of process. It was the background for the development of the theory of evolution. Back of this latter conception lies the assumption of a living process which takes on successively different forms" (127).

70. See chapter 1, pp. 25–26.

71. Mead, "A Behavioristic Account," 245.

72. Of course, there are no guarantees that we want to stand in the same position as others. But Mead would argue that if we do not attempt to share positions,

at least under certain circumstances, we run the risk of conceding too much ground to parochialism, which he views as clearly dangerous.

73. Mead, "A Behavioristic Account," 245 (emphasis added).

74. Rorty, *Contingency, Irony, and Solidarity.*

75. To achieve international-mindedness, not only must we broaden our horizons through the shifting of perspectives, but we must become positively disposed toward the shifts. How such a disposition arises is a central question that entails a turn to the developmental. That it should arise is a basic assumption of Mead's worldview. See Aboulafia, *The Mediating Self,* and chapters 3 and 5.

76. Mead, *MSS,* 270.

77. Arendt, *Lectures,* 74–75.

78. Zammito, *The Genesis of Kant's Critique of Judgment,* 272–73.

79. Quoted in Arendt, *Lectures,* 71; see Kant, *Critique of Judgement,* Part I, sec. 40.

80. Quoted in Arendt, *Lectures,* 71; see Kant, *Critique of Judgement,* sec. 40.

81. Beiner, "Editor's Commentary," in Arendt's *Lectures,* 139.

82. Arendt, *Life of the Mind,* I, 93.

83. Bernstein, *Philosophical Profiles,* 235. The distinction Bernstein alludes to between truth and meaning is a key one for Arendt. It can also be spoken of in terms of knowledge and thinking, where the former diminishes error and illusion, serves the scientifically inclined, and is the province of truth, and the latter concerns itself with interpreting and critically assessing the worlds in which it finds itself.

84. The pragmatist critique of spectator approaches to knowledge or thought should not be viewed as contradicting Mead's insistence on the importance of impartiality, as he understood it, in the making of moral decisions. I return to this issue in chapters 3 and 5.

85. Arendt, *Life of the Mind,* I, 94. Bernstein quotes the first two sentences of this passage in "Judging," *Philosophical Profiles,* 84.

86. Arendt, *Lectures,* 68–69.

87. I mention this at this juncture not to explicate the nuances of Mead's epistemology or prove its superiority to Arendt's but to suggest that he is operating with a different set of assumptions about the nature of cognition and judgment. I return to this theme in the chapters ahead.

88. See Arendt, "Crisis in Culture," 221; Beiner, in *Lectures,* 138–39.

89. Miller, *George Herbert Mead,* 172–87. How we see the past, or a past, clearly is something that can be altered for Mead. As Miller tells us, "The past, or a past, is . . . just as hypothetical as the future—we can test the validity of our hypothetical statement about the past only by future experience which may or may not confirm it, though any confirmed hypothesis may be put in question at some later date" (175).

90. Mead, *PP,* 2.

91. Although Mead would challenge the Kantian framework that differentiates determinant and reflective judgments, he could use the notion of the emergent to help suggest how one might approach the distinction. Suppose, for example, that we are attempting to understand or appreciate an object. If we focus our at-

tention on a prior system of relationships or an existing class of objects that make the object intelligible or cognizable, we may arrive at a determinant judgment, but if the accent is placed on a novel experience or object—a unique artwork, for instance—and how it interacts and transforms prior interpretive schemas, we may arrive at what we call a reflective judgment. In one case the rules that make an established class or system cognizable are emphasized; in another the remaking (creation) of a system and its new rules are accented. This is not to suggest that the relationship to novelty is all that is at stake in characterizing judgments.

92. Habermas, "Hannah Arendt," 184.

93. Derrida, "Economimesis," 3–25.

94. See Dewey, "Search for the Great Community," in *The Later Works of John Dewey*, vol. 2, 325–50.

95. Derrida, "Economimesis," 13.

96. Ibid., 18.

97. Ibid., 20.

98. Ibid., 21.

99. Ibid.

100. Ibid., 19. See also Kant, *Anthropology from a Pragmatic Point of View*, 42.

101. Derrida, "Economimesis," 19.

102. See pp. 33, 36–37.

103. Arendt, "The Crisis in Culture," 220–21.

104. Kant, "Was heisst: Sich im Denken orientieren?" quoted from Arendt, *Lectures*, 40–41.

105. Mead, "A Behavioristic Account of the Significant Symbol," 245 (emphasis added).

106. Derrida, "Economimesis," 20. See also Kant *Anthropology from a Pragmatic Point of View*, 47. An error seems to have occurred in the printing of the English translation of Derrida's piece; part of the quotation was missing. I have inserted the missing phrases using the same translation Klein uses, that is, Dowdell's. Also, the term "gesture" in the first sentence was changed to the plural.

107. Derrida, "Economimesis," 20.

108. As a matter of fact, it seems that the autoaffection of the word, which breeds closure, would have to be a source of temptation to be avoided by Kant, at least if he wants to maintain taste (and an enlarged mentality). Kant may have desired the same transcendental closure for the realm of the beautiful that he thought he had found in mathematics, but Arendt suggests that the methodological imperatives of the third *Critique* thwart such a wish. The assertion of closure, as opposed to the hope for it, becomes a temptation to be avoided by the Kant of the third *Critique*. Derrida, troubled as he is by the presence of a perennial temptation to closure, must use all his rhetorical skills to defeat it. Mead, on the other hand, would have been much less perturbed, for temptations to closure are regularly frustrated by the linguistic interaction of ordinary folk. (Perhaps Americans, for whom *The Inferno* is but a paperback, do not know how to let temptation stand in the way of experience.)

109. See the last section of chapter 1 for a discussion of disciplinary approaches to knowledge.

Chapter 3: Universality and Individuality: Habermas and Mead

1. Habermas, "Individuation through Socialization," 151.
2. Mead in Cook, *George Herbert Mead*, 31.
3. Ibid.
4. Ibid., 33.
5. Habermas, "Individuation through Socialization," 186.
6. The difficulties Mead would have with this manner of framing the process of individuation are addressed in the pages ahead; here I suggest in passing that Habermas may be placing himself in an untenable position in relation to thinkers who are willing to tread a transcendentally inspired path, such as Levinas, in the game of how one grounds or founds what Habermas calls irreducible individuality.
7. Habermas, "Individuation through Socialization," 187.
8. Ibid.
9. See Benhabib, *Situating the Self*. Several of the ideas Benhabib develops in this work bear a striking similarity to what could be called Mead's contextual universalism.
10. Mead, "The Social Self," 142.
11. Mead, *MSS*, 174. Mead goes on to say, "It is what you were a second ago that is the 'I' of the 'me.' It is another 'me' that has to take that rôle. You cannot get the immediate response of the 'I' in the process."
12. Habermas, "Individuation through Socialization," 187.
13. Ibid., 188.
14. Ibid., 187.
15. Ibid. In my view Habermas is clearly on to something here, in that Mead could have developed the anticipatory dimensions of experience more fully than he did. However, as I try to show later, there are good reasons for not taking Habermas's claims as those of Mead or as the correct extrapolations of them. For an alternative account of how the anticipatory may be related to a sense of self, see my *The Mediating Self*.
16. Mead, "The Mechanism of Social Consciousness," 141. See chapter 1, pp. 14–17.
17. I argue in *The Mediating Self* that Mead's model can be modified to accommodate a sense of self that doesn't require the full mediation of a "me." But in so doing I modify Mead's thought, as does Habermas from a somewhat different angle.
18. "In communicative action, the suppositions of self-determination and self-realization retain a rigorously intersubjective sense: whoever judges and acts morally must be capable of anticipating the agreement of an unlimited communication community, and whoever realizes himself in a responsibly accepted life history must be capable of anticipating recognition from this unlimited community." Habermas, "Individuation through Socialization," 192.
19. Ibid., 152, 200 n. 7.
20. Ibid., 186.
21. Ibid.
22. Biological endowments and dispositions also are part of this process.
23. Of course, Habermas notes the importance of particular historical circumstances for realizing autonomy and self-realization. But Habermas is much more

interested in showing the procedures and conditions behind autonomy than in addressing how the "me" can be a source of moral motivation and personal identity.

24. Habermas, "Individuation through Socialization," 182.

25. Habermas distinguishes between an epistemic and a practical relation to self in his account of Mead. He believes that this distinction is implied by Mead's work but is actually blurred in his writings ("Individuation through Socialization," 178–79). Although such a division clearly suits Habermas's account of the spheres of modernity, Mead would question the manner in which he develops it in his article. I will avoid the temptation to address this matter in any detail here. Yet given Habermas's treatment of the "me," it is worth noting a feature of this division. He claims that "unlike the epistemic 'I,' the practical 'I' forms an unconscious" (179) that manifests itself in impulses and innovations. This "I" must have limits set on its impulsiveness and creativity, and this the conventional "me" readily agrees to do. Furthermore, he writes that "in the practical relation-to-self . . . the acting subject does not want to *recognize (erkennen)* itself; rather, it wants to *reassure (vergewissern)* itself about itself as the initiator of an action that is attributable solely to it—in short, to become sure of itself as a free will. . . . It is a will that, solely as a result of socialization, constitutes itself as an 'I will,' as an 'I can posit a new beginning, for the results of which I am responsible'" (Habermas, "Individuation through Socialization," 181). In addition to hyperconventionalizing the "me" and viewing the subject in terms of the practical and epistemic, we have here another questionable move from Mead's perspective, that is, sundering reassurance and recognition.

26. Mead, *MSS*, 217 (emphasis added). The relative trust and distrust of the so-called conventional "me" in Habermas and Mead is clearly at the heart of many of their differences, and no doubt their very different historical circumstances would have to be factored into any complete study of their positions.

27. Mead was actively committed to working at the local level for expanded communities that would join people together in new ways. His involvement in the social and political affairs of Chicago may have been one of the reasons he never published a monograph.

28. Mead, "Philanthropy from the Point of View of Ethics," 404.

29. Mead, *MSS*, 167–68.

30. Mead continues, "About this problem lies the ordered community with its other standards and customs unimpaired, and the duties it prescribes unquestioned" ("Philanthropy from the Point of View of Ethics," 405). When Habermas quotes Mead in *The Theory of Communicative Action* on the universe of discourse and rationality, he conveniently leaves off these last two sentences, leaving the reader with the impression that Mead was a Habermasian "proceduralist." See Habermas, *TCA2*, 94–95.

31. Quoted from Habermas, *TCA2*, 94–95; see also "Individuation through Socialization," 184–85 (emphasis in the original).

32. In another quotation in his article Habermas replaces Mead's phrase "the universe of discourse"—which refers to a community that uses abstract symbolization, or at least more abstract symbolization than surrounding communities—with the phrase "our communication community" in German ("Individuation through Socialization," 182, 203 nn.54, 57).

33. Mead, *MSS*, 89–90.

34. Ibid., 269.

35. Ibid., 89–90.

36. See chapter 5, pp. 109–10.

37. Mead, "A Behavioristic Account of the Significant Symbol," 245. See pp. 25–26 in chapter 1.

38. The term *attitude* is used in a multitude of ways by Mead—for example, in terms of taking the attitude of specific others and generalized others—but the description given here points to a common thread. See Cook, *George Herbert Mead*, 60, 78–98.

39. Mead, *MSS*, 327.

40. Ibid., 265 (emphasis added).

41. Ibid., 326 (emphasis added).

42. See Hinkle, "Habermas, Mead, and Modernity," 325–26.

43. No doubt Habermas does not want to be viewed as an old-fashioned Kantian formalist, hence his quasitranscendentalism and proclamations about how we must consider actual historical conditions when discussing the development of autonomy and identity. Habermas is well aware that Kant's transcendental ego cannot provide the irreducible individuality that he is after. "What distinguishes the individual from all other individuals, i.e., uniqueness and irreplaceability in the emphatic sense, can at best apply to the intelligible ego; but as the addressee of the moral law, this latter is oriented precisely toward maxims that have universal validity. Furthermore, the ego qua a subject capable of moral action is a thing-in-itself and thus eludes cognition, even if it could be thought of as completely individuated" (Habermas, "Individuation through Socialization," 158). Nevertheless, the differences between Mead and Habermas are quite real, as I hope to elucidate in this chapter.

44. Abstract discourses have a role to play here, such as a logical discourse or one on rights. But in the latter Mead would especially want to emphasize how attitudes other than those geared to the reflective appreciation of procedure come into play. Our respect for rights is certainly not merely a function of their linguistic intelligibility.

45. See, for example, Bourdieu, *The Logic of Practice*.

46. Mead, *MSS*, 193.

47. See p. 20. The point here is not to deny that it is the "I" that is seen as responding but to emphasize the intimate link between the functions of the "I" and "me." The "me" is the voice we hear when we judge our actions. If this voice has imbibed universalistic assumptions, then its "reactions" to the activity of the "I" are quite different than if it is parochially inclined. Without this universalistic moment (or an inclination to it), the "I's" novel (universalistically inclined) responses will never be heeded. They will die as mutations without a home.

48. Mead, "Philanthropy from the Point of View of Ethics," 398.

49. Ibid., 398–99.

50. Ibid., 404 (emphasis added).

51. See p. 71 and note 31 in chapter 3.

52. Habermas, in Thompson and Held, *Habermas: Critical Debates*, 237.

53. Mead, *MSS*, 334.

54. Mead is willing to refer to rational procedure as setting "up an order in which

thought operates; that abstracts in varying degrees from the actual structure of society." "Philanthropy from the Point of View of Ethics," 404.

55. Habermas, in Thompson and Held, *Critical Debates*, 237.

56. Habermas, "Individuation through Socialization," 192.

57. However, in contrast to Hegel's views on conflict between states, it is important to note once again that Mead did not subscribe to the notion that warfare between nations was inevitable—quite the contrary, as we have seen.

58. Mead, *Philosophy of the Act*, 518–19.

59. Ibid., 519. We are then told that this is "an ideal of method, not of program. It indicates direction, not destination." Mead clearly does not want what he is suggesting to be confused with the program of the Marxists.

60. See chapter 5, pp. 109–10.

61. This is actually a bit more complicated than it first appears because the "I" must be understood in terms of varying degrees of spontaneity, and these different degrees of spontaneity typically are linked to specific "me's".

62. Habermas, "Individuation through Socialization," 190.

63. Dilworth, *Philosophy in World Perspective*, 30.

64. Ibid., 31.

Chapter 4: Levinas and the Other Side

1. Of course, there are institutional settings that seek to promote the suspension or adjudication of interests, such as the judiciary.

2. Taylor, *Sources of the Self*, 510.

3. These themes would warm the hearts of many postmodernists if we could find people willing to call themselves such.

4. Levinas, *Otherwise Than Being or Beyond Essence* (hereafter abbreviated *OB*).

5. Levinas, *Totality and Infinity*, 21 (hereafter abbreviated *TI*).

6. Levinas quotes Pascal in one of the epigrams for *OB* (vii).

7. Levinas, "Ethics as First Philosophy," 82.

8. Levinas, *OB*, 138.

9. Kierkegaard, *Philosophical Fragments*, 14.

10. Ibid., 15.

11. Ibid., 22.

12. Levinas, *TI*, 51.

13. Levinas, *OB*, 148.

14. Ibid., 119.

15. Sartre, *Being and Nothingness*, 252–302.

16. Hegel, *Phenomenology of Spirit*, 110.

17. Levinas, *TI*, 306.

18. "Translator's Introduction," in Levinas, *OB*, xix.

19. See "Excursus" in chapter 2, pp. 54–59.

20. Levinas, "Ethics as First Philosophy," 76–77.

21. Ibid., 78.

22. "Translator's Introduction," in Levinas, *OB*, xix–xx.

23. Levinas, "Ethics as First Philosophy," 80–81.

24. Manning, *Interpreting Otherwise Than Heidegger:* "The past of the

Other . . . cannot be made present, and even has never been present in the time of the subject. Thus, the past of the Other is always past. Since it is always past, even when revealed in the social relation, it is not revealed as a presence, but only as an absence. This is why Levinas says that the immemorial past of the Other shows itself not as a presence, but only as a *trace*, the mark only of its never having been there, and it is this trace that invades the perfect synchrony of the Said and disrupts it" (82).

25. Levinas, "Ethics as First Philosophy," 84.

26. "I believe that the site of this diachrony is the preoriginary Saying which springs from a particular subject speaking and thereby exposing himself to the other as being vulnerable." Ciaramelli, "Levinas's Ethical Discourse," 93.

27. Ibid., 98 (emphasis added).

28. Ibid., 99. Levinas writes, "There is indeed an outdoing in signification: the implication of the one in the-one-for-the-other in responsibility goes beyond the representable unity of the identical, not by a surplus or lack of presence, but by the uniqueness of the ego, *my uniqueness as a respondent, a hostage, for whom no one else could be substituted without transforming responsibility into a theatrical role*" (*OB*, 136; emphasis added).

29. Levinas, *OB*, 149.

30. Ciaramelli, "Levinas's Ethical Discourse," 89, 91. See also Levinas, *TI*, 305.

31. Levinas, *OB*, 148. "Does not the sense of sincerity refer to the glory of infinity, which calls for sincerity as for a saying? This glory could not appear, for appearing and presence would belie it by circumscribing it as a theme, by assigning it a beginning in the present of representation, whereas, as infinition of infinity, it comes from a past more distant than that which is within the reach of memory, and is lined up on the present. . . . The glory of the Infinite is the anarchic identity of the subject flushed out without being able to slip away. It is the ego led to sincerity, making signs to the other, for whom and before whom I am responsible, of this very giving of signs, that is, of this responsibility: 'here I am.'" Levinas, *OB*, 144–45.

32. See chapter 2, pp. 54–59.

33. "I am outside of any place, in myself, on the hither side of the autonomy of auto-affection and identity resting on itself. Impassively undergoing the weight of the other, thereby called to uniqueness, subjectivity no longer belongs to the order where the alternative of activity and passivity retains its meaning" (Levinas, *OB*, 118; see also 119).

34. Ibid., 138–39.

35. Ibid., 157.

36. Ibid.

37. Ibid., 158.

38. Ibid., 160–61.

39. Lingis, "Introduction," in Levinas, *OB*, xxxv–xxxvi.

40. "Justice requires contemporaneousness of representation. It is thus that the neighbor becomes visible, and, looked at, presents himself, and there is also justice for me. The saying is fixed in a said, is written, becomes a book, law and science." Levinas, *OB*, 159.

41. Ibid.

42. Ibid., 159–60.

43. In *Otherwise Than Being or Beyond Essence* only a handful of pages are given over to a discussion of justice on the level of the third.

44. "The first teaching teaches from this very height, tantamount to its exteriority, the ethical. In this commerce with the infinity of exteriority or of height the naïveté of the direct impulse, the naïveté of the being exercising itself as a force on the move, is ashamed of its naïveté. It discovers itself as a violence, but thereby enters a new dimension." Levinas, *TI*, 171.

45. Ibid., 290–91.

46. Levinas, "Ethics as First Philosophy," 83.

47. Ibid.

48. Levinas, *OB*, 118.

49. Ibid., 111–12.

50. See, for example, Llewelyn, "Am I Obsessed by Bobby?" 234–45.

51. Levinas, *TI*, 306.

52. See the quotation on p. 102.

53. Smith, *TMS*, 305. See also Skinner, "Adam Smith: Ethics and Self-Love," 149–50.

54. In an open forum at Rice University in 1993 I asked Habermas what was the most difficult challenge that his thought had to face. He replied, as expected, that it was having to defend the quasitranscendental elements of his approach. I then asked why he felt he had to defend a quasitranscendental moment. He responded immediately and emphatically, "The Holocaust." And he went on to make it clear that he was not speaking in psychological terms.

Chapter 5: Pluralism, Radical Pluralism, and the Perspectives of Others

1. Smith, *TMS*, 10.

2. Ibid., 13.

3. The contrasting ways in which Smith approaches the question of sympathy were developed by Charles L. Griswald in "Adam Smith on 'Sympathy' and the Moral Sentiments," presented at the American Philosophical Association in December 1994. His presentation and handout simplified my task here. He has since come out with a comprehensive work on Smith, *Adam Smith and the Virtues of the Enlightenment*, which unfortunately became available too late to be integrated into this book.

4. Smith, *TMS*, 317.

5. "Mankind though naturally sympathetic, never conceive, for what has befallen another, that degree of passion which naturally animates the person principally concerned. That imaginary change of situation, upon which their sympathy is founded, is but momentary. The thought of their own safety, the thought that they themselves are not really the sufferers, continually intrudes itself upon them . . . hinders them for conceiving any thing that approaches to the same degree of violence." Smith, *TMS*, 21–22.

6. Ibid., 12 (emphasis added).

7. Ibid., 22.

8. See chapter 2, pp. 37–39.

9. Editors' "Introduction," in Smith, *TMS*, 15.

10. Ibid., 16.

11. Ibid. The earlier editions of *TMS* have the impartial spectator more closely associated with popular opinion.

12. Samuel Fleischacker notes that for Smith, "If one succeeds in internalizing the ideal, internal spectator against which to judge one's own actions, one can judge oneself more or less freely, and contribute more or less freely to the social standards of judgment around one. Individually free action and the social construction of the self are compatible, for Smith, even dependent on one another." Fleischacker, *A Third Concept of Liberty*, 51.

13. Smith, *TMS*, 110.

14. Levinas, *OB*, 118.

15. We have already seen something of Smith's reply to this: "The condition of human nature were peculiarly hard, if those affections, which, by the very nature of our being, ought frequently to influence our conduct, could upon no occasion appear virtuous, or deserve esteem and commendation from any body" (Smith, *TMS*, 305). See chapter 4, pp. 103–4 for the full quotation.

16. Levinas, *OB*, 122–23.

17. Ibid., 105.

18. In chapter 3 I argued against Habermas's attempt to bind individuation and moral autonomy together through the use of a projected "I." Here I am troubled by a parallel conflation of two interrelated yet different issues, uniqueness and responsibility. One can argue that when we hold someone responsible we must presume that he or she is a unique individual (as opposed to being part of a collective conscience of some sort). However, this does not mean that one's uniqueness depends solely (or even primarily) on one's willingness to be responsible; there are clearly other variables, a number of which are addressed later in this chapter. This conflation is all the more troubling because Levinas has also managed to link the overcoming of violence to the package of uniqueness and responsibility. See chapter 3, pp. 67–68.

19. Is it accurate to claim that subjectivity depends on the kind of relationship Levinas specifies? To follow Levinas here appears to suggest that some are more subjects than others because of their ability to put into play or be put into play by the hypertranscendental, *a prioristic* conditions of the ethical, that is, the passive receptivity to the accusation of the other and the substitution of oneself for the other. It seems that such individuals can be said to be more deeply or fully individuals than others, at least to the extent that they are unique *me's* suffering their responsibility. But is Donald Trump any less of a subject, a me, than Mother Theresa? A less generous human being no doubt, but not less of a subject. In Levinas's preoccupation with finding the grounds for uniqueness in what he calls the ethical relationship, it seems he has managed not simply to say that some individuals are more ethical, which is quite reasonable, but to say that they are more unique; that is, Mother Theresa trumps the Trump as a *me*. (Do we have here one more version of the tired little continent's 200-year preoccupation with finding the core of our humanity once and for all as, for example, authenticity, spirit, or power?) Levinas could respond that there are no degrees of responsibility, that everyone is equally responsible. Do not confuse one's responsibility for substitution with living up to it. Yet this would be a difficult tack to take, for

surely being and acting in a responsible manner must be capable of some correlation, and this must be spelled out.

If Mother Theresa is more of a *me* than Trump because she acts like a *me* in a way in which he does not (that is, through the act of substituting herself for the other), then we once again have a version of the problem we saw earlier when we tried to ascertain how some are "selected" (or "chosen") to be evil or good. It seems that some do see the face of the other more clearly than others or at least manage to respond to what they see in a manner that others fail to. However, explanations for why this is so are not forthcoming, and we are left with mystery (some are blessed, open to the Good, and some aren't, and that's just the way it is).

20. To be fair, Levinas does suggest that there is an ongoing dialogue between philosophers (*OB*, 20). But it is hard to imagine the kind of dialogue he imagines given his language and concerns.

21. Quoted in Campbell, *Understanding John Dewey*, 281 n. 23.

22. Dewey, "From Absolutism to Experimentalism," 153.

23. G. H. Mead in Cook, *George Herbert Mead*, 31.

24. Hegel, *Phenomenology of Spirit*, 110.

25. Levinas, *OB*, 119 (emphasis added).

26. Levinas, "Ethics as First Philosophy," 78.

27. See chapter 1, pp. 14–15.

28. See chapter 3, pp. 67–69.

29. Levinas, *OB*, 99 (emphasis added).

30. Levinas, *TI*, 293.

31. Levinas, *OB*, 110.

32. Ibid., 113. Levinas goes on to say, "But in creation, what is called to being answers to a call that could not have reached it since, brought out of nothingness, it obeyed before hearing the order. Thus in the concept of creation *ex nihilo*, if it is not a pure nonsense, there is the concept of a passivity that does not revert into an assumption."

33. Creation is not to be confused with the sort of spontaneity one finds in a thinker such as Sartre, where creation is located in the activity of a conscious agent. For Levinas, what we do not want to do is restrict or reduce creation to the category of spontaneous freedom. What we must have is a freedom that critiques and can call itself into question, so that we are not left with a totalizing ego. "The unity of spontaneous freedom, working on straight ahead, and critique, where freedom is capable of being called in question and thus preceding itself, is what is termed a creature. The marvel of creation does not only consist in being a creation *ex nihilo*, but in that it results in a being capable of receiving a revelation, learning that it is created, and putting itself in question" (Levinas, *TI*, 89).

34. See chapter 1, pp. 16–17.

35. Mead, *PP*, 1.

36. Ibid., 23. Mead also tells us on the same page, "Given an emergent event, its relations to antecedent processes become conditions or causes. Such a situation is a present. It marks out and in a sense selects what has made its peculiarity possible. It creates with its uniqueness a past and a future. As soon as we view it, it becomes a history and a prophecy."

37. Levinas, "Ideology and Idealism," 245 (emphasis added to last two sentences).

38. Given the cultural horizons within which modern Westerners work, the "surprise factor" can be treated as a welcome addition to a host of other characteristics that participate in defining our humanity, such as self-awareness and the capacity to suffer in ways different from other creatures. But that there are other factors involved is not a problem for a thinker such as Mead. We do not need a monocausal explanation.

39. Mead, *PP*, 90.

40. Mead, "Philanthropy from the Point of View of Ethics," 397.

41. Ibid., 397–99.

42. "Ethics and Politics," in Hand, *The Levinas Reader*, 292 (emphasis added). Levinas does claim in this interview that there can be "a politics that's ethically necessary" in situations in which one must defend "those close to me" (292). I am at a loss to explain how Levinas can use the term *ethical* in this context. Even though he is clear that ethics and politics are not the same—"alongside *ethics*, there is a place for *politics*" (292)—he appears to suggest that one can have a politics that is ethically necessary. He seems to believe that such a thing is possible, perhaps to the extent that the ethical permeates the realm of the political, but it is not clear how this permeating can work given the radical disjunction between the realms. How can taking another's life, even in defense of another, be viewed as an ethical response? It seems to be a response better designated as just, and the very fact that justice allows one to take another's life under certain circumstances seems to reinforce the view that it is radically distinct from ethics.

43. See Habermas, *Between Facts and Norms*.

Bibliography

Aboulafia, Mitchell. *The Mediating Self: Mead, Sartre, and Self-Determination.* New Haven, Conn.: Yale University Press, 1986.

———, ed. *Philosophy, Social Theory, and the Thought of George Herbert Mead.* Albany: SUNY Press, 1991.

Apel, Karl-Otto. *Charles S. Peirce: From Pragmatism to Pragmaticism.* Trans. John Michael Krois. Atlantic Highlands, N.J.: Humanities Press, 1995.

Arendt, Hannah. "The Crisis in Culture: Its Social and Its Political Significance." In *Between Past and Future: Eight Exercises in Political Thought.* 197–226. New York: Viking Press, 1968; Reprint: New York: Penguin Books, 1977.

———. *The Human Condition.* Chicago: University of Chicago Press, 1958.

———. *The Life of the Mind.* New York: Harcourt Brace Jovanovich, 1978.

———. *Lectures on Kant's Political Philosophy.* Ed. Ronald Beiner. Chicago: University of Chicago Press, 1982.

———. "Truth and Politics." In *Between Past and Future: Eight Exercises in Political Thought.* 227–64. New York: Viking Press, 1968.

Beiner, Ronald. *Political Judgment.* Chicago: University of Chicago Press, 1983.

Benhabib, Seyla, ed. *Democracy and Difference: Contesting the Boundaries of the Political.* Princeton, N.J.: Princeton University Press, 1996.

———. *Situating the Self: Gender, Community and Postmodernism in Contemporary Ethics.* New York: Routledge, 1992.

Bernasconi, Robert, and Simon Critchley, eds. *Re-Reading Levinas.* Bloomington: Indiana University Press, 1991.

Bernstein, Richard J. *Beyond Objectivism and Relativism: Science, Hermeneutics, and Praxis.* Philadelphia: University of Pennsylvania Press, 1983.

———. *Hannah Arendt and the Jewish Question.* Cambridge, Mass: MIT Press, 1996.

———. *The New Constellation: The Ethical-Political Horizons of Modernity/ Postmodernity.* Cambridge, Mass.: MIT Press, 1992.

———. *Philosophical Profiles: Essays in a Pragmatic Mode.* Philadelphia: University of Pennsylvania Press, 1986.

Bourdieu, Pierre. "A Lecture on the Lecture." In *In Other Words: Essays towards a Reflexive Sociology.* Trans. Matthew Adamson. 177–98. Stanford, Calif.: Stanford University Press, 1990.

———. *The Logic of Practice.* Trans. Richard Nice. Stanford, Calif.: Stanford University Press, 1990.

———, and Loïc J. D. Wacquant. *An Invitation to Reflexive Sociology.* Chicago: University of Chicago Press, 1992.

Campbell, James. *The Community Reconstructs: The Meaning of Pragmatic Social Thought.* Urbana: University of Illinois Press, 1992.

———. *Understanding John Dewey.* Chicago: Open Court, 1995.

Canovan, Margaret. *Hannah Arendt: A Reinterpretation of Her Political Thought.* Cambridge, U.K.: Cambridge University Press, 1992.

Cassirer, Ernst. *Kant's Life and Thought.* Trans. James Haden. New Haven, Conn.: Yale University Press, 1981.

Ciaramelli, Fabio. "Levinas's Ethical Discourse between Individuation and Universality." In *Re-Reading Levinas.* Ed. Robert Bernasconi and Simon Critchley. 83–105. Bloomington: Indiana University Press, 1991.

Cook, Gary A. *George Herbert Mead: The Making of a Social Pragmatist.* Urbana: University of Illinois Press, 1993.

Deegan, Mary Jo. *Jane Addams and the Men of the Chicago School.* New Brunswick, N.J.: Transaction Books, 1988.

Derrida, Jacques. *Adieu: To Emmanuel Levinas.* Trans. Pascale-Anne Brault and Michael Naas. Stanford, Calif.: Stanford University Press, 1999.

———. "Economimesis." Trans. Richard Klein. *Diacritics* 11:2 (1981): 3–25 (originally published in French as *Mimesis des articulations* [Paris: Aubier-Flammarion, 1975], 55–93).

———. "Violence and Metaphysics: An Essay on the Thought of Emmanuel Levinas." In *Writing and Difference.* Trans. Alan Bass. 79–153. Chicago: University of Chicago Press, 1978.

Dewey, John. *The Collected Works of John Dewey, 1882–1953.* Ed. Jo Ann Boydston. 37 vols. and index. Carbondale: Southern Illinois University Press, 1969–91. References in the notes and below are to *The Early Works* (5 vols.), *The Middle Works* (15 vols.), and *The Later Works* (17 vols.).

———. "From Absolutism to Experimentalism" (1930), in *Later Works,* 5:147–60.

———. *Individualism, Old and New* (1930), in *Later Works,* 5:45–123.

———. "Search for the Great Community" (chap. 5 of *The Public and Its Problems* [1927]), in *Later Works,* 2:325–50.

Dilworth, David A. *Philosophy in World Perspective: A Comparative Hermeneutic of the Major Theories.* New Haven, Conn.: Yale University Press, 1989.

Diner, Steven J. "George Herbert Mead's Ideas on Women and Careers: A Letter to His Daughter-in-Law, 1920." *Signs* 4 (1978): 407–9.

Fleischacker, Samuel. "Philosophy in Moral Practice: Kant and Adam Smith." *Kant-Studien* 82 (1991): 249–69.

———. *A Third Concept of Liberty: Judgment and Freedom in Kant and Adam Smith.* Princeton, N.J.: Princeton University Press, 1999.

Gilligan, Carol. *In a Different Voice.* 1982. Rpt., Cambridge, Mass.: Harvard University Press, 1993.

Gould, Carol C. *Marx's Social Ontology.* Cambridge, Mass.: MIT Press, 1978.

Griswald, Charles L. *Adam Smith and the Virtues of the Enlightenment.* Cambridge, U.K.: Cambridge University Press, 1999.

Gutmann, Amy, ed. *Multiculturalism: Examining the Politics of Recognition.* Princeton, N.J.: Princeton University Press, 1994.

Habermas, Jürgen. *Between Facts and Norms: Contributions to a Discourse Theory of Law and Democracy.* Trans. William Rehg. Cambridge, Mass.: MIT Press, 1996.

———. "Hannah Arendt: On the Concept of Power." In *Philosophical-Political Profiles.* Trans. Frederick Lawrence. 171–87. Cambridge, Mass.: MIT Press, 1983 (originally published in German as "Hannah Arendts Begriff der Macht," *Merkur* 30 [1976]: 946–61).

———. "Individuation through Socialization: On George Herbert Mead's Theory of Subjectivity." In *Postmetaphysical Thinking: Philosophical Essays.* Trans. William Mark Hohengarten. 149–204. Cambridge, Mass.: MIT Press, 1992.

———. *Moral Consciousness and Communicative Action.* Trans. Christian Lenhardt and Shierry Weber Nicholsen. Intro. Thomas McCarthy. Cambridge, Mass.: MIT Press, 1990.

———. *The Philosophical Discourse of Modernity: Twelve Lectures.* Trans. Frederick Lawrence. Cambridge, Mass.: MIT Press, 1987.

———. *The Theory of Communicative Action, Lifeworld and System: A Critique of Functionalist Reason,* vol. 2. Trans. Thomas McCarthy. Boston: Beacon Press, 1987.

———. "The Unity of Reason in the Diversity of Its Voices." In *Postmetaphysical Thinking: Philosophical Essays.* Trans. William Mark Hohengarten. 115–48. Cambridge, Mass.: MIT Press, 1992.

Hall, David L. *Richard Rorty: Prophet and Poet of the New Pragmatism.* Albany: SUNY Press, 1994.

Halton, Eugene. "Habermas and Rorty: Between Scylla and Charybdis." *Studies in Symbolic Interaction* 15:3 (1992): 333–58.

Hand, Seán, ed. *The Levinas Reader.* Oxford, U.K.: Blackwell, 1989.

Hegel, G. W. F. *Phenomenology of Spirit.* Trans. A. V. Miller. Oxford, U.K.: Oxford University Press, 1977.

Hickman, Larry A., ed. *Reading Dewey: Interpretations for a Postmodern Generation.* Bloomington: Indiana University Press, 1998.

Hinchman, Larry P., and Sandra K. Hinchman, eds. *Hannah Arendt: Critical Essays.* Albany: SUNY Press, 1994.

Hinkle, Gisela J. "Habermas, Mead, and Modernity." *Symbolic Interaction* 15:3 (1992): 325–26.

Honneth, Axel. *The Struggle for Recognition: The Moral Grammar of Social Conflicts.* Trans. Joel Anderson. Cambridge, Mass.: MIT Press, 1996.

Ingram, David. *Habermas and the Dialectic of Reason.* New Haven, Conn.: Yale University Press, 1987.

James, William. "Does Consciousness Exist?" In *The Writings of William James: A Comprehensive Edition.* Ed. John J. McDermott. 169–83. New York: Random House, 1967; reprint: Chicago: University of Chicago Press, 1977.

————. *Psychology: The Briefer Course.* Ed. Gordon Allport. New York: Harper & Row, 1961.

————. "The Stream of Thought" (from *The Principles of Psychology*). In *The Writings of William James.* Ed. John J. McDermott. 21–74. New York: Random House, 1967.

Joas, Hans. *G. H. Mead: A Contemporary Re-examination of His Thought.* Trans. Raymond Meyer. Cambridge, Mass.: MIT Press, 1985.

Kant, Immanuel. *Anthropology from a Pragmatic Point of View.* Trans. Victor Lyle Dowdell. Carbondale: Southern Illinois University Press, 1978.

————. *The Critique of Judgement.* Trans. James Creed Meredith. Oxford, U.K.: Oxford University Press, 1952.

————. "Idea for a Universal History from a Cosmopolitan Point of View." In *On History.* Ed. and trans. Lewis White Beck. 11–26. Indianapolis: Bobbs-Merrill, 1963.

————. "Letter to Marcus Hertz, June 7, 1771." In *Selected Pre-Critical Writings.* Trans. G. B. Kerferd and D. E. Wolford. 108. New York: Barnes & Noble, 1968.

————. *Philosophical Correspondence, 1759–1799.* Trans. Arnulf Zweig. Chicago: University of Chicago Press, 1967.

————. "Reflexionen zur Anthropologie [Reflections on Anthropology]." In *Gesammelte Schriften*, Prussian Academy edition. Vol. 15. Berlin: de Gruyter, 1902–83.

————. "Was heisst: Sich im Denken orientieren?" (1786). In *Gesammelte Schriften*, Prussian Academy edition. 8:131–47. Berlin: de Gruyter, 1902–83.

Kierkegaard, Søren. *Philosophical Fragments or a Fragment of Philosophy.* Trans. David Swenson; trans. rev. Howard V. Hong. Princeton, N.J.: Princeton University Press, 1967.

Lavine, Thelma Z. "Modernity, Interpretation Theory, and American Philosophy." In *Frontiers in American Philosophy.* 2 vols. Ed. Robert Burch and Herman J. Saatkamp Jr. 2:26–40. College Station: Texas A&M University Press, 1996.

Levinas, Emmanuel. *Ethics and Infinity: Conversations with Philippe Nemo.* Trans. Richard A. Cohen. Pittsburgh: Duquesne University Press, 1985.

————. "Ethics as First Philosophy." In *The Levinas Reader.* Ed. Seán Hand. 76–87. Oxford, U.K.: Blackwell, 1989.

————. "Ideology and Idealism." In *The Levinas Reader.* Ed. Seán Hand. 236–48. Oxford, U.K.: Blackwell, 1989.

————. *Otherwise Than Being or Beyond Essence.* Trans. Alphonso Lingis. The Hague: Martinus Nijhoff, 1981.

————. *Totality and Infinity: An Essay on Exteriority.* Trans. Alphonso Lingis. Pittsburgh: Duquesne University Press, 1969.

Lewis, J. David, and Richard L. Smith. *American Sociology and Pragmatism: Mead, Chicago Sociology, and Symbolic Interaction.* Chicago: University of Chicago Press, 1980.

Llewelyn, John. "Am I Obsessed by Bobby? (Humanism of the Other Animal)." In *Re-Reading Levinas.* Ed. Robert Bernasconi and Simon Critchley. 234–45. Bloomington: Indiana University Press, 1991.

————. *Emmanuel Levinas: The Genealogy of Ethics.* London: Routledge, 1995.

Lyotard, Jean-François. *The Differend: Phrases in Dispute.* Trans. Georges Van Den Abbeele. Minneapolis: University of Minnesota Press, 1988.

Manning, Robert John Sheffler. *Interpreting Otherwise Than Heidegger: Emmanuel Levinas's Ethics as First Philosophy.* Pittsburgh: Duquesne University Press, 1993.

Margolis, Joseph. *The Flux of History and the Flux of Science.* Berkeley: University of California Press, 1993.

———. *Historied Thought, Constructed World: A Conceptual Primer for the Turn of the Millennium.* Berkeley: University of California Press, 1995.

———. *Interpretation Radical but Not Unruly: The New Puzzle of the Arts and History.* Berkeley: University of California Press, 1994.

McCarthy, Thomas. *Ideals and Illusions: On Reconstruction and Deconstruction in Contemporary Critical Theory.* Cambridge, Mass.: MIT Press, 1991.

McKeon, Richard. "Philosophic Semantics and Philosophic Inquiry." In *Freedom and History and Other Essay.* Ed. Zahava K. McKeon. 242–56. Chicago: University of Chicago Press, 1990.

Mead, George Herbert. "A Behavioristic Account of the Significant Symbol." In *Selected Writings: George Herbert Mead.* Ed. Andrew J. Reck. 240–47. Chicago: University of Chicago Press, 1964.

———. "The Mechanism of Social Consciousness." In *Selected Writings: George Herbert Mead.* Ed. Andrew J. Reck. 134–41. Chicago: University of Chicago Press, 1964.

———. *Mind, Self, and Society: From the Perspective of a Social Behaviorist.* Ed. Charles W. Morris. Chicago: University of Chicago Press, 1934.

———. *Movements of Thought in the Nineteenth Century.* Ed. Merritt H. Moore. Chicago: University of Chicago Press, 1936.

———. "National-Mindedness and International-Mindedness." In *Selected Writings: George Herbert Mead.* Ed. Andrew J. Reck. 355–70. Chicago: University of Chicago Press, 1964.

———. "Philanthropy from the Point of View of Ethics." In *Selected Writings: George Herbert Mead.* Ed. Andrew J. Reck. 392–407. Chicago: University of Chicago Press, 1964.

———. *The Philosophy of the Act.* Ed. Charles W. Morris. Chicago: University of Chicago Press, 1938.

———. *The Philosophy of the Present.* Ed. Arthur E. Murphy. Chicago: Open Court, 1932.

———. "Scientific Method and the Moral Sciences." In *Selected Writings: George Herbert Mead.* Ed. Andrew J. Reck. 248–66. Chicago: University of Chicago Press, 1964.

———. "The Social Self." In *Selected Writings: George Herbert Mead.* Ed. Andrew J. Reck. 142–49. Chicago: University of Chicago Press, 1964.

———. "The Teaching of Science in College." In *Selected Writings: George Herbert Mead.* Ed. Andrew J. Reck. 60–72. Chicago: University of Chicago Press, 1964.

Miller, David. *George Herbert Mead: Self, Language, and the World.* Chicago: University of Chicago Press, 1980.

Putnam, Hilary. *Realism with a Human Face.* Ed. James Conant. Cambridge, Mass.: Harvard University Press, 1990.

———. *Words and Life.* Ed. James Conant. Cambridge, Mass.: Harvard University Press, 1994.

Rasmussen, David M. *Reading Habermas.* Oxford, U.K.: Blackwell, 1990.

Rorty, Richard. *Consequences of Pragmatism: Essays, 1972–1980.* Minneapolis: University of Minnesota Press, 1982.

———. *Contingency, Irony, and Solidarity.* Cambridge, U.K.: Cambridge University Press, 1989.

Rosenthal, Sandra B., and Patrick L. Bourgeois. *Mead and Merleau-Ponty: Toward a Common Vision.* Albany: SUNY Press, 1991.

Sartre, Jean-Paul. *Being and Nothingness: An Essay on Phenomenological Ontology.* Trans. Hazel E. Barnes. New York: Philosophical Library, 1956.

Shalin, Dmitri. "G. H. Mead, Socialism, and the Progressive Agenda." *American Journal of Sociology* 93 (1988): 913–51.

———. "The Romantic Antecedents of Meadian Social Psychology." *Symbolic Interaction* 7 (Spring 1984): 43–65.

Skinner, Andrew S. "Adam Smith: Ethics and Self-Love." In *Adam Smith Reviewed.* Ed. Peter Jones and Andrew S. Skinner. 142–67. Edinburgh: Edinburgh University Press, 1992.

Smith, Adam. *Theorie der ethischen Gefühle.* 2 vols. Trans. and ed. Walther Eckstein. Leipzig: Felix Meiner, 1926.

———. *The Theory of Moral Sentiments.* Ed. D. D. Raphael and A. L. MacFie. Oxford, U.K.: Oxford University Press, 1976.

Stuhr, John J. *Genealogical Pragmatism: Philosophy, Experience, and Community.* Albany: SUNY Press, 1997.

———, ed. *Philosophy and the Reconstruction of Culture: Pragmatic Essays after Dewey.* Albany: SUNY Press, 1993.

Taylor, Charles. *Sources of the Self: The Making of the Modern Identity.* Cambridge, Mass.: Harvard University Press, 1989.

Thompson, John B., and David Held, eds. *Habermas: Critical Debates.* Cambridge, Mass.: MIT Press, 1982.

Tugendhat, Ernst. *Self-Consciousness and Self-Determination.* Trans. Paul Stern. Cambridge, Mass.: MIT Press, 1986.

Watson, Walter. *The Architectonics of Meaning: Foundations of the New Pluralism.* Albany: SUNY Press, 1985.

Westbrook, Robert B. *John Dewey and American Democracy.* Ithaca, N.Y.: Cornell University Press, 1991.

White, Stephen K., ed. *The Cambridge Companion to Habermas.* Cambridge, U.K.: Cambridge University Press, 1995.

Zammito, John H. *The Genesis of Kant's Critique of Judgment.* Chicago: University of Chicago Press, 1992.

Index

Achilles, 41, 136n.55
Action, 78, 79; free, 146n.12; habits of, 71; initiator of, 141n.25; judge, 142n.47; moral, 142n.43; political, 118; preparations for, 45, 48
Actor(s), 109, 126; communicative, 84; cosmopolitan, 87; plurality of, 56; strategic, 80. *See also* Moral; Political; Spectator(s)
Addams, Jane, 8, 129n.9
Aesthetic(s), 3, 31, 39, 89, 134nn.22, 30; evaluation, 34; judgment, 31, 38, 48; realm, 59; spheres, 40; tastes, 137n.62. *See also* Arendt, Hannah; Kant, Immanuel
Alienation, 64, 117, 127; problem of, 114–15
Alterity, 90, 93–96, 103, 106–7, 111, 115, 121–23; in the body politic, 83; Mead blind to, 117; overcome, 109; pluralism of, 114; too much, 126. *See also* Levinas, Emmanuel; Other(s); Otherness
America. *See* United States
American(s), 104, 139n.108; life, 63; philosophy, 2, 5
Anticipate, 13, 26, 78; communication, 33; recognition, 140n.18; responses, 12, 80; symmetrical relations, 67. *See also* Anticipatory
Anticipatory, 11; dialogue, 67; dimen-

sions of experience, 140n.15; nature of communication, 57. *See also* Anticipate
Antifoundationalism, 2
Arendt, Hannah, 1–5, 20, 23, 29, 87–88, 107, 126, 132n.68; career of, 133n.20; and Derrida, 56–60, 139n.108; epistemology, 138n.87; and essentialism, 136n.55; general instead of universal, 32, 133n.8, 137n.58; Habermas on, 132–33n.4; on imagination, 17, 22, 33–35, 41, 109, 136n.51; on Kant, 53, 56–59, 124, 132n.2, 133nn.14–15, 134n.24, 139n.108; and Mead, 45–53, 137n.64, 138n.87, 139n.108; meaning and truth, 138n.83; and pluralism, 39–40; the political and truth, 40–41, 48, 52, 59; reading of Kant on judgment, 30–37, 40–43, 133nn.8,10; and Smith, 39, 135n.43. *See also* General; Natality; Political; Spectator(s)
Aristotle, 21, 25, 42, 131n.59
Asymmetry, 93, 97, 100, 105, 125. *See also* Symmetry
Attitude(s), 12, 16, 26, 45, 48, 76, 81, 84, 124, 135n.44, 142n.44; biological and habitual, 75; cognitive and linguistic, 75; and language, 73; moral, 137n.62; toward new fashion, 75; particular, 72; romantic, 44; sharing of, 73–74; social, of community, 14; term used

in different ways, 142n.38; universalistic, 75, 88; of the whole community, 13; of the whole group, 79. *See also* Mead, George Herbert; Other(s)
Attitudinal, 64, 66
Audience, 49–50
Autoaffection, 54–59, 95, 98, 104, 139n.108, 144n.33; and reflexivity, 85
Autonomy, 62, 66–69, 80, 85, 98, 140–41n.23, 142n.43, 146n.18; of autoaffection, 144n.33

Behaviorism: social, 24; standpoint of, 45
Behaviorist, social, 11, 46
Behavior(s), 12, 72, 130n.31; altruistic, 111; conforming to norms, 84; influencing, 80; linguistic, 11; moral, 110, 114; nonverbal and verbal, 13; patterns of, 44, 48; problem-solving, 75; repertoires of, 15; self-interested, 81, 91; sets of, 117; social, 136n.46; spectators of our own, 38; unity of, 14. *See also* Rule(s); Science(s)
Beiner, Ronald, 42, 133n.5, 137n.58
Being, 89, 119; essence of, 97; ontology of, 121. *See also* Good(s)
Benevolence, 102–4
Benhabib, Seyla, 140n.9
Bernstein, Richard, 30–32, 48, 133n.13, 138nn.83, 85
Biological, 16, 45, 118; dispositions, 118
Bourdieu, Pierre, 75
Buber, Martin, 4, 122

Calling, 18; social, 8–9
Cassirer, Ernst, 31
Castle, Henry, 10
Cato, 41, 52
Christian, 3; household, Mead raised in, 9; sensibilities, Mead's, 10, 123–24, 131n.62. *See also* Deity; God; Religious
Ciarmelli, Fabio, 97, 144n.26
Cognition, 32, 48, 138n.87, 142n.43; objects of, 75; spectator models of, 48. *See also* Reflection; Truth(s)
Cognitive, 74–75; judgment, 134n.22; psychologist, 136n.55. *See also* Cognitive-instrumental
Cognitive-instrumental, 88

Common sense, 35, 109, 134n.24; and generalized other, 46–48; and reason, 47. *See also* Arendt, Hannah; Kant, Immanuel; Mead, George Herbert; *Sensus communis*
Communicability, criterion of, 35, 41
Communication, 27, 36, 51, 53, 55, 110, 116; anticipated, 33; anticipatory nature of, 57; community, 50, 64, 67, 74–75, 85, 141n.32; community, unbounded or unlimited, 64, 66, 68, 71, 83, 131n.50, 140n.18; development of, 73; impossible, 93; and judgment, 46; linguistic, 78; processes of, 32. *See also* Communicative action; Community; Gesture(s); Habermas, Jürgen; Language; Linguistic(s); Mead, George Herbert; Symbol(s); Universe(s) of discourse
Communicative action, 1, 3, 12, 78, 80–83, 132–33n.4, 140n.18. *See also* Communication; Habermas, Jürgen; Language; Rationality; Strategic
Communitarianism/communitarians, 4, 75–76
Communities, 5, 21, 24, 26–27; abstract, 57; actual, 72; Mead's internationally minded, 47; more universal, 14; not rational in same manner, 82; parochial, 14; particular, 46; perspective of less parochial, 83; scientific, 26; social, 20; specific, 47; and universal, 47. *See also* Community
Community, 3, 10, 23, 29, 114–16, 137n.64; and abstract symbolization, 141n.32; answer to alienation, 114–15; democratic, 74; development of, 115; within eternity, 119; ethical substance of, 104; and generalized other, 46–48; given, 71; is a good, 82; judges as member of, 36, 46; ideal, 24, 71; idealized, 67; idealized communication, 85; individuation within, 64; larger, 20, 74, 76; of logical discourse, 70–71; ordered, 141n.30; organized, 13; point of view of, 38, 135n.38; prejudices of, 70; scientific, 57; of self-respecting nations, 27; sense, 32, 36, 41, 46; sense of, 126; social attitudes of, 14; and strategic action, 82; think in, 56; of thought, 55; universalistic,

67; vital, 69; of workers, 19; world, 36, 41, 46. *See also* Communication; Communities

Conduct, 78–79; ideal human, 103; influences on, 104; and reflection, 109

Conflict(s), 71, 77, 88; and Hegel, 143n.57; moral and political, 81; of values, 124

Conscience, 135n.44; genesis of, 38; as product of social relationship, 109

Consciousness, 9, 75, 107, 135n.44; born, 99; I as, 66; of meaning, 65; of the other, 135n.44; present, 96; reflective, 97; of self, 45, 130n.38; stream of, 15, 118. *See also* Self-consciousness

Consensus, 57, 78, 80–83; with oneself, 56; rational formation of, 52

Conventional, 68–69, 110; me, 70, 76; universalistic, 69. *See also* Postconventional

Cooley, Charles H., 4, 38–39, 136n.46

Cosmopolitan, 3; actor, 87; existence, 36, 41, 46–47; individual, Kant's, 47; and novelty, 47; universalist, Mead's, 84. *See also* Enlarged mentality; International-mindedness; Universalism; Universality

Cosmopolitanism, 28; market as source of, 83; and Mead, 33, 43, 44, 45, 46, 47, 66, 105–6, 126–27. *See also* Enlarged mentality; International-mindedness; Universalism; Universality

Creation, 86, 119–22, 138–39n.91, 147nn.32, 33; diachrony of, 120; of a plural order, 94. *See also* Creative

Creative: activity, 30, 70, 141n.25; activity, Habermas and Mead contrasted, 83–86; events, 51; powers, 121; principles, 85–86, 120

Critical, 70; actor, 29; assessments, 51; check, 79; edge, 50

Critique, 29, 50, 76, 147n.33; and cosmopolitanism, 126–27; of the spectator, 138n.84; of Western tradition, Levinas's, 106–7

Critique of Judgment (a.k.a. third *Critique*; Kant), 1, 3–5, 39, 43, 66, 134n.22, 135nn.41, 43, 136n.51, 137nn.62, 64, 139n.108; Arendt's interpretation of, 31–37, 56–59; and

Derrida, 53–59 passim. *See also* Kant, Immanuel

Debate, 40, 52–53; and democracy, 126

Deconstruction, 23

Deegan, Mary Jo, 18

Deity, 38, 103–4. *See also* God

Democracy, 2–3, 5, 28–29, 126–27; and differentiation, 74; good, 126; modern, 21; nonhierarchical, 19; participatory, 9; true, 29. *See also* Cosmopolitanism; Enlarged mentality; Political; Politics; Social; Society/societies

Democratic: community, 74; context, 87; sensibility, 47; temper, 2, 30

Derrida, Jacques, 5, 30, 98; and Arendt, 53, 56–60; and Arendt and Mead, 53, 57–60, 139nn.106, 108; and Kant, 53–60, 139n.108

Development, 138n.75; of communication, 73; of community, 115; of impartiality, 45; individual, 21; progressive, 41; of rules, 12. *See also* Language; Mind; Moral; Self/selves

Dewey, John, 16, 19, 29, 53, 57, 106, 114–15, 131n.59; and Hegel, 115; influence on Mead, 62–63; and pluralism, 105

Diachronic, 97, 100, 120, 121, 144n.26

Dialogue, 29, 31; between me and myself, 33; among philosophers, 147n.20; political, dependence of democracy on, 29, 126

Dilthey, Wilhelm, 63

Dilworth, David, 23–24, 131n.60

Discourse ethics. *See* Ethics; Habermas, Jürgen

Disinterested(ness), 34–36, 55, 58, 102, 111–12, 124, 133n.16; analysis, 34; authentic, 100; bearing witness, 97; complete, 127; dimension of judgment, 48; of the Good, 87; joy, 43; and Kant, 50; observer, 41; and political, 103; question of, 88; response, 34; satisfaction, 39; spectator(s), 41, 133n.20. *See also* Impartial spectator(s); Interest(s); Levinas, Emmanuel

"Economimesis" (Derrida), 53–60

Ego, 89, 90–91, 116–17; activity of, 96, 121; alter, 67; autonomous, 68; avoidance, 97; desiring, 111; embrace of, 122; empirical, 14; equilibrated, 99; free subject, 93, 116; imperial, 86, 111; intelligible, 142n.43; and sincerity, 144n.31; totalizing, 147n.33; transcendental, 15, 68; uniqueness of, 144n.28; universal, 97. *See also* Self/selves; Subject

Ego-identity: nonconventional, 65; postconventional, 67. *See also* Identity

Egoism, 94, 102–4, 105, 111, 115. *See also* Self-interest

Emergence, 2, 10, 16–17, 65, 121–22; notion of, 83–84. *See also* Emergent

Emergent, 16, 51–52; event, 121, 147n.36; notion of, 138–39n.91. *See also* Emergence

Empirical, 4, 15, 57, 78; assessment, 45; ego, 14

Empiricism, British, 39, 103, 114

Enlarged mentality, 3, 20, 23, 33, 36–37, 42, 56, 139n.108; and cosmopolitan actor, 87; crucial to political life, 53; impetus to, 79; and multiple perspectives, 41; novelty part of, 47; of political actors, 48; and reflection, 76; share in position of others, 58; spirit of, 66; thought, 32; and views of others, 49. *See also* Arendt, Hannah; Cosmopolitan; Cosmopolitanism; Internationalmindedness; Mead, George Herbert; Perpsective(s); Universalism; Universality

Enlightenment, 2–4, 44, 61, 105

Environment(s), 73; biological, 45; social, 45

Essence(s), 42; being's, 97

Essentialism, 42, 136n.55

Ethical, 3–5, 68, 115–16, 127, 129n.1, 145n.44, 148n.42; alterity as key to, 94; conditions of, 146–47n.19; and difference, 103; and disjunction with political, 106, 114, 125–26; ground, 104; level, 97, 100; life, 5, 88, 104, 106; matters, 28, 39; problem, 71; and procedural, 76–77; relationship, 93; theory, 66. *See also* Ethics

Ethics, 105, 114, 148n.42; compared to politics, 125–26; discourse, 61, 64, 74, 110; politics and, Levinas and Mead

on, 125; realm of, 93. *See also* Ethical; Good(s)

Event(s), 57, 121, 147n.36; creative, 51; meaning of, 49; novel, 17, 47, 84; social and political, 49; world of, 121

Evolution, 44; of life, 16; philosophy of, 137n.69

Exemplary validity, 40–42, 136n.48

Existential, 15; confirmation, 75; freedom, 61; self-reflection, 67; spontaneity, 68

Existentialists, 16, 61

Experience(s), 8, 15–17, 21–22, 25, 33, 43, 81, 121, 137n.62; abstract from, 47; of another, 108; anticipatory dimensions of, 140n.15; collective, 46; 75; conscious, 14; firsthand, 82; future, 138n.89; and I, 66; immediate, 16; of individuation, modern, 62; Levinas's, 100; of nature and society, 95; novel, 138–39n.91; and other, 106; phases of, 15; purposes of, 52; rudimentary, 109; shared, 73; social process of, 72; taking positions, 23; and temptation, 139n.108; of universal meanings, 82; varied, 45

Face, 110; command of, 104; to face, 93, 99, 100, 103, 115, 123, 125; of the other, 89, 98, 101, 102, 105, 117, 127, 146–47n.19. *See also* Levinas, Emmanuel; Other(s)

Family, 13, 18, 21; life, 9, 17; as system, 17–18

Feminist(s), 7, 22–23; contemporary, 8; literature, 8–9

Fichte, Johann, 44

Fleischacker, Samuel, 39, 134–35n.33, 135nn.41, 43, 146n.12

Freedom, 15, 55, 68, 94, 96, 116, 132–33n.4, 147n.33; and action, 146n.12; of choice, 80; to communicate, 56; existential, 61; of the other, 98; productive, 54; spontaneous, 147n.33; of thought, 56; Western, 95, 117

Functional: distinctions, 15; lines of demarcation, 20; universals, 25–26

Future, 15, 51; directedness, 67; experience, 138n.89; glittering, 117; hypothetical, 138n.89; and past and

present, 51, 95–96, 121, 147n.36; and present, 95–96; wave of the, 20. *See also* Future-present; Past; Present
Future-present, 67. *See also* Future

Game, organized, 13
General, 30, 32, 34, 133n.8, 137n.58; and particular, 40–42; and reciprocity, 97; standpoint, 36; will, 137n.64. *See also* Arendt, Hannah; Universal(s)
Generality, 38; in political realm, 40
Generalized other(s), 3, 13–14, 20–23, 25–27, 44–46, 142n.38; and common sense, 46–48; complex networks of responses, 66; and family, 18; internalize, 117; network of roles, 78; roles systematically organized in terms of, 65; single standpoint, 72; as system, 65; taking the position of, 14, 23; and whole, 50. *See also* Mead, George Herbert; Other(s)
Gesture(s), 10–13, 65, 73; exchange of, 78; significant, 72; vocal, 10–11, 65. *See also* Symbol(s)
God, 5, 10, 54, 92–93, 97–99, 115, 122–23. *See also* Deity
Goethe, Johann Wolfgang von, 31
Good judgment. *See* Judgment(s)
Good(s), 71, 102, 112, 123, 146–47n.19; beyond being, 98, 127; common, 9; community as, 82; disinterestedness of, 87; ethic of, 115; good enough, 127; life, 77; personal, 81; self-actualization as crucial, 114
Goodness, 102, 107. *See also* Good(s)
Griswald, Charles L., 145n.3
Group(s), 21, 23, 25–27, 72; abstract, 20; concrete, 67; organized, 13, 44; perspective of, 25; social, 13, 17, 26–28, 65, 77–78; solidarity, 45; unified, 14; whole, 79; of women, 22. *See also* Social

Habermas, Jürgen, 1–5, 29–30, 43, 45, 60, 88–89, 106, 120, 132n.68, 140n.18, 145n.54; conditions for autonomy, 140–41n.23, 146n.18; criticizes Arendt, 52–53; and ethical life, 104; and Kant, 142n.43; as Kantian, 66; on law, 125–26; and Levinas, 104, 110,

129n.1, 140n.6; and Mead, 12, 21, 53, 61–86 passim, 88, 110, 129n.1, 130n.29, 131n.52, 132n.1, 132–33n.4, 140nn.6, 15, 17, 141nn.25, 26, 30, 32; Mead's influence on, 64; and modernism, 106; not a pragmatist, 81; and Smith, 110. *See also* Autonomy; Communication; Communicative action; I; Individual(s); Individuation; Me; Reason; Reflexive; Strategic; Universality
Habermasian, 50
Habit(s), 71, 75. *See also* Habitual
Habitual, 14, 45, 66, 81, 122. *See also* Attitude(s); Habit(s)
Hearing, 33; one's own speech, 54–55, 58–59
Hegel, Georg Wilhelm Friedrich, 5, 62, 85; and conflict, 143n.57; and Dewey, 115; and ethical life, 104; influence on Habermas, 64; and Levinas, 114–17; and Mead, 43–44, 63, 70, 106, 114–17, 120; physiological psychology applied to, 63; system of, 61, 90, 116; and universals, 82; and universality, 61. *See also* Alienation; Hegelian; Hegelianism; Idealism; Recognition
Hegelian, 88; neo-, 4; post-, 66; quasi-, 63; sympathies, Mead's, 81
Hegelianism: democratized, 62–63; empiricized and pluralized, 66
Heidegger, Martin, 90, 101, 131n.59
Heideggerian, 30, 88; turn, 42
Hertz, Marcus, 36–37, 134n.30
Historicism, 85
Holocaust, 101, 104, 145n.54
Hume, David, 38–39, 131n.59, 135n.40
Hutcheson, Francis, 38
Hypertranscendental, 146–47n.19

I, 13–17, 65–70 passim, 84, 118, 130n.29; account of, Habermas's, 67–69, 84, 132–33n.4; actualizing implicit principles, 70; distorted by Habermas, 66; epistemic, 141n.25; fictitious, 15, 67; future directed, 131n.55; initiator of the novel, 70, 132–33n.4; in Mead's thought, 13–16, 61, 66–68, 70, 120, 140n.11; non-reflective, 130n.38; novel responses

of, 14–17; practical, 141n.25; projected, 146n.18; projects, for Habermas,
65, 67; and responsibility, 91; that is
"we," 94, 116; transforming, 25; and
universalistic moment, 142n.47. *See
also* Me; Novel; Novelty; Spontaneity
Ideal: community, 24, 71; counterfactual, 72; human conduct, 103; of method, 143n.59; of rationality, 95; of rational society, 82–83; spectator,
146n.12; world, 70–71, 77
Idealism: German, 4, 31, 44; romantic,
137n.62
Idealization, 54, 59
Idealizing, 58; supposition of universalistic form of life, 64
Identification, 124–25
Identity, 5, 66, 69; anarchic, 144n.31;
perpetuation of, 84; personal, 140–
41n.23; postconventional, 68; reconstruct conventional, 65, 67; uniqueness of, 102. *See also* Ego-identity;
Individuality; Individual(s); Self/selves
Illeity, 93, 98, 99
Imagination, 134n.22, 135n.44, 145n.5;
Arendt on, 17, 22, 33–35, 41, 109,
136n.51; and critical judgments, 17;
faculty of, 33; provides examples for
judgment, 41; and Smith, 107–9; sympathetic, 136n.46
Impartiality, 19, 28–29, 31, 36, 49–50,
62, 72–73, 124; absolute, 123; conditions for, 35; development of, 45;
Mead on, 30, 45, 83, 87, 138n.84; and
moral and political, 79, 126; question
of, 88; and social, 38; sought by Levinas, 103. *See also* Disinterested(ness);
Impartial spectator
Impartial spectator, 3, 29, 45, 135n.38,
146n.11; empirically minded, 83;
Smith's notion of, 30, 37–39, 72–73,
83, 109–11; sympathy of, 39. *See also*
Spectator(s)
Impulse(s), 15–16, 118, 130n.31,
141n.25, 145n.44; ameliorationist,
Mead's, 10; to assist others, 76–77;
ethical, 3–5; kindly, 124
Independence, 10; intellectual, 18; of
mind and self, 8–10, 18
Individual(s), 4–5, 10, 13–15, 20, 24, 26,
29–31, 130n.31; and attitude of the

other, 45; biological, 15–16, 118; charitable, 9; cosmopolitan, Kant's, 47;
and death, 107; development, 21; different, 102; dignity of, 41; future-
directed, 131n.55; and group participation, 23; highly developed, 74;
initiative, 30; integrity of, 30, 61; interaction among, 75; interest of, 63,
115; and international-mindedness,
47; and judgment, 49; and justice,
103; limitations, 56; morality located
in, 110; potentialities of, 82; resent-
ment of those who cause distress, 76;
and shared selfhood, 22; and society,
131n.52; Socratic view of, 92; speaking, 11; spontaneity among, 84; and
sympathy, 109; terms, 52; totality, 62;
two, 25, 44, 57, 80; uniqueness of, 29,
31, 91–92, 106, 112–13, 118–19,
142n.43, 146nn.18–19; and universal,
61–86 passim; voice, 118; whole
group, 78–79. *See also* Identity; Individuality; Individuation; Subject
Individuality, 2–5, 21, 97; irreducible,
65, 140n.6, 142n.43; and universality,
Habermas and Mead on, 61–86
passim. *See also* Identity;
Individual(s); Individuation; Subject
Individuation, 3, 62, 64–71 passim, 80,
84, 102, 146n.18; within community,
64; modern processes of, 15; roles a
source of, 64; and socialization, 21,
61, 131n.52. *See also* Identity;
Individual(s); Individuality
Interaction(s), 51, 69, 73, 115, 121; of
agents, 25; communicative, 11, 20;
context of, 65, 67; ideal of, 66; increased, 27; among individuals, 75;
linguistic, 10–11, 44, 80, 139n.108;
networks of, 65; nonstrategic, 78;
pattern(s) of, 48, 65–66; social, 64;
symbolic, 65; systems of, 21. *See also*
Communication; Communicative action; Social
Interdependence, 27, 74
Interest(s), 27, 29, 59, 83, 100, 106, 111–
12; adjudication of, 143n.1; of all, 63;
appeal to, 125; balancing of, 80; competing, 103; distance from, 42; expansion of, 124; of fame or gain, 49; generalized, 28, 80; grappled with, 50;

individual, 63, 115; one's own, 87, 124, 126; of others, 29, 88, 111; partial, 114; satisfy, 82; weighing of, 125. *See also* Disinterested(ness); Pragmatist(s); Self-interest
International-mindedness, 3, 19–20, 27–28, 45, 46–47, 74, 138n.75; and positions of others, 58; and warfare, 130–31n.46, 132n.69. *See also* Communities; Cosmopolitan; Cosmopolitanism; Enlarged mentality; Mead, George Herbert
Intersubjective, 12, 33–34, 36, 43, 56, 136n.55, 140n.18; conditions for valid judgments, 42; linguistic, 84; relations, 80; of selfhood, 9; theory of mind, 9. *See also* Self/selves; Social

James, William, 15–16, 22, 131nn.59, 62
Joas, Hans, 129n.1
Judaism, 98. *See also* Deity; God; Levinas, Emmanuel; Religious
Judgment(s), 50, 55, 58, 134n.24, 135n.41, 138n.87, 146n.12; Arendt's reading of Kant on, 30–37, 40–43, 133n.8; cognitive, 134n.22; and communication, 46; critical, 17; determinant, 31–32, 44, 48, 138–39n.91; faculty of, 35, 47; fair, 28; good, 2, 28–29, 79, 87; good, genesis of, 29; of hypothetical observer, 109; imagination provides examples for, 41; and individual, 49; logical, 134n.22; Mead on, 30; moral, 37, 110, 135n.44; of others, 18; political, 48, 135n.43; political and moral, 28; possible, 47; reflective, 32, 41–42, 44, 47, 138–39n.91; on situation, 76, 124; of taste, 56, 134n.22; valid, 40–42; of value, 124. *See also* Aesthetic(s)
Justice, 77, 79, 103, 112, 144n.40, 145n.43; guarantee, 104; the third and, 99–100, 105. *See also* Symmetry

Kant, Immanuel, 1, 3–5, 23, 29, 30–43, 49, 87, 131n.59, 132n.68, 134n.24; and *a priori*, 36, 44, 47, 75; and the beautiful, 32–36, 47, 134n.22, 139n.108; categorical imperative, 81; on the cosmopolitan, 47; and Derrida, 53–60, 139n.108; and English, 37, 134n.31;

influence on Habermas, 64, 66; and Mead, 44, 138–39n.91; and perpetual progress, 30; philosopher of the revolution, 43, 137n.64; and Smith, 37–39, 134–35n.33, 135nn.38, 40–41; transcendental self (ego) of, 15, 142n.43; transcendental unity of apperception, 137n.62; underhanded Christian, 67; and war, 132n.69. *See also* Arendt, Hannah; *Critique of Judgement*; Judgment(s); Kantian(s); Universal(s)
Kantian(s), 43, 66, 142n.43; modern-day, 60; notion of disinterestedness, 50; tradition, 68; transcendentally inspired, 43
Kierkegaard, Søren, 4, 61, 98; and Levinas, 92–93

Language, 17, 33, 53, 55, 58–59; attitudes, 73; and bearing, 78; development of, 10–13; evolution of, 12; fabric of, 57; Levinas's, 89; Mead's, 137n.64; of ontology, 89; rational, 78; self-conscious, 12; strategic uses of, 83. *See also* Communication; Gesture(s); Linguistic(s); Mead, George Herbert; Speech; Symbol(s)
Law, 125–26, 144n.40; and democracy, 126; Habermas on, 125–26; modern, 81; moral, 142n.43; and morality, 125–26
Leibnizian monad, 51, 118
Levinas, Emmanuel, 1, 2, 50, 51, 53, 62, 86, 88–104, 105–7, 131n.59, 133n.16, 143–44n.24, 144nn.28, 31, 33, 40, 145n.44, 147nn.32–33; challenge from, 4–5, 29, 105; conflation of uniqueness and responsibility in, 146n.18; degrees of subjectivity for, 146–47n.19; and dialogue, 147n.20; distrusts of political, 103; on ethics and politics, 125–26, 129n.1, 148n.42; and Habermas, 104, 110, 129n.1; and Hegel, 114–17; Jewish thinker, 5; and Kierkegaard, 92–93; language of, 89; and Mead, 110–12, 114–27, 129n.1; Orthodox Jew, 88; religious thinker, 105; and Smith, 110–12; unsatisfied with Smith on sympathy, 108. *See also* Alterity; Asymmetry; Disinterested(ness); Good(s); Impar-

tiality; Other(s); Pluralism; Plurality;
Said; Saying; Substitution; Symmetry;
Theme(s); Totality
Liberal(s), 9; ironist, 87; theory, 9
Life, forms of, 82
Life history, 64, 67–68, 130n.31,
140n.18; individuated, 66; unique,
118. *See also* Individual(s)
Life-world, 78, 80
Lingis, Alphonso, 95, 96
Linguistic(s): and attitude, 75; behavior,
11; construct, gender as, 22; interac-
tion, 10–11, 44, 80; intersubjective,
84; meanings, 45; and rights, 142n.44;
rules, 12; symbols, 13. *See also*
Gesture(s); Language; Symbol(s)
Logocentrism, 53, 59, 89, 103, 104
Logos, 54, 79, 89
Lyotard, Jean-François, 5

Manning, Robert John Sheffler, 143–
44n.24
Margolis, Joseph, 1
Marx, Karl, 21
McKeon, Richard, 23
Me, 14–17, 61, 65–70 passim, 117, 118,
120, 131n.55, 140n.11, 142n.47; born
in responsibility, 96; conventionality
of, 70, 141nn.25–26; distorted by Habermas, 66, 69–70, 141n.25; habits of,
84; mediation of, 140n.17; and moral
motivation, 140–41n.23; new, 25; the
other as, 93; and reflection, 130n.38;
source of universality, 76; and spontaneity, 143n.61; as system, 16; uniqueness of, 112–13, 146–47n.19. *See also*
I; Mead, George Herbert; Novelty;
Spontaneity
Mead, George Herbert, 1–5, 7–31, 36,
43–53, 92, 111, 130n.38, 131n.60,
132nn.68–69, 142n.38, 147n.36; and
Arendt, 45–53, 137n.64, 138n.87; and
Arendt and Derrida, 53, 57–60,
139n.108; and dialectical method,
131n.62; epistemology, 138n.87; and
Hegel, 43–44, 63, 70, 106, 114–17,
120, 143n.57; Hegelian sympathies of,
81; on humanity, 148n.38; on impartiality, 30, 45, 83, 87, 138n.84; on instinct, 130n.31; internationalist, 19;

and Kant, 138–39n.91, 139n.108; lectures of, 137n.63; and Levinas, 110–
12, 114–27; and Levinas on ethics and
politics, 125, 129n.1; and Marxists,
143n.59; modernist, 117; naturalist, 3;
neo-Hegelian, 4; and physiological
psychology, 63; pluralist and universalist, 87; and political, 7–31 passim,
111; and pragmatism, 3, 5, 30, 81; as
progressive, 83, 129n.9; and rights,
142n.44; on romantic idealism,
137n.62; and Smith, 37–39, 82–83,
106, 108, 110, 112, 135n.44, 136n.46;
summary of key ideas, 65–66; texts of,
131n.59. *See also* Attitude(s); Christian; Communities; Cooley, Charles
H.; Cosmopolitanism; Democracy;
Future; Gesture(s); Habermas, Jürgen;
I; Impulse(s); International-mindedness; Judgment(s); Me; Mind; Novel;
Other(s); Past; Perspective(s);
Pragmatist(s); Present; Rationality;
Role(s); Self/selves; Social; Symbol(s);
Universalism; Universality;
Universal(s); War
Mead, Irene Tufts (daughter-in-law), 7–9,
17–21
Meaning(s), 10, 26, 50–51, 132n.2; abstract universality of, 83; awareness
of, 11; common, 72, 82; confirm, 12;
consciousness of, 65; identities of, 12;
linguistic, 45; quest for, 49; same, 73;
of significant symbols, 45; similarities
of, 26; slippage in, 57; and truth,
138n.83; universal, 25, 44, 57–58, 82
Memory, 95–96, 144n.31
Metanarrative(s), 89. *See also*
Narrative(s)
Miller, David, 136n.46
Mind, 9, 109, 136n.55; *a prioristic* processes of, 47; and body, 64; development of, 10–13, 17; enlarging itself, 37;
and hearts, 114; independence of, 8–10,
18; intersubjective theory of, 9; life of,
48; Mead's understanding of, 10–13,
17; openness of, 90; perspectival, 19
Modern, 3; individuation, 15, 62; law,
81; self, 43; world, 19, 23, 46, 64–65,
123, 132n.69
Modernism, 106, 117

Modernist(s) 2, 53, 106, 116; Mead as, 117; obsession, the new as, 119
Modernity, 3, 67, 95; spheres of, 89, 141n.25
Moral, 68, 73–75; absolutism, 30; action, 142n.43; actor(s), 29, 79; attitude, 137n.62; autonomy, 67, 146n.18; behavior, 110, 114; conflicts, 81; criticism, 38; decisions, 79, 138n.84; development, 78; ideals, 19; imperatives, 102; intuitions, 78; judgment, 28, 37, 110, 135n.44; law, 142n.43; life, 102; motivation, 140–41n.23; philosophy, 4, 37; and political beings, 123; problems, 114; realm/sphere, 59, 126; theory, 38, 135nn.41, 43; universe, 114. *See also* Ethical; Ethics; Morality; Moral-practical
Morality, 4, 37, 54, 74, 76, 79, 86, 110–12, 140n.18; condition for, 89; lack of, without alterity, 107; law and, 125–26; political action linked to, 118; realm of, 121; and self-interest, 107, 126–27; summon me to, 101; war suspends, 90; Western, 32. *See also* Ethical; Ethics; Moral; Postconventional
Moral-practical, 88. *See also* Practical
Mutuality, 78, 81, 98, 116–17. *See also* Reciprocity; Recognition

Narrative(s), 69, 89, 118. *See also* Metanarrative(s)
Natality, 51–52, 122
Nationalism, 20, 74; power of, 27
Natural: benevolence, 102; world, 84, 122
Naturalism, 15–16
Nature, 16, 115, 117; experience of, 95; spiritualizing of, 63, 115
Negation of the negation, 85
Neo-pragmatism, linguistic, 12. *See also* Pragmatism
Nietzsche, Friedrich, 17, 67, 131n.59
Nonreflective. *See* Reflective
Nontheme(s), 89
Nontranscendental, 64, 105, 126
Normative, 12, 78
Norms, 132–33n.4; behavior conforming to, 84; universalization of, 65
Novel, 51; events, 17, 47, 84; experience, 138–39n.91; I initiator of, 70; responses, 14–17, 66, 68, 120–23, 142n.47. *See also* Creation; Creative; I; Novelty
Novelty, 16, 119–23, 138–39n.91; and the cosmopolitan, 47; sham, 123; varying degrees of, 15, 84. *See also* Creation; Creative; I; Novel

Ohrbach, Harold, 135–36n.44, 136n.46
Ontology, 89, 90, 107, 117, 119–20; of being, 121; language of, 89; of presence, 121
Otherness, 30, 56, 90, 117, 121; irreducible, 61; jejune, 123; of the neighbor, 123; overcoming, 124–25; species of, 122; too much, 126; transcendent, 5. *See also* Alterity; Other(s)
Other(s), 1, 4–5, 13, 17, 26, 38, 54, 65, 106; absence of, 73; absolute, 122; accusation of, 146–47n.19; action of all, 79; alterity of, 106, 111, 115, 122–23; assist, 125; attitude(s) of, 21, 43, 45, 72, 79; behavior of, 80; communication with, 19, 33; displacing, 115; disregard for, 112; force of, 113; freedom of, 98; infinite, 92–93; judgments of, 18; and Levinas, 1, 50, 86, 88–104; multiplicity of, 69; as neighbor, 83; not solely as means, 81; organized, 20, 74; past of, 143–44n.24; in place of, 47, 53; positions of, 45, 58; presence of, 33, 56; respect for, 105, 126; role of, in self-education, 59; sanctity of, 60, 117, 125; and self, 107, 110, 116, 123, 131n.62; specific, 67, 142n.38; standpoint of, 36, 47; surprises, 122; sympathy and, 76–77, 109, 124; taking attitude(s) of, 11, 14, 46, 72, 74, 136n.46; taking position of, 11, 13, 124; truly, 121; uniqueness of, 62, 117; viewpoints of, 36; views of, 49; weight of, 144n.33; words of, 87. *See also* Alterity; Disinterested(ness); Face; Generalized other(s); Interest(s); Perspective(s); Recognition; Response(s); Responsibility; Role(s)
Otherwise Than Being or Beyond Essence (Levinas), 89–102 passim, 112–13, 116, 119–20, 145n.43

Parmenides, 121
Parochial(ism), 14, 76, 83, 88, 126, 137–
38n.72, 142n.47
Particularity, 4, 32, 49, 136n.48
Particular(s), 42, 133n.20; and general,
40–42; and universal, 31–35, 40–42,
48, 49, 50, 51, 52
Pascal, Blaise, 90–91
Past, 15, 43, 117; always already, 93;
finalized, 122; hypothetical, 138n.89;
one's own, 23; personal, 91; and
present, 51–52, 90, 94–96, 98, 143–
44n.24, 144n.31; and present and future, 51, 95–96, 121, 147n.36
Peace, 90, 98, 111; alterity as key to, 94;
pluralism of, 103; starts from an I, 103
Peirce, Charles Sanders, 24, 131nn.59,
62; influence on Habermas, 64
Perspectivism, 2–3, 22, 87; Mead's 19,
73, 74, 75, 76
Perspective(s), 17, 20, 25–26, 28, 33, 56,
133n.14, 136n.55; alternative, 70; authorial, 24; of circle of addressees, 67;
disciplinary, 24–25, 27, 131n.60,
132nn.66, 68; enlarged, 78; of everyone
else, 64; of groups, 25; Habermas's, 52–
53; in and out of, 46; internalizing, 78;
of less-parochial communities, 83;
Mead's, 48; multiple, 41, 45, 79; objective, 24; of other(s), 43, 78; pragmatist's, 50; reverse, 65; share, 74; shifting of, 138n.75; system as, 66; taking,
of other(s), 2, 5, 13, 27–29, 39, 42, 53,
66, 106, 115, 127; of unified group, 14;
various, 19, 77; viewing ourselves from
others', 38. *See also* Other(s); System(s)
Phenomenologist(s), 5, 61
Philosopher(s), 1, 49–50, 57; dialogue
among, 147n.20; of the revolution,
Kant as, 43; romantic, 3, 43–44; transcendental, 3
Philosophical, 4, 7–8; spectator,
132n.68; Western, tradition, 56, 119;
works by Levinas, 90
Philosophy, 1–2, 63, 92, 100; abstract,
63; contemporary, 62; of evolution,
137n.69; history of, 120; moral, 4, 37;
ontological, 119; romantic, 43; U.S.,
2, 5; Western, 90, 120
Physiology, 63–64
Plato/Platonic, 40, 42, 126, 131n.59

Pluralism, 2–5, 7, 28–30, 58; of alterity,
114; and Arendt, 39–40; becomes impossible, 116; and interpretation of
Kant, 36; Mead's position on, 62, 105–
6, 127; of peace, 103
Pluralist(s), 82; Mead as, 87; radical,
106; systematic, 23–24, 85–86
Plurality, 30–31, 53; of actors, 56; disengaged, 50; ensure, 81; guarantee, 83;
Levinas's approach to, 105; real, 94;
true, 123
Political, 4–5, 26, 31, 42, 43, 48, 73–75,
129n.1; action, 118; activity, 94; actors, 3, 48–52, 79; agenda, 28; arena,
52; Arendt's views on, 30, 40–41, 83;
conflicts, 81; decisions, 79; and difference, 103, 106; disjunction with ethical, 106, 114, 125–26; events, 49;
judgment, 28, 48, 135n.43; Levinas's
distrust of, 103; life, 12, 32, 46, 51,
53, 116; matters, 28–29, 41; and
Mead, 7–31 passim, 111; and moral,
123; parties, 13, 23; philosophy 1;
practice, 8; realm, 105; speech, 57;
systems, 126; and thirds, 105;
thought, 37; tools, 9; universalism,
25; universality or generality in, 40–
41; value sphere, 89; world, 47, 51,
59, 125, 126. *See also* Democracy;
Politics; Truth(s)
Politics, 7, 148n.42; city, 10; compared
to ethics, 125–26; defined by phenomenality, 42; and ethics, Levinas and
Mead on, 125, 129n.1; Mead's interest
in, 10; spectator models of, 29; U.S.,
9. *See also* Democracy; Political
Postconventional: I, 69; morality, 65, 78;
self, 64, 69; selfhood, 65; terms, 67.
See also Identity
Postmodern, 1, 2, 4, 106; camps, 30; pluralists, 82; tracts, 9
Postmodernists, 4–5, 95, 103, 143n.3
Practical: plans, 76; reason, 79; relation
to self, 141n.25; wisdom, 46. *See also*
Moral-practical
Practice(s): actual, 57; daily, 76; everyday, 75; political, 8; reasonableness of,
75–76
Pragmatic: method, 50; pluralists, 82;
tradition, 53, 62, 68; world, 66. *See*
also Pragmatism; Pragmatist(s)

Pragmatism, 1, 4; classic U.S., 1; history of, 2; linguistic, 1; Mead's, 3, 5. *See also* American(s); Pragmatic; Pragmatist(s)

Pragmatist(s), 18, 22, 29, 60, 105–7, 114, 116; and Arendt, 43, 48, 50–51; critique of spectator, 138n.84; and Derrida, 57; and goods, 127; and habit, 75; impartiality for, 87; and interests, 29, 87, 125; Mead as, 30, 81; and novelty, 119; strategic, 132n.1; term not applied to Habermas, 81. *See also* American(s); Pragmatic; Pragmatism

Presence, 53–59, 89, 95, 98, 104, 107, 143–44n.24, 144nn.28, 31; ontology of, 121

Present, 15, 93, 99, 117, 120, 121; immediacy of, 17; just-past, 15; and past, 51–52, 90, 94–96, 98, 143–44n.24, 144n.31; and past and future, 51, 95–96, 121, 147n.36; privilege granted to, 95; specious, 121. *See also* Future-present

Problem(s): ethical and political, 114; moral, 114; requiring reflection, 76; solving, 75, 127

Procedural, 64, 70; and ethical, 76–77; rationality, 77. *See also* Proceduralists

Proceduralists, 125, 141n.30. *See also* Procedural

Procedure(s), 73, 89, 140–41n.23, 142n.44; rational, 71, 73, 79, 142n.54

Progress, 2, 9, 59–60; idea of, 30; perpetual, and Kant, 30

Progressive, 8–9; development, 41; ideas, 9; Mead as, 83

Proximity, 94–95, 99, 100

Psychological, 4, 7

Putnam, Hilary, 1

Quasitranscendental, 61, 78, 82, 88, 106, 132n.1, 142n.43, 145n.54

Rational, 18; being(s), 71–72, 79, 137n.64; beings, commonwealth of, 77–78; communities not, 82; formation of consensus, 52; language, 78; reflection, 78; society, 82–83. *See also* Procedure(s); Rationality; Reason; Reflection

Rationality, 53, 66, 75; communicative,

76, 80; degrees of, 79; forced, 82; ideal of, 95; Mead on, 77–79; procedural, 77; strategic, 76, 80. *See also* Communicative action; Rational; Reason

Reality, 17, 109, 132n.67; of mixed motives, 112; of others, 26; Parmenidean, 121; unsophisticated, 16

Reason, 29, 54, 76–79, 95; cognitive, 32; and common sense, 47; of humanity, 36, 47; practical, 59. *See also* Habermas, Jürgen; Practical; Rational; Rationality

Reasonable(ness), 2, 87; nonreflective, of practices, 75–76

Reciprocity, 78, 93, 96, 97, 98, 99, 105. *See also* Mutuality; Recognition

Recognition, 13, 65, 93–94, 114, 136n.55, 141n.25; anticipating, 140n.18; Hegel's dialectic of, 64, 93–94, 116–17; Levinas on, 116; mutual, 94; of the other, 116; by others, 80; reciprocal, 64, 67; on the watch for, 116. *See also* Mutuality; Reciprocity

Reflection, 16, 19, 32, 35, 47, 54, 90, 124; before, 98; on conduct, 109; and critical edge, 70; and me, 130n.38; moments of, 86; not an act of, 91; operation of, 34, 134n.24; prior to, 97; in problem solving, 75–76; rational, 78. *See also* Problem(s); Rational; Reflective; Self-reflection, existential

Reflective: appraisal, 74; consciousness, 97; not, 14, 81, 118, 130n.38; and procedure, 142n.44; thought, 19; turn, 45; type, 70. *See also* Reflection

Reflexive: and life history, 64; principles, 85–86, 120; self, 118

Reflexivity, 11, 65; and autoaffectivity, 85; autonomous, 68; of systems, 86

Relativism, 28, 104

Relativist(s), 73, 87

Religious, 5; ideals, 19; texts, 24; thinker, Levinas as, 105. *See also* Christian; Deity; God; Judaism; Levinas, Emmanuel

Re-presentation, 95–96

Representation(s), 33–36, 47, 90, 99, 120, 133n.16, 144nn.28, 31, 40; of God, 98; natural, 55

Response(s), 10–11, 65, 78–79, 84; anticipating others', 12; call out, 73; complex networks of, as generalized others, 66; different, 102; disinterested, 34; ethical, 148n.42; functional, 12; functional identity of, 65; of I, 131n.55; identity of, 45; immediate, 34; kinds of, 81; new, 75; of other, 12, 80; process of, 15; response to, 110; roles as complex sets of, 13; shared network of, 46; similarity of, 44; to symbol, 44; sympathetic, 77; system of, 14. *See also* Anticipate; I; Novel

Responsibility, 96–100, 104, 110, 141n.25; degrees of, 146–47n.19; for myself, 100; for the other, 91, 93, 99, 102, 113, 116–17, 122, 144nn.28, 31; precedes violence, 98; and uniqueness, 112–13, 146n.18, 146–47n.19. *See also* Levinas, Emmanuel; Substitution

Rights, 21, 99; and Mead, 142n.44; system of, 65; universal, 21; women's, 3, 8

Role(s), 14, 17, 65–67, 84, 97; assumption of, 44; complex sets of responses, 13; different, 45; exchange of, 78; internalized, 117; of judicious observer, 109; and me, 140n.11; Mead's theory, 65; in moral life, 102; of the other in self-education, 59; source of individuation, 64; of the spectator, 133n.20; taking, 13, 44, 69, 78, 136n.46; of the wretched, 76. *See also* Generalized other(s); Mead, George Herbert; Perspective(s); Self/selves

Romanticism, 2, 43–44, 106, 114, 137n.62; philosophy of evolution, 137n.69

Rorty, Richard, 1, 12, 87

Rousseau, Jean-Jacques, 43, 137n.64

Royce, Josiah, 44, 63

Rule(s), 48, 138–39n.91; behavioral, 65; explicit, 44; implicit, 13, 44; linguistic, 12; pattern of interaction, 65–66; universal, 134n.24

Said, 89, 92, 98–100, 101, 118, 144n.40; realm of the present, 98–99; synchrony of, 143–44n.24. *See also* Saying

Sartre, Jean-Paul, 94, 147n.33

Sartreans, 55

Saying, 89, 96–98, 100, 101, 117–18,

144nn.31, 40; and diachrony, 144n.26. *See also* Said

Schelling, Friedrich, 44

Science(s), 19–20, 24, 26, 53, 59, 63, 79, 105, 144n.40; behavioral, 44; empirical, 2; inform political life, 53; possibilities of, 118

Scientific, 46, 89, 122; analysis, 105; communities, 26; community, 57; discipline, 132n.67; hypotheses, 16; matters, 25; method, 18–19, 24; realm, 59; standing, 19

Scientist(s), 24; social, 18

Segregation: of sexes, 8, 18; voluntary, 21

Self-actualization. *See* Self-realization; Self/selves

Self-assertion, 101, 113

Self-conscious, 11, 22, 66, 118; communication, 25; ego, 91; language, 12

Self-consciousness (awareness), 11, 90, 102, 118, 148n.38; born, 99; independent, 94, 116; and selfhood, 14

Self-deception, 109–10

Self-determination, 70, 77, 80, 140n.18. *See also* Self/selves

Selfhood, 22, 65; genuine, 113; intersubjective theory of, 9; and self-consciousness, 14

Self-interest, 81, 88, 89, 91, 104, 106–13, 115; enlightened, 92, 100; expanded, 124; imperial, 123; and morality, 107, 126–27; and violence, 101. *See also* Egoism; Interest(s); Self/selves

Self-reflection, existential, 67. *See also* Reflection

Self-realization, 70, 77, 80, 114, 125, 126–27, 140n.18, 140–41n.23. *See also* Self/selves

Self/selves, 2–4, 68–70, 88, 90–92, 97, 135n.44; actual, 15; as cognitive object, 14, 118; consciousness of, 45, 130n.38; constituted, 27; development of, 13–17, 21, 44–45, 64–66, 82, 87, 117; diremptions of, 90; dislocation of, 114; epistemic relation to, 141n.25; forgetting of, 100; free, 137n.62; genesis of, 13, 28, 64; as hostage, 102; independence of, 8–10, 18; isolation of, 115; larger, 70, 74; looking-glass, 38–39, 136n.46; love, 108; as me, 65; Mead's understanding of, 9, 13–22, 28, 44, 65, 114, 115; modern, 43; multiplicity of, 23; and other, 107, 110, 116, 123, 131n.62; postconventional, 64, 69; premodern, 65; reflexive, 118; sense of, 140nn.15, 17; social, 7, 10, 28, 39, 124; social conception of, 37, 61, 110, 131n.55; social construction of, 146n.12; transcendental, 15; unique, 110, 118; unity of, 13. *See also* Ego; Generalized other(s); I; Me; Self-interest; Social; Subject

Senses, 33–35, 55, 59, 133n.20

Sensus communis, 3, 32–36, 41, 46–47, 56. *See also* Common sense

Shalin, Dmitri, 129n.1

Significant symbol. *See* Symbol(s)

Smith, Adam, 1, 3–5, 72, 92, 124, 126, 134n.30, 145nn.3, 5, 146nn.12, 15; and Arendt, 39, 135n.43; on benevolence, 103–4; and Habermas, 110; and imagination, 107–9; and Kant, 37–39, 134–35n.33, 135nn.38, 40–41; and Kant and Mead, 37–39; and Levinas, 110–12; and Mead, 37–39, 82–83, 106, 108, 110, 112, 135n.44, 136n.46; on sympathy, 106–14, 145n.1. *See also* Impartial spectator; Sympathy

Social, 10, 87, 118; activities, 19; attitudes, 14; behaviorism, 24; behavior(s), 117, 136n.46; calling, 8–9; communities, 20; and conscience, 109; consciousness, 135n.44; constitution, 15; environments, 45; events, 49; givens, 84; goal of, 123; and impartiality, 38; life, 5, 44, 46, 53, 106; matters, 29; and plurality, for Levinas, 105; process, 11, 72; psychological, 8–9, 12; psychology, 4, 7, 8, 62, 135–36n.44; reconstruction, 77; reform, 124; role, 44; scientists, 18; structure, 77; theorists, 61, 110; theory, 1, 62, 66, 78; world, 25, 59. *See also* Communities; Generalized other(s); Group(s); Interaction(s); Self/selves; Social

Sociality, 5, 16–17, 84; state of, 47

Society/societies, 2–3, 8–9, 18, 21, 100,

102, 110–11, 117, 137n.64; abstracts from, 142–43n.54; actual structure of, 71; advances, 63, 115; consumer, 42; democracy as order of, 21, 74; democratic, 126; experience of, 95; implied, 70; and individual, 131n.52; at large, 29; larger, 70; potentials, 77; projected form of, 64, 68; rational, 82–83. *See also* Community; Social

Socrates, 32–33, 92; reflective type, 70

Spectator(s), 28–29, 43, 126, 133n.20, 136n.48; and actors, 48–52; critique of, 138n.84; disinterested, 41; external, 109; internal, 146n.12; judge as, 109; judging, 49; models of knowledge, 29; in moral theory, 38; of own behavior, 38; philosophical, 132n.68; world, 41. *See also* Impartial spectator

Speech, 54–59, 78; free, 56, 59. *See also* Communication; Gesture(s); Language; Linguistic(s); Symbol(s)

Spontaneity, 24, 55, 132–33n.4, 147n.33; existential, 68; and I, 15, 61, 84, 132–33n.4, 143n.61. *See also* Freedom; I; Novel; Novelty

Stimulus/stimuli, 11–12, 16, 130n.31; to assist, 124

Strategic, 29; action, 80–83, 132n.1; not, interactions of, 78. *See also* Communicative action; Rationality

Subject, 2, 92, 142n.43, 146–47n.19; acting, 141n.25; and anarchy, 98, 144n.31; decentered, 1; free, 93; incomparable, 99; outside, 88; responsible, 91; social, 3; socialized, 80; time of, 143–44n.24; unique/uniqueness of, 94, 96, 112–13. *See also* Ego; Individuality; Individual(s); Other(s); Self/selves; Subjectivity

Subjective, 34, 80; reasons, 115

Subjectivity, 61, 93, 98, 99, 112–13, 144n.33; degrees of, 146–47n.19; lose, 94

Substitution, 91, 93, 96–99, 102–3, 111, 116, 119, 123; and uniqueness, 112–13, 146–47n.19. *See also* Levinas, Emmanuel; Responsibility

Symbol(s), 44, 65; abstract, 141n.32; greater universality, 79; range of, 79; sharing of, 73–74; significant, 11–13,

20, 25, 44–45, 57–58, 73–74; system, 57; as universal, 72–73, 78. *See also* Communication; Gesture(s); Language; Linguistic(s)

Symmetry, 99–100, 105, 116, 125. *See also* Asymmetry; Justice; Reciprocity

Sympathy, 23, 76–77, 102–3, 106–15, 123–24, 145nn.3, 5; immediate, 124; of impartial spectator, 39; for spectators, 49. *See also* Imagination; Other(s); Smith, Adam

System(s), 13, 61, 65–66, 92, 98, 101–2, 104, 121, 132n.67; autoaffective, 59; called a perspective, 66; closed, 54–55; of common meanings, 72; different, 17; entwinement in, 94; generalized other as, 65; Hegel's, 61, 90, 116; intelligibility of, 99; me as type of, 16–17; of money and power, 81; movement among, 47; not isolated, 51; political, 126; prior, 138–39n.91; reflexivity of, 86; of rights, 65; symbolic, 57; theorist, 61; totality of, 55. *See also* Family; Perspective(s)

Taste, 31–36, 41, 133n.14, 137n.62, 139n.108; judgment(s) of, 56, 134n.22; kind of *sensus communis*, 32

Taylor, Charles, 88–99

Theme(s), 89–93, 97–99, 100–102, 117–19, 144n.31; as idol, 98

Theory of Moral Sentiments (*TMS*), 4, 37–38, 107–12, 134n.30, 135nn.38, 43, 146n.11. *See also* Smith, Adam

Third(s), 99–100, 105, 125, 145n.43; realm of, 103; world of, 102. *See also* Justice; Symmetry

Time. *See* Future; Past; Present

Totality, 26, 89, 100, 105, 110, 119–21, 125; concept of, 90; creation foils, 119; individual, 62; obviate, 83; prevent, 81; of system, 55

Trace, 93, 96, 123, 143–44n.24

Transcendence, 98, 105, 119–20, 122–23; absolute, 86, 123

Transcendental, 81, 87, 110, 140n.6; aspirations, 66; closure, 139n.108; conditions, 82; counterpart, 14; ground, 4, 74, 104; and Kantians, 43; modernists, 106; musings, 60; purely, 67; self of Kant, 15. *See also* Ego; Hypertran-

scendental; Nontranscendental; Quasitranscendental

Truth(s), 16, 45, 49, 54, 95, 132n.66; cognitive, 40, 48; eternal, 92; and meaning, 138n.83; not in political world, 40–41, 48, 52, 59; not recollected, 92

Tufts, James Hayden, 114–15

Unbounded/unlimited communication community. *See* Communication

United States: seeming materialism of, 115; socialism in, 10

Universalism, 2, 5, 7, 25, 28–29, 88; contextual, 63, 78; Mead's position on, 73–79 passim, 106, 140n.9; nontranscendental approach to, 105; political, 25. *See also* Attitude(s); Cosmopolitan; Cosmopolitanism; Enlarged mentality; International-mindedness; Universal(s); Universality

Universality, 3–4, 23, 55, 87, 134n.22; of the beautiful, 36; functional, 57–58; and individuality, Habermas and Mead on, 61–86 passim; and Hegel, 61; Mead's position on, 30, 39, 43, 44, 45, 46, 47, 57–58, 76; notions of, 88; in political realm, 40; possibility of, 58; unity of, 45. *See also* Attitude(s); Meaning(s); Universal(s); Universalism

Universal(s), 3, 30, 55, 73, 133n.8, 137nn.58, 64; abstract or concrete, 82; agreement, 41; circles of, 83; and communities, 47; conditions, 78; functional, 25–26, 44–45, 57–58, 73; Mead on, 25–26, 43, 44, 45, 46, 47, 57–58, 66, 72–73; meaning, 25, 44, 57–58; more, and communities, 14; and particular, 31–35, 40–42, 48, 49, 50, 51, 52; problem of, 72; progress, 60; and reciprocity, 97; rights as, 21; rule, 134n.24; sole source of, 45. *See also* Meaning(s); Symbol(s); Universalism; Universality

Universe(s) of discourse, 71–72, 77, 131n.50, 141nn.30, 32; logical, 20; logicians', 72. *See also* Communication

University of Chicago, 8, 10, 18, 114

Value(s), 65; conflict of, 124; judgments of, 124; restatement of, 71

Violence, 5, 89–91, 94, 97–99, 101–3, 111–13, 124, 145nn.44, 5; lessening, 127; overcoming, 112, 146n.18; and power, 125; responsibility precedes, 98
Vocal gesture. *See* Gesture(s)

War, 19, 90, 93–94, 99, 110–11, 116, 143n.57; of all against all, 100, 111; and international-mindedness, 130–31n.46, 132n.69; original, 102

Watson, Walter, 23–24, 132n.66
Westbrook, Robert, 129n.9
Will, 137n.64; altruistic, 102; autonomous, 67; free, 67, 141n.25; general, 137n.64
Wittgenstein, Ludwig, 1; understanding of rules, 12
"World that is there," 75
Wundt, Wilhelm Maximilien, 63, 65

Zammito, John H., 134n.31

MITCHELL ABOULAFIA is professor and chair of the philosophy department at the University of Colorado at Denver and director of the graduate interdisciplinary programs in humanities and social sciences at the same institution. He is the author of *The Mediating Self: Mead, Sartre, and Self-Determination* (Yale University Press, 1986) and *The Self-Winding Circle: A Study of Hegel's System* (W. H. Green, 1982), the editor of *Philosophy, Social Theory, and the Thought of George Herbert Mead* (SUNY Press, 1991), and has published numerous articles on social theory, American philosophy, and Continental thought.

Typeset in 9.5/12.5 Trump Mediaeval
with Trump Mediaeval display
Composed by Jim Proefrock
at the University of Illinois Press
Manufactured by Thomson-Shore, Inc.

University of Illinois Press
1325 South Oak Street
Champaign, IL 61820-6903
www.press.uillinois.edu